3 812(

MW01109293

A Conspicuous Life:

George B. Christian Sr. and the Rise of Industrial Marion

JOEL MIYASAKI

ZEA MAYS

PUBLISHING

SYCAMORE, ILLINOIS

ZEA MAYS
PUBLISHING

Edited by Kelly Unger

ISBN 978-0-9897167-1-0

Table of Contents

Foreword

My middle name is Christian, my dad's mother's maiden name. But the name was almost all I knew about the Christian line when I was younger, other than that the family was from Marion, Ohio. My family and I visited Marion several times while my grandmother was still living there. Over the years, I also heard tales of a connection between the Christian family and Warren G. Harding, twenty-ninth president of the United States.

I'm a late bloomer when it comes to my passion for family history and genealogy. I wish I had been more interested when I could have personally asked my relatives about our history. Fortunately, my father and his two brothers kept in close contact after they left Marion in the years following World War II. Through their conversations, I continued to learn more about Marion, the Christians, and the Hardings.

Several years ago, with the help of some of my cousins, I connected with a number of history students at the University of Illinois to research my Marion relatives, including the Christians and the Robertses. This book reveals what we discovered about the Christians, and it is local history at its best.

Our research found that my great-grandfather, George B. Christian Sr. and his ancestors and descendants were deeply involved in the growth and development of Marion. The family was politically, socially, and economically active in the city, which included owning a newspaper and stone quarry. Local newspapers recorded the family's accomplishments and activities, providing ample sources to review when creating this manuscript.

One interesting footnote to the Christians' story was their close relationship with Warren and Florence Harding and the role they played in the front porch campaign that launched Harding to the presidency. Another is that my grandmother's sister and her husband were long-time caretakers of the Harding home after the president's death.

We learned enough about Marion history to want to publish our findings in hopes that others might appreciate the story of our ancestor and the city in which he lived. The fact that this is a family story makes it extra special for us. One thing is for sure, my middle name means much more to me today than it did a few years ago!

I want to thank my paternal Roberts family members (my mother's last name was also Roberts, but her family settled in Illinois) for their participation and perspective. My cousins and I took a couple of field trips to Marion in search of family history and enjoyed meeting some present-day Marionites.

I also want to thank the University of Illinois and the history students who helped assemble the resources that resulted in this manuscript. Most especially, I want to thank author Joel Miyasaki for his endurance throughout this project. It began when he was a doctoral candidate at U of I and continued as he worked in Utah, managing research assistants there while continuing to write this family history project for our family located back in Illinois.

Enjoy the read.

Douglas Christian Roberts
Sycamore, IL
March 2016

Acknowledgments

When writing any work of history, the logistical and intellectual debts extend well beyond the quality or character of the manuscript. I can only begin to thank the many people who made this biography possible. First and foremost, I am grateful to the Roberts family, and Doug in particular, for sharing their ancestor and family with me. In the past few years, I feel that I have come to know and respect George B. Christian Sr. While his life and story did not follow the path of national fame, fortune, or power that might demand a traditional biographical study, the observations in this book make a strong case that every person's life is conspicuous and can offer insight into the history through which he or she lived. I appreciate the Roberts' patience and patronage. They allowed me to follow the history where it led and placed no restrictions on the nature of the narrative produced. I feel confident that Christian would be proud of his descendants and the good they do in the world.

I would also like to express my gratitude to Tom Matya and Sue Breese at Zea Mays Publishing. Both have exerted significant energies to assist my work. Tom was the principal shepherd of this research, making sure the process moved forward and putting me in contact with helpful friends. Sue, an accomplished historian in her own right, helped with research, images, and logistics. Any value found in the visuals began with her able assistance. Mary Stuart, their contact at the History, Philosophy, and Newspaper Library at the University of Illinois, first recruited me to this project and provided library resources to help launch the book.

In addition, I am thankful to the diligent researchers who tediously combed through rolls of microfilmed newspapers. Danielle Gomm and Antonia Keller provided the building blocks for much of the story of George B. Christian Sr., and their help permitted me a breadth and depth impossible without such comprehensive examinations of evidence. They probably know the history and story of Marion and its citizens better than I do. I consider them both friends and colleagues of significant ability. In addition, Dr. David Bates and I worked together on the newspaper research that became the basis for the chapter about Christian's time at the *Marion Democratic Mirror.*

I am also very grateful for the help I received at the various archives and historical centers I visited in Marion. Sherry Hall of the Harding House offered an excellent primer into the scholarship and understanding of the Harding presidency. She also directed me to some crucial images that appear in the manuscript. Her book about Warren G. Harding's publishing background helped me better understand the newspaper business in Marion. Brad Bebout, formerly of the Marion Community Foundation, helped orient me in Marion and assisted me in my quest to access Quarry Park. Gale Martin, director of the Marion Historical Society, offered insight and advice about Marion and its history. She also gave me a tour of their excellent museum and archives. Many thanks to the True-Stengel Museum, which provided access to priceless family paintings that appear in the book. I am also indebted to the helpful staff at the Marion County Recorder's office for their help searching through county deed and mortgage records.

Many other scholars and archivists provided important assistance. Diane Gagel, Melinda Gilpin, and Sally O'Connor did much of the preliminary genealogical and historical research on the Christian line in Ohio, and their work served as an excellent jumping-off point for this biography. I am indebted to the archivists at the Ohio Historical Society Archive/Library in Columbus, who assisted me in my research and helped me obtain microfilm and images. Jennie McCormick at the Worthington Historical Society provided research help from afar, and Rebecca Jewett at the Rare Books & Manuscripts Library at Ohio State University assisted my research efforts there. I also owe a debt of gratitude to the volunteers of the Delaware County Historical Society, who helped me at the Cryder Historical Research Center. Marie Bouic of Ostrander, Ohio, provided valuable information and images of the White Sulphur Quarries in Delaware County in spite of my overly persistent efforts to contact her. Donald Keller kindly offered insight and background about the master's thesis he wrote more than forty-three years ago about George B. Christian Jr. and Warren G. Harding. Ben DiBiase of the Florida Historical Society, Rebecca Felkner of the Grandview Heights Library, and Michelle Gullion at the First Ladies National Historical Site helped secure image permissions.

Kelly Unger edited this manuscript, and her outside perspective and meticulous attention to detail made this book much better than I could possibly have managed on my own. More than anything, she helped me understand when my historical training was getting in the way of my ability to share the riches of history. All authors should be so lucky to have such a capable editor in their corner. I am also very grateful to Stephen Anderson, who formatted and designed the book. Its attractive display owes everything to him.

I especially acknowledge my mentors and colleagues in the various history departments along my academic journey. The fundamentals of historical inquiry that I have developed through their instruction and collaboration made this work possible. I am grateful to the professors at the University of Illinois Urbana-Champaign, Utah State University, and Brigham Young University-Idaho for their belief in me and my work.

Finally, I cannot begin to thank my family enough. I am appreciative that my parents and siblings fostered an atmosphere of intellectual inquiry and love throughout my life. I owe a profound debt to my lovely wife and partner, Ashley. During these years, she has also cohabited with George Christian—though sometimes with less affection. She is my biggest supporter, and this work was possible because of her patience and love.

Introduction

"Biography is history seen through the prism of a person."
Louis Fischer, in a 1965 speech accepting the National Book
Award for History and Biography for *The Life of Lenin*.

In late November of 1909, many of the pious residents of
Marion, Ohio, gathered in two of the city's churches to celebrate an
important anniversary. One year earlier, a new Ohio law had
empowered local communities to choose whether or not to close their
saloons, an option which the people of Marion subsequently exercised.
To celebrate the law, Sunday schools around the state had designated
November 24 as Temperance Day.
At the Marion Free Baptist
Church on Main Street,
businessman George B. Christian
Sr. was one of the orators who
spoke to an ecumenical crowd

Fig. 2. Photo of Trinity Baptist (formerly
known as the Marion Free Baptist) Church
in Marion, Ohio, which served as the site of
George B. Christian Sr.'s prohibition speech.
(Courtesy of the Library of Congress)

Fig. 1. George B. Christian Sr. (Courtesy of
the Roberts Family Library)

about the positive effects that had resulted from the ban. Christian had been chosen because of his reputation as a rousing public speaker and committed churchgoer, and he carefully navigated the moral and pragmatic arguments for the temperance cause. He began that night by reassuring the crowd that he felt no hatred toward any saloon owner. Instead, Christian directed his condemnation toward the saloon as an institution and the tawdry activities that occurred there. He recounted the story of a friend who had frequented these institutions, lost a battle to alcoholism, and committed suicide in the far-off state of Wyoming. He used this tragedy as an opening argument to support his conclusion that saloons served as breeding grounds for law breaking and spiritual degeneracy. At the time, national papers had broken the story of sex traffickers in New York City, and Christian tied the plots to enslave young white women to saloons. He also argued that many violent anarchist schemes, instigated by rogue workers' unions, had come together within the walls of such establishments. He finished his speech by praising the changes experienced under Marion's dry mandate, which had lowered crime and improved the physical and mental health of the people. That evening, Christian's audience responded enthusiastically to his words and the cause for which he spoke.[1]

Although the prohibition of alcohol would fail spectacularly as a constitutional mandate more than twenty years later, Christian actively embraced the temperance cause at a time when this longstanding moral crusade was transforming into one of the most successful issue campaigns in the history of the nation. The movement culminated with the passage of a constitutional amendment which banned the production and sale of alcohol in the United States for more than ten years. From the beginning of the nineteenth century, the temperance movement had sought to eliminate the consumption of alcohol. Nevertheless, early religious and women's campaigns struggled to accomplish the universal changes supporters believed this moral hazard merited. Christian's state of Ohio served as a central battleground for fights against the brewing industry, which had grown significantly in the years after the Civil War. The development of a national railroad network had allowed alcohol producers to manufacture for and participate in a national market. One commercial innovation inspired by this increased competition was the creation of proprietary saloons to sell brewers' spirits. As saloons became ubiquitous, their reputation as sites of moral degeneracy spread as well. Organized in 1893, the Ohio Anti-Saloon League, which eventually became a part of the more nationally-minded Anti-Saloon League of America (ASLA), identified saloons as the new principal target of the temperance movement.[2]

The organization's savvy advocacy against saloons convinced George B. Christian Sr., a Marion industrialist and leader, to assist the cause. Because the ASLA worked successfully outside political parties to lobby for its moral goals, historians have identified it as the first modern pressure group. The ASLA modeled their organization along corporate lines, with state branches and departments that all received direction from a national board. Local church members, traditional temperance advocates who targeted alcohol and its purveyors as advocates of evil, staffed much of the ground-level organization and provided most of the financial support for the league. Nevertheless, Christian businessmen like George B. Christian Sr., whose backing more often focused on the pragmatic goal of reducing drunkenness, contributed a disproportionate amount of money, legitimacy, and direction to the movement on a national level. Applying the Progressive Era principles of scientific improvement and reasoned change, the national organization soon determined that the most efficient course to limit alcohol consumption in the United States would be to encourage local communities to ban saloons. Such bans would slowly cripple brewers' distribution networks and eliminate the sites where public drunkenness was acceptable. This was a modern solution to a longstanding moral question, and it proved attractive to those without strong moral objections to drinking.[3]

Christian had spent his adult years negotiating the rapid tide of economic change and development that occurred in Ohio, the Midwest, and the United States over the last half of the nineteenth and first half of the twentieth centuries. As a concerned employer in the limestone processing industry, speechmaker Christian was drawn to the anti-saloon movement primarily for pragmatic reasons. Limestone quarrying, processing, and transportation presented potentially fatal consequences for impaired workers at Christian's production facilities. Although his father, John Christian, had supported the temperance movement in the 1870s, Christian had previously shown little inclination to support the restriction of alcohol. In fact, he had sometimes mocked rigid temperance stances during his tenure as a small-town newspaper editor many years before. In addition, the punch bowl at his Christmas parties had become legendary among his Marion friends, including future president Warren G. Harding, for the potency of its hot rum punch. While he gave lip-service to the moral imperatives of the movement, business-minded Christian became a temperance supporter out of paternalistic concern for his quarry workers in Marion and Delaware Counties and materialistic concerns for his profit margins. Consequently, Christian always added a caveat to his advocacy, pointing out that he held no objection to the consumption of alcohol within one's own home; the saloon as an institution was his true enemy. The strategies of the Anti-Saloon League of America allowed Christian to support shutting down public purveyors of alcoholic beverages without completely accepting the many moral arguments for the restriction of spirits. Christian embraced this modern solution to the temperance question and became a de facto spokesman for the ASLA's cause in the city of Marion.[4]

The story of Christian's temperance speech and advocacy demonstrates one of the ways in which he engaged with the important historical forces of his time. His oration also illuminated three central themes that appeared again and again in the course of his accomplished life. First, Christian's speech captured one of the many ways in which industrialization and development affected him and his community at the turn of the twentieth century. Second, his discourse illustrated the leadership and service he offered to his community. Third, his talk revealed his desire to inform and interpret important events for his friends and colleagues.

Christian's conversion to the temperance cause was motivated by the central role that industrial and corporate development occurring throughout the nation played in his decisions and destiny. Christian spent much of his youth trying to find his niche within the post-Civil War economy, and his faux-military title of "Colonel" emerged from his many economic endeavors during this period. As a young journalist and publisher at the *Marion Democratic Mirror,* Christian prioritized the promotion and development of Marion companies and industries. Later, Christian's lime and stone companies succeeded because developments in the railroad industry allowed for the easy transportation of goods throughout the nation. The growth of the construction industry offered a market for the many limestone-related products offered by the quarries. This meant that Christian's financial fate as a business owner often depended on the fluctuating conditions of the national and world economies. Christian embraced the industrial, technological, and financial fluidity of the years after the Civil War, and his efforts to navigate the changing tides of economic development offer one unifying theme for the many stories that follow.

While George B. Christian Sr.'s temperance activism demonstrated his commitment to his workers and business, the invitation to speak at this countywide event illustrated how people in the city of Marion respected his oratorical skill, economic leadership, moral judgment, and piety. Christian knew how to captivate an audience with humor and storytelling—especially in Marion. He enjoyed the people of his city; he liked commanding their respect even more. He spent significant time developing friendships in the community, and he sought various opportunities to run for public office to assist his friends and neighbors. In his mature years, Christian became a vocal advocate for veterans, and he used his oratorical skill to help organize and fund numerous groups and causes within the city. Consequently, a second significant theme developed within subsequent chapters is Christian's relationship with and efforts to serve in the community of Marion, Ohio.

In his speech about temperance, Christian tried to educate the people of Marion about the various ills that occurred within saloons. He also explained the benefits that had resulted from local restrictions on alcohol. Christian loved to describe and analyze events and developments in the world around him. He spent a little more than half a decade as a small-town newspaperman. With his editorial pen, he attempted to educate his readers and persuade them to understand problems and issues the same way that he did. Even after Christian left the *Marion Democratic Mirror*, his drive to record his observations and share his analyses persisted. While Christian eventually directed most of his efforts toward his entrepreneurial interests, he never completely buried his journalistic sensibilities. Christian's public speaking drips with description and analysis, and this book explores Christian's educational and journalistic efforts as an important lens for understanding the story of his life.

These three themes, introduced through Christian's temperance speech, appeared in various ways within the different stages of Christian's life. Christian sought to adapt to changing economic forces, to serve in his community, and to document his observations and perspectives about the past, present, and future. While the themes are key to understanding the way he perceived the world, the world around him was constantly changing. Christian's life encompassed more than eight eventful decades of U.S. history. Born in 1846, he lived until 1930. As the economic, political, and social dynamics of the nation shifted, Christian formed a family, raised children and grandchildren, worked to support them, and found ways to contribute to the growth and well-being of Marion.

The setting of the speech is important because the story of George B. Christian Sr.'s life is as much a story about the community of Marion as it is about the man himself. The city provided the backdrop for most of the events recounted within this book. At the time of Christian's birth, Marion was a tiny village located in the center of Ohio, approximately sixty miles north of the state capital, Columbus. Until 1820, the land that eventually became the village of Marion lay within the territory ceded to Native American inhabitants of the region in a late eighteenth century treaty. The city opened for white settlement when the federal government made a new agreement with the region's indigenous peoples. Like most treaties made with the Native Americans, the coercive pact benefited the white settlers and squatters who took over the land. The small village of Marion was fortunate to be named the seat of Marion County, which was formed as people moved into this newly opened section of Ohio. Early settlers focused on the agricultural potential of the region, and the city of Marion remained somewhat isolated following the county's incorporation.[5]

Fig. 3. Photo of downtown Marion, Ohio, taken during the city's centennial celebration in 1922. (Courtesy of Scripps-Howard Newspapers/Grandview Heights Public Library/ Photohio.org)

Four years after Christian was born in 1846, the U.S. census reported that the city of Marion housed a population of 1,311 people. Through the 1850s, Marion remained the center of a county devoted to agriculture. Nevertheless, the village's fortuitous geographical position along routes between major Ohio and midwestern cities created opportunities for the growth of industry. The development of manufacturing in this era depended primarily on the vast expansion of railroad infrastructure throughout the nation. Important Marion leaders understood the significance of the rails and worked to convince various railroad companies to make Marion a stop on their routes. Marion's efforts to attract railroads were largely successful. In 1852, the Bellefontaine and Indiana Railroad (eventually known as the Big Four Railroad) reached the city of Marion and connected it to Cleveland, Columbus, Cincinnati, Indianapolis, and even St. Louis—major manufacturing and metropolitan centers of the region. The Atlantic and Great Western Railway arrived in 1865 and eventually connected Marion to upstate New York. A third railroad, the Columbus and Toledo, connected Marion to the coal fields of southeastern Ohio and West Virginia and stretched north to the city of Toledo. In 1883, the Chicago and Atlanta Railroad (eventually named the Chicago and Erie) connected the city directly with two more major urban centers. A fifth and final railroad connected Marion to both southeastern Ohio and the port of Sandusky on Lake Erie in the 1890s. Thus, Marion became a regional hub offering access to major markets throughout the country.[6]

This access, which vastly exceeded that of other moderately sized cities in the region, gave Marion businesses an advantage over these other urban centers. Shipping availability, in combination with a good local supply of lumber and vast limestone deposits, supported the development of Marion's three biggest industries: farm implements, limestone, and steam shovels. The Huber Manufacturing Company formed in the 1860s and initially produced Huber's revolving hay rake, a significant technological improvement in the bundling of hay. The company soon moved into the manufacture of earth-moving scrapers and farm engines. From 1870 through 1890, Huber was the city's largest and most important production facility. It had anticipated the national turn toward mechanized farming as well as any company in the United States. At the same time, work in limestone quarries throughout Marion County employed many workers and produced lime, stone, and macadam for construction projects nationwide.[7] By the end of the nineteenth century, however, the Marion Steam Shovel Company had become the city's most important business. This enterprise sold steam shovels to construction sites all over the world and, until Harding's election in 1920, represented the county's most recognizable feature. Marion's three major industries produced heavy goods that required easy railroad access for transport, and the industries prospered as demand for their products grew together with shipping capacity. During the latter half of the nineteenth century, this success attracted workers to Marion.[8]

One way of measuring the shift in Marion County from an agricultural to industrial economy is to track the change in the percentage of the county population living in its seat. In 1860, Marion's residents represented approximately twelve percent of the county's inhabitants. By 1890, the city's share of the population had grown to a massive thirty-four percent. This trend toward urbanization continued until the Great Depression stunted growth everywhere. When George B. Christian Sr. passed away in 1930, the percentage of the county populace living in the city of Marion had reach sixty-eight percent, and the city boasted a population of more than 31,000. During the years encompassed by Christian's life, the population of the city had multiplied almost twenty-four times. Although Marion's growth had not approached the levels seen in Ohio's more dynamic cities, such as Cleveland, it had become the largest commercial hub in six surrounding counties. Marion companies had begun selling goods to national and international markets, and its steam shovels had become world renown.[9]

Christian's life offers the reader a first-hand view of the way that the economic and cultural changes that occurred between the Civil War and the Great Depression affected families and communities in small-town America. His life was altered by the many tensions and contradictions created through such transformation. For example, he opposed the expansion of the U.S. government and modern rejections of Christian morality while eagerly embracing the benefits of industrial and technological development in his business. He also dedicated much of his life to memorializing his fellow veterans, yet he opposed foreign military interventions such as World War I. Christian took great pride in supporting a large contingent of workers and their families in his community, but he also exposed those workers to daily physical dangers and opposed any collective or governmental action on their behalf. He built a fortune by riding the wave of industrial expansion, but the unyielding surge of progress eventually left his business behind. Although Christian's belief in the inferiority of other races seems jarring to the modern reader, his dedication to hard work and service inspire admiration. In short, Christian's experiences encapsulated the messiness and triumphalism of modern life.

How would George B. Christian Sr. have written his own life story? The historical record suggests that he would have told a series of anecdotes from his past. His unpublished biography of Warren G. Harding reads as a sequence of descriptive vignettes connected by informative interludes. In some ways, the life history told here seeks to emulate that narrative style. This book offers a more comprehensive examination of Christian's life than he ever wrote himself. His biography can be broken thematically into a mosaic of smaller overlapping and interconnected stories. Each chapter in this history tackles one aspect of Christian's life. Chapters appear in a rough chronological order, but occasionally aspects of the chapters' timelines fall outside a strict sequential narrative. This biography provides context for Christian's words and actions while presenting a "warts and all" portrait of his humanity.

Chapter one, "Roots and Branches," offers a genealogical portrait of George B. Christian Sr.'s family. By examining Christian's ancestors and posterity, the chapter seeks to understand the origins and florescence of Christian's beliefs, character, and position in society. In many ways, Christian's ancestors chose the context for his story by settling in Marion, Ohio, before the Civil War. The chapter also describes Christian's immediate family, including his three adult children. It presents the antecedents of Christian's story and the cast of characters who appear throughout the rest of the narrative.

Chapter two, "Christian Plays the Soldier," examines George B. Christian Sr.'s Civil War service. The chapter pushes beyond a simple narrative of his time as a soldier and examines how his service affected him throughout the rest of his life. Christian entered the army at a very young age, and his service during the Civil War occurred in the mostly inconsequential border state of Kentucky. For years after the war, Christian struggled with his ambiguous feelings toward his unexceptional military service, yet he eventually came to treasure his identity as a Union soldier. When new government regulations allowed Christian to obtain a veteran's pension, such official recognition seems to have helped Christian embrace his place in the brotherhood of ex-soldiers. He not only became an active participant in veterans' organizations, he became a leader as older veterans became incapacitated and passed away.

Chapter three, "Christian Becomes the Colonel," depicts Christian's efforts to make a living after the end of the Civil War, a time of vast economic upheaval. Christian received the nickname "the Colonel" after a famous Mark Twain literary character, and the name described his manic approach toward making a living in these tumultuous years. His entrepreneurial efforts mirrored those of many industrialists attempting to negotiate the manufacturing revolution introduced through the ubiquitous growth of railroads in the Midwest. Nevertheless, Christian's lofty ambitions met with general failure during this era.

Chapter four, "A Trip to Summerland," offers the reader a chance to accompany George B. Christian Sr. on his first journey to the almost uninhabited Atlantic Coast of central Florida in 1877. In the wake of the disputed presidential election of 1876, Christian traveled with friends and relatives through the defeated South by railroad, boat, and carriage to the Indian River. Like many writers of the day, Christian employed the conventions of travel writing to share his adventure with his friends and colleagues in Marion. Along the way, Christian commented on the potential for post-war reconciliation and growth that he observed in transit to the southern paradise.

Chapter five, "The Mirror Man," explores Christian's time as an editor of the *Marion Democratic Mirror*. The paper, along with its Marion rivals, described how politics functioned in the years after Reconstruction. The chapter argues that ownership of the *Mirror* allowed Christian to indulge his humanistic impulses. When economic travails pushed Christian away from his former role as a civil engineer, he pursued a different passion by becoming a conduit for information and opinion. Christian's writing for the *Mirror* offered him a chance to make sense of his changing world and to exert influence in the way economic growth remade his community.

Chapter six, "The Rise and Fall of a Limestone Tycoon," narrates Christian's ascension to the ranks of Marion's manufacturing elite. The chapter follows the development of the lime and stone industry in the city, as well as the growth of Christian's holdings as part of this important Marion enterprise. While Christian's quarrying and processing facility succeeded mightily for many years, his decision to sell the quarries and try to develop a new plant in Delaware County suffered from the manufacturing controls imposed during World War I. Government restrictions in combination with poor investments caused Christian to lose much of what he had gained during the successful decades of the late nineteenth and early twentieth centuries. Ultimately, Christian experienced the highs and lows that accompanied the fast-moving industrial economy enveloping the United States during his lifetime.

Chapters seven and eight, "Christian the Campaigner" and "Exposition Lost," both examine Christian's forays into the political mess that characterized Ohio governance near the turn of the twentieth century. In 1897, a revitalized local Democratic Party nominated Christian as its candidate for state senator in a district that was overwhelmingly Republican. Although Christian initially feigned disinterest and reluctance to become a candidate, the prospect of this elected position aligned perfectly with his long-term commitment to public service. Christian campaigned energetically, but he ultimately lost a close and competitive race. With this defeat he abandoned his dream to become a national politician. His loss also opened an opportunity for a young newspaper editor named Warren G. Harding to run for the same seat two years later—enabling, in part, Harding's meteoric political success. In the meantime, Christian served on the planning committee, appointed by the governor, for an exposition to celebrate Ohio's centennial. The process was exhausting and frustrating as political intrigue undermined the hard work of centennial commissioners such as Christian. The failure of this venture seems to have soured Christian's ambitions for all elective office.

Chapter nine, "Warren G. Harding: From Mentee to Colleague to Senator," examines the relationship between the Christian family and future president Warren G. Harding. George B. Christian Sr. mentored Harding in publishing and politics during Harding's early days as an editor of the *Marion Star*. This chapter and the next utilize the Christian family as a lens for understanding the much-maligned president. Marriage and experience transformed the Christian-Harding mentorship into a friendship of equals. When Harding left his job as a newspaper editor to enter the world of politics, his relationship with Christian changed again. Harding accomplished what Christian had unsuccessfully courted: political recognition. Harding's attainment garnered Christian's admiration. Christian began to imagine Harding's achievements in the Senate as vicarious personal victories, and Christian became invested in Harding's continual upward trajectory as a vindication of his own worth.

Chapter ten, "The Life and Death of a Political Friend," juxtaposes the rise of Warren G. Harding to the presidency with George B. Christian Sr.'s economic decline. Harding's success became the cause on which Christian focused as his economic prospects darkened, because his presidential election allowed Christian to more easily downplay his personal failures. Christian's investment in Harding continued even after his friend passed away and scandal besmirched his legacy. At that time, Christian took up his pen to defend the fallen leader. He championed Harding so passionately because he felt that his own legacy was wrapped in that of the former commander in chief.

Chapter eleven, "A True Christian Gentleman," examines Christian's life in the 1920s. Despite the cultural and social upheavals occurring throughout the nation during the Roaring Twenties, Christian seemed insulated from those events. During his final ten years, Christian turned once again to his historical and journalistic impulses. He wrote a variety of manuscripts that contained his impressions and ideas for posterity. He also continued to remind the people of Marion about the debts they owed to the city's veterans. Finally, Christian worked to draw closer to his family as he began to feel his mortality. During his final years, Christian grew introspective about his past, present, and future; his community; and his world.

While the great majority of Marion County residents lived in happy anonymity throughout their lives in rural Ohio, Christian's personality, ambition, and status placed him at the front of the crowd gathered at the Marion Free Baptist Church to celebrate Temperance Day in 1909. The Anti-Saloon League of America had made saloons a national issue of importance, and Christian always seemed to find a way to engage in significant debates. The narrative of Christian's life forms windows for examining the events unfolding all around him. This biography explores the ways in which George B. Christian Sr. lived through history, understood history, and became history during his lifetime, which traversed many crucial transformations of modern American society.

1 George H. Busby Property
2 John M. Christian Home
3 West Church Street Home of George B. Christian Sr.
4 East Church Street Home of George B. Christian Sr.
5 McGruder Building
6 Warren G. Harding Home
7 George B. Christian Jr. Home

Fig. 4. This adapted map shows the city of Marion in 1878. Properties associated with George B. Christian over the course of his life have been highlighted. (Map by H.G. Howland, from *Atlas of Marion County Ohio from Records and Original Surveys* [Philadelphia: Harrison, Sutton, and Hare, 1878])

CHAPTER 1

Roots and Branches

"Everyman is a quotation from all his ancestors." Ralph
Waldo Emerson, *Representative Men. Nature, Addresses and
Lectures* (Boston and New York: Houghton, Mifflin and
Company, 1855), 44.

Telling the story of George B. Christian Sr. would be impossible
without acknowledging the key role that his family played in the
development of his personality and character. Patterns of behavior,
values, and belief appear across generations. This chapter focuses
primarily on the stories of Christian's grandparents, parents, wife,
and children because they most closely influenced Christian or were
influenced by him. Like many other immigrants, Christian's ancestors
came to North America from various backgrounds, traditions, and
locations during the seventeenth and eighteenth centuries. Their
examples established a legacy of courage, ambition, and drive
that would characterize Christian's personal and professional life.
Unfortunately, his family tree also incorporated the stench of slavery
and the culture of racism. The story of George B. Christian Sr.'s
family, and his connections to them, offers context for understanding
his actions and achievements in subsequent chapters of his life.

Christian's grandparents descended from four families with
distinct paths to central Ohio. They came from different geographical,
religious, and ethnic backgrounds. While few first-hand accounts
from Christian's earliest American ancestors have survived, regional
histories and vital records offer snapshots into their lives. The
chronicle of Christian's ancestors divides into two genres of origin
stories. Christian's paternal grandparents, who descended from the

17

Miller and Christian lines, came from old and established families in Virginia. From these Old Dominion relatives, Christian inherited a sense of self-importance as well as his Democratic politics. He also gained sympathy for the South and belief in the racial hierarchies of slavery. From his maternal grandparents, who represented the Busby and Welsh lines, Christian learned about business and trade. They offered him a model of innovation and risk taking in vocation and relocation. Christian's forbearers taught him principles of leadership as they served their country, their communities, and their families. Even though all the similarities running through Christian's family tree were not passed from generation to generation, many correlations demand attention and analysis. The following paragraphs explore the ancestral lines of each of Christian's four grandparents.

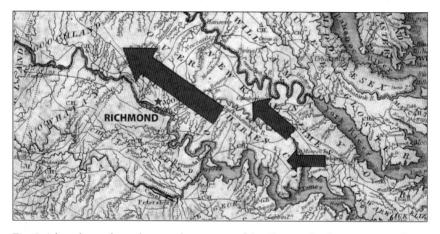

Fig. 5. Adapted map shows the general movement of the Christian family into interior of peninsular Virginia. (Map by Samuel Lewis, *A New Map of Virginia with Maryland, Delaware, etc.*, 1814. Courtesy of the Library of Congress)

George B. Christian Sr.'s great-great-great-grandfather Thomas Christian Sr. emigrated from the Isle of Man to the colony of Virginia around 1655.[1] As Thomas Christian and his family settled in the New World, they changed their Manx surname McCristyn to the Anglicized *Christian*. The family first established itself in James City County, in the area southeast of present-day Richmond. This region lies inland on the Virginia Peninsula, which is bordered to the south by the James River and to the east by the York River. Some members of the Christian family eventually moved to Charles City County, on the opposite side of the Chickahominy River. Over time, branches of the family continued to expand their settlements along the peninsular region of Virginia called the Southern Slope. Some Christians settled to the west in Goochland County, while George B. Christian Sr.'s direct ancestors landed in New Kent County located north of Charles City and James City Counties and east of Richmond. Overall, the Christian family expanded their land holdings in a northwestwardly direction toward the interior of the colony of Virginia.

The Christians entered Virginia as a family of some means, having served as judges on the Isle of Man. Thomas Christian Sr. and his father, William Christian, settled and patented land in Charles City County before 1657. In 1676, the family seems to have avoided participating in Bacon's Rebellion, which pitted many interior landholders and their indentured servants against Governor William Berkeley and the leadership of the colony. The Christians' stability helped them prosper. They eventually acquired large land holdings and slaves to accommodate their property. Members of the Christian family played a prominent role in the early history of Virginia by serving on committees of correspondence before and as officers during the Revolutionary War. Others served in the Virginia state assembly and as local justices of the peace. They even intermarried with families as famous as those of Presidents James Monroe and John Tyler.[2]

While certainly not belonging to the most influential branch of the Christian family, George B. Christian Sr.'s paternal grandfather, John Hunt Christian, built a name for himself in New Kent County. Born in 1774, John Hunt Christian served in the War of 1812 and commanded the Fifty-Second Virginia militia regiment as its lieutenant colonel. This meant that he directed the volunteer soldiers from his and a neighboring county. John Hunt Christian's commission as lieutenant colonel came from the state of Virginia for one of two reasons: either because of his service and prominence in the state militia or because of his connections to state leaders. While the early campaigns of the war had occurred in Canada and the Great Lakes region of the United States, in the spring of 1813 British Admiral Sir John Warren and his second in command, Rear Admiral Sir George Cockburn, led a flotilla of British ships that bottled up trade in the Chesapeake Bay. They also conducted periodic raids on various Virginia cities and towns including Norfolk and Hampton. The U.S. army recruited local militia regiments, including Christian's Fifty-Second, to defend the tidewater region from this British threat. Throughout the course of the War of 1812, Christian's regiment consisted of eighteen companies and possibly as many as two thousand soldiers from Charles City and New Kent Counties. Future president John Tyler, who had married one of John Hunt Christian's cousins, even commanded a company of elite riflemen within the regiment.[3]

Christian's position as a regimental commander was one of many markers of his family's influence in the region surrounding Richmond. In many ways, John Hunt Christian embodied the Southern cavalier tradition that imagined southern planters as a class of noble warrior-gentlemen. Beyond military service, members of this elite oversaw large plantations dependent on slave labor. John Hunt Christian owned fifty-eight slaves in 1820 which represented about 1.5% of all of the slaves in New Kent County. Slave ownership signified wealth and status because the slaves served as huge repositories of capital in the Antebellum South. This standing meant that plantation owners like Christian were often chosen to provide leadership in their communities. George B. Christian Sr.'s paternal family heritage connected him to this long tradition of Southern elitism that developed and lived by hierarchal and paternalistic attitudes about race and class.[4]

John Hunt Christian married Mary Heath Miller on February 26, 1811. Mary Heath Miller had been widowed with two children from her previous marriage, and she probably brought some property into the family from this earlier union. While no known records designate the geographic origin of the Miller family, property records place them in Lancaster County, Virginia, in the mid-seventeenth century. George B. Christian Sr.'s great-grandfather William Miller served as the Goochland County sheriff in the 1740s.

Fig. 6–7. Paintings of the Miller-Guerrant Family. Heath Jones Miller is the father on the left sitting beside his son John Guerrant Miller. Elizabeth Porter Guerrant Miller is seated in the other painting holding little Elizabeth Miller. George B. Christian's grandmother, Mary Heath Miller holds her bird and Jane Miller her doll. (Images courtesy of the Stengel-True Museum, Marion, OH)

The family must have enjoyed a certain amount of economic success, because in 1799, Mary Heath Miller sat with her parents and siblings for a family portrait—an option open only to the wealthy. Her mother, Elizabeth Guerrant, came from a family of Huguenots, French Protestant followers of John Calvin, many of whom fled France to avoid the religious persecutions of Louis XIV in the seventeenth century. Goochland County had become a gathering place for the descendants of the Huguenots, and the French immigrants rapidly assimilated into their surroundings. George B. Christian Sr. often invoked his Huguenot heritage, knowing that his great-great-grandfather Jean Guerrant served as a major in the American Revolution under George Washington at Valley Forge.

Christian's French ancestry, passed to him through the Miller line, connected him to a strain of devout religious pilgrims whose association with the foundation of the nation played a significant role in Christian's own identity and origin story.[5]

Of all his grandparents, George Henry Busby most inspired George B. Christian Sr.'s admiration and emulation. Busby was also probably the only grandparent Christian ever met. Busby was born in Darston/Derrstown (present-day Lewisburg), Pennsylvania, on July 10, 1794.[6] His father had emigrated from Ireland, and the family settled in the huge but sparsely populated county of Northumberland, Pennsylvania. Busby eventually moved with his family to Fairfield County, Ohio, around 1810.

Fig. 8. Portrait of George Henry Busby (Courtesy of the Roberts Family Library)

Shortly thereafter the War of 1812 broke out. A year into the conflict, the British and their Native American allies threatened the Ohio frontier after defeating U.S. forces in Michigan. General William Henry Harrison, future president of the United States, constructed Fort Meigs

Fig. 9. Fort Meigs was located southwest of Lake Erie. (Richard W. Stewart, *American Military History: The United States Army and the Forging of a Nation, 1775–1917* [Washington, D.C.: Center of Military History, 2005])

overlooking the Maumee River near present-day Perrysburg, Ohio, as a vanguard against a potential invasion into the state.

Fig. 10. Illustration depicting General William Henry Harrison who spoke to the young George H. Busby, winning the soldier's support when he ran for president. (Courtesy of the Library of Congress)

The Maumee River had strategic value because it offered one of the most convenient waterways from Canada through Lake Erie to the Old Northwest.[7] Almost immediately after engineers completed the fort, it was threatened by the loss of troops whose enlistments had expired as well as an impending British and Native American attack. The fort withstood a siege near the end of April 1813. With the help of reinforcements from the Kentucky militia, Harrison and his troops slowly repelled the invaders. During this moment of peril, Busby was among the Ohio volunteers raised by a Captain Hooker to march to the relief of Fort Meigs. Fatefully, the British-led troops had been defeated and left Fort Meigs on May 8, 1813—a day after Busby had joined the state militia. The Ohio volunteers had no way of knowing the threat had ended, so they marched to the relief of the fort. Nonetheless, the retreat of the enemy meant that Harrison had little need for the thousand militia volunteers. He gave a rousing speech thanking the troops for their sacrifice and sent them home. This single interaction made Busby a loyal supporter of the general when he ran for president years later as the Whig Party candidate. Because of these fortuitous events, Busby returned to Fairfield County after a mere eighteen days of military service.[8]

Busby's enlistment in the War of 1812 was short and mostly insignificant. He was recalled and served for thirty-seven days, beginning in July of 1813, when it appeared that the British and their allies might renew their attack on Fort Meigs. Even though the danger proved overstated, the Ohio volunteers guarded the countryside, while more experienced troops pushed the enemy out of the region. This victory allowed Harrison to dismiss the Ohio volunteers permanently. Thus, Busby's military service in the War of 1812 added up to less than two months of actual time as a soldier. Busby eventually received a bounty of land for his service—though his short participation in the conflict, consisting of two abbreviated and unnecessary calls to aid an Ohio fort, was probably insufficient to legally qualify him for this perk. Military records show that Busby never achieved a rank higher than private during his time in the War of 1812. Consequently, his nickname of Major must have emerged out of civilian life. Busby possibly gained this mock rank during his time in the U.S. House of Representatives or as he outlived other veterans and became a symbol of the War of 1812 in his community. An article in the *Marion Independent* once complained about the tendency of Marion Democrats to give military titles to their leaders as a means to combat the perception of the party as disloyal which emerged out of the Civil War. Busby used his faux-military rank to remind others of his service and to maintain a sense of importance as a leader in the community of Marion.[9]

In 1818, shortly after his military service, Busby met and married his first wife, Elizabeth Welsh. The historical record offers limited insight about the ancestry of Christian's maternal grandmother. Elizabeth Welsh's grandfather emigrated from England sometime before the Revolutionary War and settled in Maryland, where Elizabeth's father, Zachariah, was born. His daughter, Elizabeth Welsh, was probably born in present-day Charles Town in Jefferson County, West Virginia, sometime around the turn of the nineteenth century. She moved with her family to Ross County, Ohio, around 1810. Consequently, she arrived in Ohio at about the same time that George Busby and his family relocated there. In 1818, Welsh and Busby married in Fairfield County. They moved to Marion County sometime in the 1820s after a new treaty pushed

Native Americans out of a reservation partially situated within the county's future boundaries. Both the Busby and Welsh families came to the United States in the eighteenth century and followed a path of gradual migration to the interior of the new nation until they reached central Ohio. Elizabeth passed away in 1825, and Busby struggled to raise his young family for several years until eventually marrying Eliza Kennedy.[10]

George H. Busby and his family became some of the founding settlers of the town of Marion. In the fledgling village, he worked as a trader—a vocation that likely involved providing goods to both white and indigenous residents. A biographical sketch, probably written by George B. Christian Sr., recorded that Busby's "energy and push laid the foundation of a handsome fortune, that was far more speedily destroyed by the unfortunate tendency that characterized our father of 'going bail.'" The phrase *going bail* referred to Busby's tendency to offer his property as security for criminals' release. If any of those offenders jumped bail, Busby had to sell his property to cover the debt. While the historical record offers no other verification of Christian's willingness to gamble with his resources in this manner, contemporary literature confirms that many wealthy individuals suffered from the liabilities of going bail in the nineteenth century.[11]

In the long run, George Busby built a reputation in the community because of his public service more than his business dealings. When the Ohio legislature passed the bill forming Marion County in 1822, it appointed three judges to create a county charter and appoint officers to serve in the new jurisdiction. The judges chose George H. Busby to serve as the county's first clerk. This appointment probably came because Busby's education rendered him suitable for a position that required substantial record keeping. Busby prevailed in Marion County's first elections in 1823 when the people chose to retain him as the county clerk. The name of his position changed from county clerk to county recorder in the fourteen years he served. As part of his job, Busby logged land transactions and documented the actions of the county and court. Even after he left office in 1837, Busby could not stay out of the limelight for long. He ran as the Democratic candidate for the Ohio House of Representatives in 1845, but lost the nomination in a close race to another Democrat. Despite this setback, Busby ambitiously ran for the U.S. Congress in 1850 and won. He served a single two-year term in the House of Representatives from 1851–1853 as part of the Thirty-Second Congress.[12]

Busby's election occurred in the wake of the Compromise of 1850, which admitted California to the nation as a free state while creating the territories of Utah and New Mexico and allowing them to choose their own path regarding slavery. The settlement also abolished slavery in the District of Columbia and created a national fugitive slave law.[13] While the agreement tried to mitigate the most explosive tensions over slavery, it eventually led to the regional bifurcation of both the Democrats and Whigs. Busby's campaign and short stint in Congress came during this tumultuous sectional strife. His victory marked the last time that a Democratic candidate from Marion prevailed in a Congressional race for many years. During his time in Congress, Busby generally voted with his fellow Democrats. He opposed government efforts to subsidize railroad expansion but favored plans to give away federal land to settlers willing to develop it. Politicians ultimately rejected both ideas, at least until the emerging Republican Party resurrected them for political gain in the 1860s. The major issues facing the Thirty-Second Congress seemed small compared to the massive compromises that had taken place in the previous two years or the Kansas-Nebraska controversy that would tear the country apart in the next legislative session.[14]

Busby relinquished his seat at the end of his term to Democrat Thomas Ritchey from neighboring Delaware County. He continued to garner respect in the community, however, for his actions during the deadly cholera outbreak of 1854. During this time, immigrants brought the dreaded disease into the country and spread it as they moved west. Busby gained a reputation for compassion by remaining in the city to tend to the sick and dying while many fled in fear for their lives. In future years, Busby ran for state senator, probate judge, justice of the peace, and county auditor but suffered defeat in each election. Busby's political career floundered as conflicts over slavery tore the Democratic Party asunder in the North. Like many other Democrats, Busby held mixed feelings about the conflict. He had always opposed abolitionists, and in 1864 he supported Lincoln's opponent George McClellan. It was only after the Civil War, in 1866, that the people of Marion once again chose the Democratic Busby for elected office, as probate judge for Marion County. His judicial service generally garnered little notice in the local newspapers, but he did create controversy when he unwittingly issued a marriage license for a black man and a white woman. The ensuing storm of condemnation demonstrated how the conclusion of the Civil War had not erased racism within American society. In a post-emancipation world, Americans had to find new ways to organize their perceptions of race. American society and law governed racial boundaries by limiting sexual contact between the races, and Busby had accidentally permitted this couple to defy such societal norms. Despite the controversy, Busby held his judicial position until he passed away in 1869 at the age of 75.[15]

George B. Christian Sr.'s parents represented a merger of Southern aristocracy and entrepreneurial trailblazing, and Christian and his siblings lived with the ironies, tensions, and creativity which resulted from the union. On March 21, 1821, George B. Christian Sr.'s father, John M. Christian, was born in New Kent County, Virginia.

Fig. 11. John Christian attended Rumford Academy, a prestigious preparatory academy in King William, Virginia. Rumford served as a conduit to the state's premier educational institution, the College of William and Mary. (Courtesy of King William Historical Society)

Christian received a preparatory education at the Rumford Academy, one of the oldest in the state. The school was founded in 1775 to prepare students for the College of William and Mary, Virginia's greatest educational institution at the time. Unfortunately, Christian's family soon faced economic setbacks associated with the Panic of 1837. The origins of this financial strife were in the government's decision not to renew the charter of the Second Bank of the United States in 1832.[16] Consequently, the bank dissolved in 1836, and U.S. markets lost this principal stabilizing force of the country's money supply.[17]

With the demise of the Second Bank of the United States, local banks grew rapidly. Their unregulated lending standards created an economic bubble during the 1830s. In the South, new banks offered slaveholders the ability not only to mortgage their land but also their slaves. This permitted slaveholders to monetize both the labor and the perceived economic value of their slaves. Because intense demand for cotton had inflated the crop's value, planters anticipated large returns as they borrowed to expand its cultivation. Easy credit and high crop yields inflated the value of everything associated with the Southern plantation: land, slaves, and supplies. Despite the appearance of prosperity, slave owners' assets were dangerously leveraged. The bubble of land speculation and growth collapsed when the federal government announced that it would no longer accept local bank currencies in payment for federal land. The government's demand for payment in gold or silver quickly sucked up large quantities of precious metals and deflated the value of bank-issued paper money. Credit became very difficult for both banks and their customers to acquire. Commodity prices fell as the money supply dwindled both at home and abroad, which left planters unable to pay their debts. Banks tried to foreclose on mortgaged property and slaves, but collapsing markets led to institutional failures. With the Christian family fortune tied into land and slaves, the effects of the Panic of 1837 proved devastating. The family's prospects darkened even more when patriarch John Hunt Christian passed away in 1839.[18]

John M. Christian departed from Virginia because the family estate had eroded during these difficult years. Christian left his ancestral Virginia roots to work as one of Marion's first postal clerks, an appointment he probably received because of his family connections. Christian's uncle, John Guerrant Miller had moved to Columbus, Ohio, in 1830 and had served as the mayor and postmaster of the city, a job he received when his brother-in-law John Tyler became President of the United States. Whether Tyler also gave Christian, who was the president's cousin, a similar appointment is difficult to surmise, but it seems plausible. Christian's government earnings afforded him an education from Ohio University, in Athens, Ohio. This university was the first institution of higher education in the Old Northwest, and it had become a reputable college by the time John M. Christian arrived there in 1843. He received a classical education, which meant that he studied ancient languages, philosophy, literature, history, natural science, and mathematics. After graduating in 1844, Christian became the principal of the Marion Academy where he also taught. He then returned to Ohio University and received a master's degree in 1848.[19]

Fig. 12. Illustration depicting Ohio University (Athens) in 1847. (Henry Howe, *Historical Collections of Ohio: History Both General and Local, Geography with Descriptions of its Counties, Cities and Villages, Its Agricultural, Manufacturing, Mining and Business Development, Sketches of Eminent and Interesting Characters, Etc., With Notes of a Tour Over It in 1886*, Vol. 1 [Cincinnati: State of Ohio, 1888])

In Marion, John M. Christian became acquainted with Pauline Busby, daughter of George Busby, and they married on March 26, 1846. The birth of their first son, George Busby Christian, occurred nine months and one day later. A second child, Mary Heath Christian, came two years after that. Christian's career as a teacher took him to Madison County, Ohio, after completing his master's degree. Nevertheless, he must have felt unsettled in his vocation as an educator, because he relocated his family to Lawrenceburg, Indiana, in 1851 to begin practicing as a homeopathic physician.

The field of homeopathic medicine originated with a German physician named Samuel Hahnemann, who theorized that illnesses should be remedied by medicines that caused similar symptoms to the maladies being treated. Thus, a homeopathic doctor might treat nausea with a small dose of ipecac syrup. While this theory of treatment has since been discredited, homeopathic doctors became popular in the United States at the time because their relatively unobtrusive methods often allowed the body to heal itself much more gently and effectively than the unhygienic bloodletting and overmedicating practices of traditional doctors. Homeopaths generally treated patients with very small dosages of drugs that were finely catered to their individual symptoms. When it came to injuries, the doctors employed the same techniques as traditional physicians, but were less likely to resort to surgery to repair damaged bones and tissues. Homeopathic physicians' ability to customize their treatments made them the doctors of choice for the rich and powerful.[20]

John M. Christian began studying and practicing homeopathic medicine as it was gaining credibility among the general public. While the precise chronology of his training and the initiation of his practice remain vague, Christian came to Indiana to study or apprentice in homeopathy. Either learning scenario might explain the short duration of the Christian family's stay in Indiana. Lawrenceburg is located across the river from Cincinnati, Ohio, which hosted several medical schools specializing in homeopathic methods. This proximity made Lawrenceburg a prime location for learning the vocation. After three years away, John M. Christian returned to Marion to practice medicine in his wife's hometown. Interestingly, the Christian family's sojourn in Indiana almost directly coincided with George Busby's time serving in Washington, DC, as a part of the Thirty-Second Congress. When Busby returned to Marion, his daughter was not far behind in her homecoming. It seems that Busby might have offered to help Christian develop a medical practice in the city in order to bring his daughter and grandchildren closer to home. John and Pauline Christian went back to Marion with three children—Pauline had given birth to Carrie Christian in 1854. The family never moved away from the city again.[21]

As the Christians put down roots in Marion, John M. Christian became involved in city politics. Busby's prominence in the Marion Democratic Party probably helped Christian achieve acceptance and leadership within that group. As early as September of 1858, John M. Christian appeared with his father-in-law and Philip Dombaugh as an author of a notice from the members of Marion's Democratic Central Committee. By 1859, Christian had become the chairman of this committee. In addition, he often served as a delegate in local, state, and national nominating conventions. As the Civil War approached in 1860, Christian worked intensely to promote the causes of the Democratic Party despite growing Northern animosity toward slaveholders. He became one of Stephen F. Douglas's "invincibles," the name given to organized advocates and demonstrators on behalf of the Democratic presidential candidate, who they claimed was unbeatable. Christian visited other Ohio communities to discuss the necessity of Douglas's election. Having grown up in Virginia, Christian assuredly held some of the biases and political resentments that characterized the South in the years leading up to the Civil War. Christian probably supported Douglas because the "Little Giant" (a nickname that referred to the senator's stature) felt that slavery should not become a regional and economic wedge between North and South.[22]

Unfortunately, war broke out in 1860, and John M. Christian displayed mixed feelings about the justice of a fight he believed the Union was waging to suppress the free will of Southern citizens. With most of his cousins and siblings still living in the South, Christian felt a more personal connection with the Confederacy than most of his friends and neighbors. He had not supported President Abraham Lincoln's election and, like many other Democrats, proved quite critical about wartime decisions made by the commander in chief. Nevertheless, many of Christian's Ohio relatives and family members, including his oldest son, served as part of the Union forces or advocated for the Union cause. In the end, Christian served as a part of the loyal opposition to the war effort, which claimed devotion to the Union while criticizing the sectionalism and abolitionism undergirding the conflict.

John M. Christian's Southern heritage and leadership in the Democratic Party made him a target for overly enthusiastic Republican conspiracy theorists. In the aftermath of the attack on Fort Sumter, which lit the fires of conflict between North and South, Ohio Republican Unionists began to attack Ohio Democrats both verbally and physically for their supposed disloyalty. In the wake of mob action, Marion Democrats came together in a pledge to defend one another in the event of even

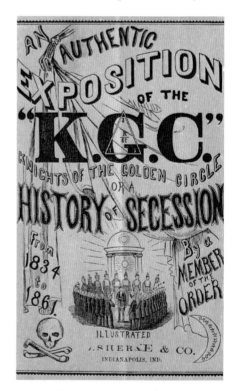

Fig. 11. This tract was written by a supposed member of the Knights of the Golden Circle. (*An Authentic Exposition of the K.G.C., Knights of the Golden Circle: or a History of Secession from 1834 to 1861* [Indianapolis, IN: C.O. Perrine, 1861])

greater violence or persecution. This mutual defense pact became an open secret, because the Democrats wanted Republican bullies to know they stood ready to protect themselves.[23]

Local Republican reactions to this Democratic pledge soon pulled John M. Christian into a national wartime controversy. In 1861, Marion Republicans accused John M. Christian and Thomas Hodder, the editor of the *Marion Democratic Mirror,* of covenanting to commit treason as part of the Knights of the Golden Circle, a fraternal organization devoted to destroying the Union. The Knights descended from the tradition of semisecret brotherhoods, tied together through ritual, oath, and gesture, which had become quite common in the years leading up to the war. Almost all these groups borrowed aspects of their ceremonies from the Freemasons. Like the Masons, these societies tried to keep their rituals away from public scrutiny. One prominent group molded in this fashion was the Know-Nothings, created in the 1850s as a fraternal organization built around anti-immigrant and anti-Catholic sentiments and actions. In Texas, another secret brotherhood developed to support filibusterers who sought to expand the practice of black slavery into Mexico, Cuba, and Central America through conquest. Both the Know-Nothings and the Southern filibusterers offered a model, as confidential societies formed to advocate specific causes, for the Knights of the Golden Circle.[24]

George Bickley, a Virginia native who had moved to Cincinnati, founded the Knights to acquire the resources and manpower to conquer a Latin American country and make him a military ruler over a new cotton kingdom. Bickley created a series of oaths and ceremonies to bind supporters together and vowed to keep the identities of members secret. Bickley had failed in his other business ventures, and the Knights became his desperate attempt to reimagine himself as a gladiator for expanding the slave-holding South. As relations between North and South deteriorated in early 1860, Bickley sought to repurpose his Knights to promote Southern rights and self-defense. He traveled to the rebel capital in Montgomery, Alabama, and unsuccessfully offered his services to the Confederacy. Undaunted by this rejection, Bickley struck out on his own and set up his society's wartime headquarters in Knoxville, Tennessee.

Bickley desperately promoted his organization not only because he was a true believer in the Southern cause, but because he depended on the dues of members for his livelihood. Consequently, he made exaggerated claims that the group boasted a roster of thousands and played a significant role as secret soldiers for the Confederacy within Union territory. While historians disagree about the actual reach and scope of the Knights of the Golden Circle among groups that opposed the Civil War in the North, most agree that the perception of the Knights as a vast paramilitary organization was overblown and created, in part, out of Bickley's self-interest. His efforts to publicize them eventually caught the attention of Northern journalists who wrote exposés about this underground army. The reporters used the source materials created by Bickley, often uncritically, as the primary evidence for their profiles. By writing about Bickley's sensational claims and his previous residence in Cincinnati, journalists drove midwestern Republicans' fear of traitors within their communities. Some Northern alarmists even claimed that the Democrats who opposed the war, commonly known as copperheads because their treachery could poison the North like a venomous snake, secretly belonged to the militarized Knights. War blurred the line between the perception of threat and actual danger.[25]

In Marion, Republicans saw an opportunity to harness the general fear of sedition for their political ends. Some local Republicans felt that Democrats exercised traitorous sympathies for the South, and this conviction allowed the Republicans to justify framing their rivals. After the closed meeting where Marion Democrats made their mutual defense pledge, a Republican presented city officials (also Republicans) with a second oath supposedly sworn by John M. Christian, Thomas Hodder, and other Democrats as part of the proceedings. Purported witnesses claimed that each person who took the second oath promised, "I will not rest or sleep until Abraham Lincoln, now President, shall be removed from the Presidential chair; and I will wade in blood up to my knees, as soon as Jefferson Davis sees proper to march with his army to take the city of Washington and the White House."[26] Accusers claimed that the combined oaths of self-defense and militant resistance were part of the secret rituals through which Marion Democrats entered the notorious Knights of the Golden Circle. Consequently, Marion officials promptly arrested oath participants Christian and Hodder for sedition. Even though others participated, Marion Republicans targeted Hodder for his open criticism of Republicans, the president, and the war effort in the pages of the *Mirror*. They focused on John M. Christian because of his effective leadership among local Democrats. These accusations were groundless. No credible evidence survives that ties either of the two men to the Knights of the Golden Circle.[27]

The two Democrats' arrests soon made national headlines. While journalists had depended on George Bickley's propaganda campaign when they broke the story of the society's existence, its secret practices meant that reporters had very little idea about how many people belonged to the organization and the nature of its rituals. While all surviving evidence suggests that the membership of the group was quite small, wartime anxiety fueled irrational fears of a massive Democratic conspiracy to fight against the Union cause. The official court proceedings against mainstream Democrats like Christian and Hodder for their alleged membership in the Knights seemingly gave legitimacy to concerns about Democratic perfidy. Consequently, newspapers throughout the country commented on the Marion arrests as real evidence of the Knights' pervasiveness within the Union.

Nevertheless, Republicans soon learned the truth about Marion's Democrats. When the district court held hearings for Hodder and Christian in Cleveland, where they had been imprisoned, the defendants presented evidence of politically motivated false testimony.

Because the prosecution's entire case rested on this faulty testimony from partisan witnesses, the U.S. commissioner dismissed both cases without trial. Christian and the Democrats of Marion continued to face accusations of traitorous behavior, but the case proved that political sympathy for the Confederacy was not synonymous with treason. Christian's integrity during the whole affair allowed him to maintain the respect of most Marionites and continue his role as an esteemed physician after the war ended.[28]

John M. Christian maintained his position as a leader in the local Democratic Party after the war. His participation in Democratic conventions remained unchanged, and his fellow party members in Marion and surrounding communities sought him out for his eloquent oratory. In December of 1867, Christian ran for school commissioner in Marion, but was defeated. A year later he ran for mayor of Marion, but lost when controversy arose about whether his house and property actually rested within the city boundaries. In 1869, he even gained some traction as a candidate for Ohio state treasurer, but he was beaten out in the early ballots of the nominating process. Though he continued to play a role in the Democratic Party itself, Christian must have decided that he suffered from bad luck as a candidate, because he stopped seeking public office for about ten years after his candidacy for this statewide office ended.[29]

Christian's failures at the ballot box contrasted with his renewed family life. After Pauline Busby Christian passed away sometime during the Civil War, John M. Christian married Josephine Elizabeth Norris on September 12, 1867. Eleven months later the couple welcomed their first child, George Christian's half-brother Daniel Norris Christian. Two more children joined the family in the next eight years. The Christians' youngest daughter, Berenice, was born in January of 1876, shortly before John M. Christian's fifty-fifth birthday and six years before he passed away. Thus, Christian's second marriage greatly increased his familial responsibilities in his mature years as he and his spouse raised a trio of young children.[30]

Although John M. Christian left no known records about his medical practice, a few facts emerge from newspaper accounts about his professional life. Like most other country physicians of the era, Christian made house calls. Marion newspapers recorded several accounts of Dr. Christian's horses getting away from him or throwing him off. While Christian probably dealt with a spirited team of horses, the many accidents attested to the bad road conditions faced by a country doctor forced to travel quickly through rural areas to treat his patients. Christian cared for a variety of conditions from broken bones to major illnesses. His medical expertise even caused county officials to recruit him to serve on the local board of health. While his training in homeopathy triggered his pharmaceutical minimalism and his hesitancy to turn to surgical techniques, his treatments also developed through observation as well as trial and error. Christian believed that attitude and optimism played a significant role in the recovery of the infirm, so he employed laughter and positivity in his medical practice. Though Christian's treatments offered little medical benefit to his patients, his careful concern for them probably served them as well as the efforts of more traditional doctors who had generally not yet adopted antiseptic techniques. He readily embraced the medical maxim found in the Hippocratic oath "*Primum non nocere*" or "First, do no harm."[31]

Christian's success as a physician aided in his election as county coroner in 1878. This position served both a medical and judicial role during this era. Christian conducted and supervised autopsies to determine the causes of all deaths in Marion County. If the reason for a death was in doubt, he could convene an inquest, a legal proceeding with subpoena power where evidence was presented and he determined the official cause of death. Christian's decisions might establish whether a suspicious death would lead to an investigation for murder. He also settled matters of liability in workplace accidents. Christian's election as coroner seemed to vindicate his many previous political failures and allowed him to serve in a public office that used both his medical talents and his education. He had worked as a leader within the Democratic Party ever since he came to Marion, but his Southern background and perceived wartime disloyalty probably held him back from winning any of the elective offices he sought over the years. By the end of his life, the political tide in Ohio had turned against Republican Reconstruction efforts and in favor of Democrats like Christian. Unfortunately, Christian passed away before his term as coroner expired.[32]

John M. Christian died on June 29, 1882, and his son George B. Christian Sr. offered a detailed account of John Christian's illness and death in a short article the son wrote as the editor and publisher of the *Marion Democratic Mirror*. According to George Christian, John M. Christian found a black spot near his left ear, which doctors diagnosed as skin cancer approximately a year before his death. A short time later a red lump appeared on Christian's neck, which his doctors treated through medication. Nonetheless, his health continued to deteriorate as he suffered from severe digestive problems and pain in his left hip. Through further examinations it became apparent that his body was riddled with cancer—especially throughout his digestive system. Even though Christian's health had quickly declined, the timing of his passing shocked his family.

His death also affected the city of Marion. Even though many people might have disagreed with his politics, Christian had become a beloved member of the community. Presbyterian Reverend E. B. Raffensperger summarized the doctor's character through his eulogy, in which he remarked:

> There was not a member of our Church whose presence added so much to the cheer and enjoyment of our social meetings, and it is seldom our privilege to listen to a man in the prayer meeting whose utterances are so full of the grace of Christ as were the prayers of Doctor Christian, which are now ended.[33]

The people of Marion honored Christian for his service to the community and his optimism. Both were traits George B. Christian Sr. sought to integrate into his own life.[34]

While attributing all of George B. Christian Sr.'s personality and character traits to his family tree seems too deterministic, too many attributes persisted through generations to completely ignore the man's antecedents. Christian's ancestors helped build the colony of Virginia after leaving their homes in Great Britain and France. They participated in the struggle for independence and in the building of the early republic in Virginia, Pennsylvania, and Ohio. From his father's side of the family, Christian learned about the South: its institutions, hierarchies, and successes. On his mother's side he found a model of trailblazing and entrepreneurship in the Old Northwest. From the combined experiences of his forbearers, Christian discovered the value of public service and party loyalty. He emulated his ancestors' patriotism and military service. He also witnessed the benefits of hard work and friendship. Like his relatives who served in their communities, Christian showed leadership throughout his life. His ability to connect with others and his relentless innovation helped him become one of the most successful businessmen and public figures in Marion—at least for a time.

George B. Christian Sr. was the oldest of John M. Christian's six children. Born on December 27, 1846, in Marion, Ohio, Christian moved with his parents to Indiana and back to Marion as his father established his medical practice. Christian Sr. left very little record of his childhood. His early years would have been framed by the small-town setting of Marion in the 1840s and 1850s. Before the Civil War, the town housed fewer than two thousand people and found distinction principally as the county seat. As with most children of his era, Christian probably grew up facing a mix of school, work, and play. His father invested in a great deal of property, and

Christian surely spent much of his time cleaning, repairing, and building. Such efforts may have fueled his aptitudes for construction and business. Christian graduated from Marion Grammar School, under the tutelage of Reverend J. M. Heller, with many friends and future Marion leaders. Even as a teenager, Christian exhibited signs of his precocious nature. On March 30, 1860, he delivered a formal speech at the closing exercises of Marion High School. The irony of the speech's title—"Thoughts of the Future"—became apparent in subsequent years, with the onset of the Civil War.[35]

Christian, like most of his contemporaries, quickly became lost in the anticipation of fighting for his country. He later recalled that most of the town's male youth drilled as soldiers during their free time and dreamed of marching off to war. While he might have previously served as a drummer boy before his official enlistment, at seventeen, Christian became a private in the war effort. He was fortunate to serve in Kentucky—far away from the brutality and carnage of more traditional battlefields. Christian came home in early 1864 because of illness and avoided the final, bloody standoffs of the war. In later years, Christian embarked on a variety of business ventures and also spent time working in the county recorder's and surveyor's offices. Later chapters address both Christian's Civil War service and early career in greater detail.

George B. Christian Sr.'s ancestors influenced the person he became, and he sought to similarly affect his wife and children through his roles as husband and father. In many ways, Christian's love and devotion toward his spouse and children permeated the other aspects of his life examined throughout this book. Christian's wife, Lydia, and his three children served as central characters in his life story.

In 1869, a short time after
George H. Busby passed away,
George B. Christian Sr. married
Lydia Ellen Morris. She came
from a family of early settlers
in Green Camp (also called
Berwick), Ohio, several miles
southwest of Marion on the
Scioto River. The Morris family
had settled in Green Camp in
1824, less than a year after Lydia
Morris's father was born. By
the time George B. Christian
Sr. married Lydia Morris, her
family's farm, located across the
river and to the south of the

Fig. 14. Young Lydia Morris Christian.
(Courtesy of the Roberts Family Library)

village of Green Camp, had become one of the most prominent in the
area. The Morris family had originally emigrated from Wales in the
early eighteenth century and had settled temporarily in Maryland and
Delaware before moving to Ohio.[36]

While no records survive that describe how Lydia and George
Christian met or the nature of their courtship, their paths probably
crossed along one of several junctures. For example, John Riley
Delbert Morris, the family patriarch, attended the Marion Academy
at the same time that John M. Christian directed and taught there.
Morris would have been one of John Christian's first students
at a time when the future doctor was little more than a student
himself. Morris and John Christian could have maintained a long-
term acquaintance that allowed them to introduce their children.
George Christian also engaged in a variety of road-building
projects throughout Marion County as an engineer, surveyor, and
contractor. Morris had contracted for similar projects. Christian
possibly met Lydia Morris as he and his crews built roads to isolated

villages such as Green Camp. In addition, George Christian and John Morris might have worked together on a building project that created the opportunity for the couple's paths to cross. They could not have met in church, because she was Methodist and he was Presbyterian. Also, John Morris came from an abolitionist background and belonged to the Republican Party, while Christian was a Democrat. However Lydia Morris and George Christian met and fell in love, they married on October 14, 1869, at the Morris family estate. Reverend Leroy A. Belt, a Methodist minister who later became the second president of Ohio Northern University, officiated over the wedding.[37]

The historical record contains tragically little about Lydia Christian, mother of four. The *Marion Democratic Mirror*, when reporting about her wedding to Christian, described her as accomplished, meaning highly trained, educated, or skilled with many achievements. In typical fashion, the paper declined to list any of the things that made her accomplished. Throughout the nineteenth century, women were haunted by what historians have identified as the cult of domesticity. Producers of popular culture developed feminine ideals that middle-class women sought to incorporate in their lives and identities. Concepts such as piety, purity, submission, and domesticity became the standards by which society judged women. Social norms portrayed marriage as an agreement where the wife assented to the labors of the home, including the rearing of children, in exchange for the monetary support provided by her husband. Husbands expected wives to stay out of the public sphere where politics, salaried work, and male socialization took place.[38]

While Lydia Christian, like most women, rarely complied completely with the expectations society placed on her, these values set the boundaries of behavior for respectable women. George B. Christian Sr.'s responsibilities as a husband forced him into the workplace and the realm of public discourse, where he left a significant historical footprint in public records, newspapers, and public correspondence. On the other hand, the expectations that domesticity exerted on Lydia Christian made her less visible in the public records which repositories collect. The few accounts we have about Lydia Christian either come from her private correspondence or in descriptions of her participating in what were perceived as acceptable women's activities. Despite the dearth of records about Lydia Christian, she played an essential role in the lives of George B. Christian Sr. and her children.[39]

Tragedy struck the family a few years after the Christians' marriage. Their first-born child, Pauline "Lena" Christian, passed away a month before her second birthday. As a result of this loss, the Christians often reached out to comfort others when illness or accident claimed a child's life. Lydia Christian gave birth to a second child, George B. Christian Jr., less than a year after Lena's death. Mamie Christian was born two years after her brother, and Mildred Christian came eight years after her older sister. Like most women of the era, Lydia Christian probably spent much of her time overseeing the family household. George B. Christian Sr. seems to have dedicated significant time to his various economic projects. Lydia Christian showed patience as her husband moved from scheme to scheme and the family faced the difficulties of dealing with his businesses' inconsistent income streams.

Despite any hardships Lydia Christian faced as the wife of a serial entrepreneur, she and her husband seem to have participated in an active social life. The Christians often traveled to see friends and family as far away as Florida and as close as the surrounding townships. In addition, they participated in the Marion social scene, interacting with families of similar means and status. They fulfilled some of these obligations as a couple and others separately. Social expectations required them to host events in their home and visit the homes of their friends. The couple also attended various fundraisers, meetings, parties, and other public gatherings. Women often planned and coordinated these activities, which allowed them to demonstrate their leadership capacity at a time when they were still expected to spend most of their time at home taking care of their children and household.

As their children grew and George Christian's income increased, Lydia Christian found more time to engage with other women in the community. While her name was not actively associated with some of the more controversial feminine causes of the day such as temperance or suffrage, Lydia Christian served quite actively with the Marion Relief Society, which worked to alleviate the suffering of the city's poor and sick. For example, she played a leadership role in an 1890 potato drive, overseeing the society's efforts to distribute donated money to poor farmers to buy the potatoes they grew but could not store or sell by conventional means. Lydia Christian also engaged in relief efforts for Marion's veterans and their wives who suffered from disabilities and poverty.[40]

Fig. 15. Lydia Morris Christian. (Courtesy of the Roberts Family Library)

One interesting way to analyze Lydia Christian's role within the Marion community is to consider a series of formal teas given at her home in 1909. Afternoon teas were fashionable social affairs among middle-class women of the time. At a five o'clock tea on December 7, 1909, Lydia Christian and her daughter Mildred hosted fifty-five callers. An article in the *Mirror* described the elaborate decorations, which included chrysanthemums and carnations picked and arranged by the hostesses. Place cards at each table with intricate watercolor sketches of flowers not only dictated seating but also demonstrated the level of detail expected at such events. In addition, such formal teas allowed the hostesses to

44

display expensive and ornate tea sets to their peers. At the follow-up tea a few days later, the Christian home was draped with a different floral décor of sweet peas and wild roses. The guest list included a slightly different roster of invitees. Guests at these social occasions often reached beyond the Marion region. For example, among Lydia and Mildred Christian's guests were several acquaintances from the state of New York. The meticulous planning, decorating, and cooking that went into these events demonstrated the importance of social obligations in the lives of the Christian family. Social events cemented friendships and set expectations for inclusion among this group of women. Accommodating this kind of event proved that the Christian family had the discretionary income to afford to feed so many visitors and the time to prepare such elaborate spectacles. While the Christians assuredly just wanted to throw a good party for their friends, these gatherings also carried implicit social meaning about the Christian women's place within the community.[41]

No letters penned by Lydia Christian have survived, but her letters from Warren G. Harding show the depth of her friendship with the future first family. Harding generally wrote to George Christian, but on occasion he directed his correspondence to Lydia Christian, whom he had nicknamed "Coonie Calvin."[42] For example, during the Hardings' trips to Europe in 1907 and 1909, Warren G. Harding directed his letters to Lydia Christian to share with her a taste of their transatlantic travels. Lydia had never visited Europe, and Harding probably wanted to let her travel vicariously with him and his wife. Two other letters from Harding came in 1916 and 1922. Both arrived at Christmastime and sought to uplift Lydia Christian from poor health. It seems that she suffered from what she thought were nervous attacks, a common diagnosis of the era. Harding's desire to encourage and share experiences with Lydia Christian offers a window into the affection and respect Harding felt for her. These letters also prove that the relationship between the Hardings and the Christians extended beyond masculine and feminine boundaries.[43]

While newspapers and community histories generally focus on events instead of relationships, a few observations offer a glimpse into the bonds of family love that existed in the Christian marriage and home. George and Lydia Christian's marriage endured until the end of their lives, and they maintained close contact with their children and extended family. While the social stigma associated with divorce served as a powerful disincentive in the nineteenth century, the Christians' nearly sixty years of marriage still represented a significant accomplishment and commitment. Although no letters between George and Lydia Christian have survived, the couples' correspondence with others offers a window into their relationship. For example, in a letter written on Christmas Day, 1920, from Warren G. Harding to Lydia Christian, Harding joked that George B. Christian's potential appointment as hugmaster general had revitalized his old friend. He followed this jest with a rather telling compliment. He told Lydia Christian, "I pay tribute to your wonderful eyes, keen today as of yore, that holds [sic] him safe."[44] Whether Harding was referring to the beauty of her eyes, which continued to attract her husband's attention, or her ability to watch over George Christian and keep him from straying, Harding obviously respected the strength of the Christians' relationship—an ironic stance considering Harding's philandering.

One example of George B. Christian's concern for his wife appeared in a letter to his son near the end of the elder Christian's life. On November 8, 1928, Christian admonished his son to write frequent letters to his mother, who was ill and would pass away in the coming weeks. Even in his graying years, Christian worried about his wife's happiness and anticipated the joy that letters from her children might bring in her delicate state of health. An important gesture that served as a commentary on the Christians' relationship involved their house on East Church Street. When George and Lydia Christian moved into the home in 1915, Christian bought the property in his wife's name. While such an arrangement was not an uncommon strategy to protect and provide for a spouse, the act points to the deep affection and concern shared by the now elderly couple.[45]

George and Lydia Christian raised three children who lived to adulthood. Their eldest, George B. Christian Jr., initially followed in his father's career footsteps. Christian Jr. studied engineering at Chester Military College in Pennsylvania. His military career ended before the outbreak of the Spanish-American War, but his service paid tribute to his father's martial efforts during the Civil War. After discharging his military obligations, Christian Jr. joined the family business in the limestone quarries and served as his father's secretary and right-hand man. Christian Jr. married Stella Farrar of Shelby, Ohio, in 1897, and they soon settled in a house near that of Warren G. Harding in Marion. He and wife Stella had two boys: Warren and John. Like his father, George B. Christian Jr. became a leader in Marion's Democratic Party. He also dedicated part of his time to public service. He even followed his father's political trajectory by serving on the local school board. At one time he even worked as one of the clerks for the national Democratic convention. Christian's devotion provided stability to his father's business endeavors, but he never loved the quarrying business to the same extent as his father.[46]

Fig. 16. George B. Christian Jr. (Courtesy of the Roberts Family Library)

47

In 1914, Harding offered George B. Christian Jr. the opportunity to serve as his personal secretary in the Senate. Christian's loyalty and proficiency became so invaluable to the future president that they became fast friends and unquestioning political teammates. Christian probably knew Warren G. Harding better than any other man and assuredly carried many of the president's secrets to his grave. After Harding's tragic death, Christian struggled to find the right place for himself in Washington. His bureaucratic career ended when he was struck with blindness later in life.[47]

George and Lydia Christian's second child, Mary (Mamie) Christian, married Fred Dombaugh, a son of one of George B. Christian Sr.'s close Freemasonry colleagues. They married just a few months after George Christian Jr.'s wedding in 1897. They had a daughter and a son, but both of their children passed away at a young age. The death of six-and-a-half-year-old Ruth Christian Dombaugh in 1905 might have affected the family most traumatically. Ruth was George and Lydia Christian's only granddaughter, and she died from a debilitating condition diagnosed at the time as acute gastritis. Attacks of this stomach condition had left her frail and undernourished. Even though she had suffered from periodic illness, her death caught many

MR. J. FRED DOMBAUGH AND BRIDE.

Fig. 17. Sketches from Fred and Mamie Dombaugh's wedding announcement. (*Marion [OH] Daily Star,* Oct. 8, 1897)

Fig. 18. Ruth Christian Dombaugh. (Courtesy of the Roberts Family Library)

of her closest relatives by surprise. The pain of her passing probably reminded George and Lydia Christian of their little Pauline, who had died at an even younger age.

Like George B. Christian Jr., Fred Dombaugh worked for George B. Christian Sr. in the quarrying business—his employment demonstrated the extent to which the lime, macadam, and stone business was a family affair. When George B. Christian Jr. left his job at the White Sulphur Stone Company to work for Warren G. Harding in the Senate, Dombaugh assumed the role of secretary at the plant. Much later, the Dombaughs became caretakers of Harding's home and memorial, keeping the connections strong between the fallen president and the Christian family.[48]

Alice Mildred Christian (generally known as Mildred) was born eight years after Mamie and remained in her parents' home until she was in her thirties. She traveled with them to Florida three times in her youth and generally reaped the benefits of their prominence and affluence. She graduated with high marks at Marion High School— offering, as her father had before her, an address at the school's commencement and a toast at the seniors' banquet. Mildred Christian went away to National Park Seminary in Maryland near Washington, DC, for finishing school. Dr. John A. I. Cassedy

MARION. ❋ Vail. ❋ OHIO.

Fig. 19. Young Alice Mildred Christian. (Courtesy of the Roberts Family Library)

opened the National Park Seminary in 1894 to teach future wives and mothers advanced homemaking skills and an appreciation of the arts and culture. It became one of the best-known finishing schools in the country because of its vibrant sorority culture in which each house had been elaborately constructed with its own architectural style. The school drew female students from all over the country. Mildred Christian, vice president of her class of ten, formed many deep friendships with her classmates before graduating around 1904. She went to California in 1911 to serve as a bridesmaid to one of her classmates, and another friend from the school served in Mildred's own wedding as the maid of honor.[49]

In 1918, Mildred Christian met and fell in love with a military captain named Chester Roberts who had come to Marion to manage his family's many land and livestock holdings in central Ohio while on leave. They were married on April 20, 1918, at the home of George and Lydia Christian. Captain Roberts wore his uniform during the ceremonies—a poignant reminder that he had received orders to serve the remainder

Fig. 20. Chester Roberts. (Courtesy of the Roberts Family Library)

of World War I at an army base in Georgia. For their honeymoon, the couple drove out East on their way to Georgia, stopping to see Senator Harding and his wife as well as her brother along the way. While stationed at Camp Gordon near Atlanta, Chester Roberts received a commission as a major, but saw no combat. After the war, the couple returned to Marion, and Chester Roberts eventually became president of the Marion Reserve Power Company. Though her husband passed away in the 1940s, Mildred Roberts remained involved in the community by serving on hospital and library

50

boards. She was the only child of George and Lydia Christian to have grandchildren.[50]

While the biographical sketches in the preceding paragraphs offer only a brief glimpse into the family of George B. Christian Sr., they reveal that he passed some of the same values and character traits to his children that he learned from his ancestors. His wife, Lydia Christian, stuck with him through his economic and political endeavors. His children worked hard and strove to serve their communities and friends. George B. Christian Jr.'s commitment to civic duty and friendship led him to the White House to serve the president. Christian Sr.'s oldest daughter, Mamie Dombaugh, and her husband dedicated much of their lives to the memory of that president. Mildred Roberts advocated for important civic institutions in Marion for most of her life—even after her husband passed away at a young age. While the family also encountered significant tragedy and disappointment, their desire to build communities and serve their neighbors was a consistent goal across generations.

Subsequent chapters examine many events, accomplishments, and themes from George B. Christian Sr.'s more than eighty years in Marion, Ohio. Nevertheless, Christian himself probably would have considered his family to be his greatest achievement. While he might not have passed on a significant amount of wealth to his children or grandchildren, Christian left them an inspiring legacy of service, work, and innovation. His commitment to family was one of the few constants in his eventful life.

CHAPTER 2

Christian Plays the Soldier

"For Americans broadly, the Civil War has been a defining event upon which we have often imposed unity and continuity; as a culture, we have often preferred its music and pathos to its enduring challenges. The theme of reconciled conflict to resurgent, unresolved legacies." David W. Blight, *Race and Reunion: The Civil War in American Memory* (Cambridge: Harvard University Press, 2001), 4.

The American Civil War was the transcendent event of the nineteenth century in the United States. Not only did the war and its aftermath end slavery throughout the nation, but this era forged a cohesive American identity. Instead of a federation of semi-autonomous states, Union victory meant that states became permanently subordinate to the national government. In addition, the Thirteenth, Fourteenth, and Fifteenth Amendments, passed after the war ended, declared that African Americans should enjoy full rights of citizenship—though such rights would not be granted in practice for many years. The scope and impact of the conflict marked the lives of virtually every citizen on both sides of the struggle.

The impact of the Civil War in George B. Christian Sr.'s life was much more ambiguous. Christian confronted the meaning of the Civil War in three distinct stages of his life. First, Christian served in the Union army for a little less than eight months. While he served during a critical juncture in the conflict, his own deployment was short, inconsequential, and sometimes unpleasant. The hearing impairment he suffered during his term of service inconvenienced him throughout the rest of his life and served as a constant reminder of his short time in the army. Second, Christian struggled to understand the meaning of the war in his own life and the trajectory of the nation after the peace made at Appomattox Courthouse. While Christian was proud of his service during the war and the fraternal bonds it helped him forge with fellow veterans, the short duration of his enlistment and his survival sometimes created a sense of guilt, defensiveness, and isolation from his fellow soldiers. In the aftermath of the struggle, the government rejected his application for a pension to help him cope with his hearing loss. Despite his personal war baggage, Christian also attempted to influence his community's understanding of the war's meaning. He became an apologist for the Democratic Party and its Southern members. Finally, Christian began to embrace his role as a veteran as he joined with and spoke for his fellow former soldiers. Governmental recognition of his service in the form of a disabled soldier's pension later in life helped him embrace his limited participation in the conflict despite the larger brutality and tragedy of the war. In the end, Christian's Civil War story demonstrated the complicated and shifting meaning linked to the tragic struggle.

Fig. 21. Depiction of Abraham Lincoln giving the Gettysburg Address. The Battle of Gettysburg, along with with other victories in 1863, turned the tide of the war. (Courtesy of the Library of Congress)

Christian enlisted in the Union army during the summer of 1863 as a short-term volunteer. While some evidence suggests he might have served temporarily as a drummer boy before this time, Christian's official enlistment as a private occurred during this active summer of the conflict. He and his fellow recruits entered the war at a critical turning point. War had raged for over three years and both sides had suffered casualties on a scale never before experienced in American combat. Emboldened by his convincing victory at Chancellorsville, Virginia, Robert E. Lee and the Confederate army invaded Pennsylvania on June 3, 1863, with 75,000 Confederate troops hoping to sap the Union's will to fight. At about the same time, Union General Ulysses S. Grant remained bogged down in a difficult siege of the apparently impregnable but strategically important town of Vicksburg, Mississippi. Such military setbacks appeared especially grim since Lincoln's Emancipation Proclamation, signed earlier that year, had helped change the stakes of the struggle. The proclamation had freed all slaves located in the Confederacy, and this action affirmed that slavery and its abolition were the central struggle of the Civil War. Many Union soldiers and citizens questioned the importance of emancipation, and military setbacks caused these detractors to call for a peaceful resolution to the conflict while rejecting any changes to slavery. When Union forces ultimately halted the Confederates' advance into Union territory through the bloody fighting at Gettysburg and forced Vicksburg's surrender in July of 1863, these victories represented a crucial turning point in the overall course of the war. Whereas Union supporters had bemoaned emancipation and military reverses during the early part of the year, the summer events initiated the long road toward Union victory and assured that the effort to halt slavery would move forward.[1]

For Christian and his fellow recruits, the conflict had recently entered their own backyard. Confederate General John Hunt Morgan had raided Indiana and Ohio during the spring and summer of 1863, looting the countryside and creating fear in the minds of the people. Morgan's raid stretched farther north than any other Confederate incursion. The general had initially thought to meet up with Lee, who had moved into Pennsylvania, but the Confederate rendezvous faltered at Gettysburg. Despite Lee's failure, Morgan continued his movements throughout the Midwestern countryside with Union armies in hot pursuit. He finally surrendered in July of 1863, and the capture of his animals provided mounts for the

Fig. 22. Portrait of General John Hunt Morgan whose raid into the Midwest terrified the populace and served as the backdrop for Christian's enlistment in the army. (Courtesy of the Library of Congress)

coalescing Ohio Fifth Independent Cavalry. Morgan's daring raid had terrified the people of the region and inspired many volunteers who wanted to protect their homes and families.[2]

Fig. 22. This *Harper's Weekly* illustration depicts Morgan's attack on the town of Washington, Ohio. (*Harper's Weekly* 7, no. 346 [1863]: 513)

Christian enlisted in the Union army in the early summer of 1863, when the prospects of Northern victory seemed tenuous. Recruited by Captain William H. Garrett, who had come to Ohio from the front lines of the war, Christian and many of his fellow trainees in the Ohio Fifth Independent Cavalry were young and naive. Looking back on his time as a soldier, Christian described himself as a seventeen-year-old boy who weighed 111 pounds upon his entry into the military. He claimed that no

Fig. 24. Portrait of George B. Christian Sr. as a boy soldier. (Courtesy of the Roberts Family Library)

uniform fit his tiny frame. He enlisted with other Marion boys who had trained with wooden swords and guns in anticipation of their call to arms and the excitement of the battlefield. Although he might have exaggerated his puniness, Christian served as one of the war's 250,000 to 420,000 underage soldiers. The virtues of brave child-patriots became sensationalized through the press's treatment of the war's most famous underage soldier, Joseph John Klem (aka John Lincoln Clem or Johnny Shiloh), who had also joined the army as a boy in Ohio. Klem's drum was supposedly destroyed at Shiloh, and the drummer boy proved adept for combat and intelligence duty, using his size and innocence to undermine Confederate movements and plans.[3]

Despite Christian's fervent desire to fight for the Union, he and his family must have looked toward the conflict at times with uncertainty. As discussed in the previous chapter, Christian's father was a Southerner by birth and a Democrat by choice, and John Christian was jailed as a suspected member of the Knights of the Golden Circle. Ohio had become a center of Democratic opposition to the war and emancipation—the infamous copperhead congressman Clement Vallandigham hailed from Dayton, Ohio. Christian stated, probably with some embellishment, that of the forty-five men in his extended family who died in the Civil War, half fought for the Union and half for the Confederacy. One of his prominent Southern relatives even married the great Confederate General Stonewall (Thomas) Jackson. Thus, the Christian family, like many others, felt the reality of divided loyalties between North and South.[4]

Even though his heritage and politics might have created intellectual objections to the war, the emotional force of peer pressure and patriotism trumped such rational concerns. Christian entered the military on June 19, 1863, in Marion, and served as part of Company B of the Fifth Independent Cavalry Battalion of Ohio until February 15, 1864. Major John Ijams commanded the Fifth Battalion of Ohio, and, within that battalion, Captain Garrett led the Marion soldiers of Company B. Consequently, Christian entered the army with many of his friends and served under an officer from his hometown who had recruited them. During his training, Christian occasionally participated in the types of spectacles that generated pride in the military enterprise and the adoration of the communities that the volunteers represented. One highlight of the recruits' training in the fall of 1863 involved their marching in a parade at the Franklin County Fair. Such occasions allowed these young men to play soldier. Military processions served to solidify volunteers' identities as soldiers and projected a sense of security and success to the spectators of these events. Holding such a parade at a

5" REGIMENT OHIO VOLUNTEER CAVALRY

Fig. 25. Colors of the Fifth Regiment of the Ohio Volunteer Cavalry to which George B. Christian Sr. belonged. (Reproduced by permission of the Ohio History Connection)

Fig. 26. This illustration shows a Civil War era parade involving soldiers in Hamilton County, Ohio. (Howe. *Historical Collections of Ohio*)

county fair, an event that served as a celebration of the community's achievements, offers a platform for understanding these young men as the region's best and brightest contributions to the war effort. Upon completion of their training, the troops participated in another spectacle when they marched along High Street in Columbus as they left for their first battlefield deployment.

Despite the emotional and social rewards that came from military service, the harsh conditions of army life quickly tested Christian's resolve. On his first night as a private, Christian slept with other recruits between two stone pillars on the cold floor of the statehouse. His battalion soon came together at Camp Todd in Columbus along the Scioto River. In their camp, they slept with twelve men crowded in a teepee, lying on the hard, cold ground with their feet toward the center to facilitate the greatest number of occupants. After leaving Ohio, Company B of the Fifth Battalion first camped in Maysville, Kentucky, on the Kentucky-Ohio border. Christian complained that the Tenth Kentucky Mounted Infantry, which had previously occupied their campsite in Maysville, left an infestation of bedbugs for the Ohio soldiers, which caused them great distress whenever they attempted to rest. The military life extracted young men from the comforts of home and forced them to adapt to the difficult conditions inherent in the military lifestyle.

Christian later wrote about the exceptional cold he and his fellow soldiers faced during the winter of 1863–1864. He commented that the government provided few supplies to help troops deal with the elements. In fact, under the direction of Captain Edward Cooper, Christian and eleven other men built their own shack out of scrap lumber to endure the winter weather. The most extreme weather occurred on New Year's Eve of 1863 when the temperature dropped from a daytime mark in the sixties to a nighttime temperature of negative twenty-five degrees

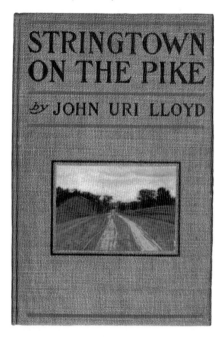

Fig. 27. Cover of the 1900 edition of *Stringtown on the Pike.* (John Uri Lloyd, *Stringtown on the Pike: A Tale of Northernmost Kentucky* [New York: Grosset & Dunlap, 1900])

Fahrenheit. Throughout the region people remembered this day as the Cold New Year's Day. To help readers understand the magnitude of the cold, Christian referenced a nineteenth-century novel called *Stringtown on the Pike,* which described the same night as being so cold that it killed animals and humans throughout the area. Christian remembered the chill so vividly that he labeled it one of the unsung horrors of the war.[5]

In addition, Christian blamed the cold for an infection he acquired in the late fall of 1863, the effects of which became one of his lifelong frustrations. In a legal affidavit filed as part of his pension application after the war, Christian detailed the health problems he encountered when patrolling the Kentucky countryside. In the application, using the legalistic third-person perspective, he detailed that "he [Christian] commenced becoming deaf from exposure and severe cold which caused a catarrh [an inflammation of the mucous membranes] in the head causing almost total deafness; this deafness continued to grow worse from that 19th of November until the time of his discharge and has never become any better."[6] Christian's illness was not unusual; historians have pointed out that many more Civil War soldiers died from sickness and disease in camp than wounds received on the battlefield. In these years before the discovery of microbes, physicians wielded few tools for fighting the rampant spread of infections between soldiers.[7]

Despite this supposedly debilitating condition, Christian tried to play the good soldier. He recounted that his company spent most of its time patrolling the countryside and chasing the Southern guerrillas and vigilantes known as bushwhackers. Soldiers with Confederate sympathies quickly adopted guerilla warfare after their initial defeat by formal Union forces. Christian's battalion guarded counties in the area known today as Daniel Boone National Forest. Their watches, which patrolled twelve hours on and twelve hours off, sought to dissuade the Confederates from causing trouble for Union supporters and soldiers. Kentucky, though a slave state, never left the Union, but its slave-holding populace held mixed loyalties during the conflict. Christian later observed that General Boyle, commander of the Department of the Ohio, often discussed sending the Ohio Fifth Cavalry into combat zones, but Union loyalists persuaded him to leave the Ohio troops in Kentucky to protect its vulnerable Unionist population.

While these guerrillas caused anxiety for Kentuckians who supported the Union, they usually posed little danger to the Union troops. Christian later recalled, "Our clashes with the bushwhackers, although frequent and sometimes exciting, were generally bloodless."[8] Because the Confederate vigilantes normally retreated when faced with danger, the Ohio infantrymen suffered few casualties. The company saw so little serious fighting that Christian joked about the skirmishes in which they did engage. He later parodied his and his comrades' participation in "the greatest scuttle of the war—the charge at Phillips, KY." During the skirmish, "four men went down, rolled on by their horses amid heavy firing, one man was drowned, and after the fight was over it was discovered that not a soul on either side was hit by lead."[9] By definition, Southern bushwhackers avoided confrontations with regular Union forces, causing frustration and apathy among their pursuers.[10]

The Union army started recruiting soldiers from the Fifth Ohio Independent Battalion to transfer to the developing Thirteenth Ohio Volunteer Cavalry Battalion only when the volunteers' terms of service began to expire at the beginning of 1864. Union recruiters offered month-long furloughs and bonuses as incentives for reenlisting. Despite the temptation, it seems that Christian felt that he could not physically continue as a soldier and chose not to reenlist. His former comrades who moved into the Thirteenth Battalion later

THE CRATER, AS SEEN FROM THE UNION SIDE. FROM A SKETCH MADE AT THE TIME.

Fig. 28. Depiction of the Battle of the Crater at Petersburg. (Courtesy of the Library of Congress.)

participated in the siege of Petersburg and the infamous Battle of the Crater. Almost one in every eight males from Marion County, a total of 1,700 soldiers, served in the Union army. Very few homes avoided sending a husband, son, or brother to the battlefront.[11]

When he exited the army, George B. Christian Sr. had mixed feelings about his service. Christian and his comrades who chose not to reenlist were discharged on February 15, 1864, in Cincinnati, Ohio. Other than his illness, Christian had avoided the traumas of combat and survived when many other soldiers he knew died in the heavy fighting that took place as Grant attempted to grind the Confederate army into submission. Christian seems to have felt some mix of relief and regret that he avoided Grant's final, bloody Virginia campaign. He inevitably felt a measure of survivor's guilt. In the years immediately after his service, Christian appears to downplay his war record. While Christian's actions in the year or two after he left the army remain mostly unknown, one of his affidavits stated that he was "going to school and doing odd jobs, but owing to deafness ha[d] been unable to do any business requiring an ounce of hearing."[12] Thus, illness and the trials of civilian reintegration made Christian's early years after the war difficult.

On May 11, 1865, Christian submitted an application for an invalid pension, swearing that he had become hard of hearing during his time in the army. Christian hoped to receive a government pension under the provisions of the Pension Act of July 14, 1862, which allotted soldiers "disabled by reason of any wound received or disease contracted while in the service of the United States . . . eight dollars per month."[13] This act also created a National Pension Board with a commissioner to allocate funds for the nation's first entitlement program. After reviewing Christian's application on September 26, 1865, Pension Commissioner Joseph H. Barrett asked the adjutant general's office to submit paperwork regarding the scope of Christian's military service. Several weeks later, the assistant adjutant general wrote back that he had found no evidence of Christian's service in the Fifth Ohio Cavalry Battalion. This ruling, based on incorrect governmental recordkeeping, halted Christian's application at that time. Because Christian joined the army as an underage boy, he might have lied about his age or identity on his initial enlistment paperwork, which would have made his records difficult to find.[14]

Why did Christian accept the government's ruling, based on incorrect information, about his service? At times, especially in the early years after his military career, Christian seemed to find his military service wanting when compared to Marion soldiers who reenlisted for the duration of the war. Consequently, he might have believed that the pension commissioner would decline his request, even if the records could be found, by ruling that his hearing loss was not a disability worthy of governmental support. This seems like a legitimate concern since Christian had played up the seriousness of his deafness for his application, and he seemingly functioned in the workplace for the next fifty years with only an occasional mention of his hearing struggles. Speculation aside, something made him hesitant to question the obviously incorrect findings of the U.S. pension officials, and Christian delayed his quest to receive government compensation for his hearing loss for the next sixteen years.

During this long gap between pension applications, Christian played an active role in the way his community remembered the war. He worked hard to help Marionites understand the meaning of the Civil War on his terms, because alternate interpretations might have triggered his insecurities. Christian defended the positions and goals of the Democratic Party in the post-war world, in part, because he needed reassurance about his own loyalty and patriotism. As the editor of the *Marion Democratic Mirror* from 1876–1882, Christian condemned Reconstruction efforts in the South as ineffective and unnecessary. He also downplayed or defended the South's efforts to disenfranchise black voters. Christian fought to combat the waving of the bloody shirt by Republicans who constantly reminded Americans about the death and destruction suffered by Union soldiers. Republicans pointed out that the Democrats, who populated the Confederacy and the Northern opposition during the Civil War, had the blood of many valiant Union soldiers on their hands. Consequently, Republican partisans attempted to condemn the party of Jackson and Jefferson by associating it with disloyalty and death.

To refute Republican claims of Democratic treachery, Christian used a variety of tactics. For example, he cited the service records of many Democratic soldiers, including himself, from Marion and throughout the country. The 1880 Democratic presidential candidacy of Winfield Scott Hancock, a Union hero of Gettysburg, offered Christian an especially powerful rhetorical tool to refute Republicans' attempts to assert their opposition's inherent disloyalty. In addition, Christian encouraged Marion's Democratic voters to flood the polls and demonstrate their patriotism by participating in the election process. Finally, Christian employed humor to downplay accusations of Democratic betrayal. In one 1879 editorial, he joked that the blood on Republicans' shirts was really regurgitated huckleberry pie, which Republicans embraced because they had no other winning strategies. Whether toeing a party line or expressing his own opinions, Christian's writing in the *Mirror* demonstrates how the contentious issues of Reconstruction caused both parties to constantly litigate the legacy of the Civil War. Overall, Christian defended the loyalty of the Democratic Party and downplayed the role of slavery as the cause of the conflict. Nevertheless, his need to stridently defend party and ideology might also have revealed Christian's insecurities about the war and his service.[15]

Consequently, Christian sought ways to forge his identity as a veteran among his peers. For example, Christian participated as a member of the local post of the Grand Army of the Republic (GAR), and he helped plan Marion's annual Memorial Day celebration. The GAR, founded in Decatur and Springfield, Illinois, in 1866, sought to foster camaraderie among and support for veterans of the Union army. In addition, it supported widows and orphans of deceased soldiers and vowed to protect the reputation of Union soldiers from the revisions of history. Christian served as a founding member of Marion's GAR post. He also worked as president of Marion's Memorial Day festivities, serving as the master of ceremonies for local programs and overseeing celebration planning. Memorial Day had become an important tool in creating new narratives about the Civil War. The holiday began as "Decoration Day" in May of 1868 when the national commander in chief of the GAR ordered veterans to decorate

Fig. 29. Celebration of the first official Decoration Day, the precursor to modern Memorial Day, at Arlington National Cemetery. President Ulysses S. Grant gave the keynote address. (Courtesy of the Library of Congress.)

the graves of deceased soldiers. Memorial Day eventually became an opportunity for elaborate displays of patriotism within a community marked by placing flowers on veterans' graves and solemn oratory. Historian David Blight has argued that Memorial Day offered the American people an opportunity to celebrate heroism on both sides of the conflict and to downplay the economic, political, and cultural differences that had caused the war. Slavery took a back seat to tales of bravery and suffering. Americans had found their own Homeric tales of defining conflict. Along these lines, Christian's Memorial Day celebrations sought to honor the bravery of all Civil War soldiers. This focus on mutual valor, suffering, and death served to downplay regional differences and to focus on reconciliation between North and South.[16]

Despite his very limited service in the war, or perhaps because of it, George B. Christian Sr. felt obligated to publicly testify of the profound heroism exercised by many of his comrades in arms. While a later chapter will more fully cover Christian's efforts to help his community remember its veterans in his mature years, some preliminary observations are helpful. In 1902, Christian memorialized the Marion soldiers who had reenlisted for the duration of the war in 1864 when he wrote, "Their voices and presence come oft back to me now, and the tears unbidden come in spite of the years that have passed since then."[17] Christian eloquently described his role as a surviving soldier to a gathering of the Marion branch of the GAR. He observed:

> To him [the surviving soldier] will befall the lot to
> look upon the vacancies occasioned by the absence
> of nearly 4,000,000 of men; it will be his heritage;
> in his memory there will pass before him a ghostly
> multitude, reminders of the men who carried the flag
> of this nation in a time of great peril from Gettysburg
> to Appomattox—from Atlanta to the sea. If his mind
> shall be clear and there shall be something of the
> dreamer in his personality, he may see before him the
> banners, the leaders, and me thinks hear the tramp
> of myriads of marching men, the drum beat of many
> decades long ago, the shouting of the host of the
> victors and the vanquished, all before him like some
> modern picture show.[18]

Christian considered himself a keeper and purveyor of Civil War memories. He wrote and spoke about his fellow soldiers to keep the recollection of their bravery alive, to give meaning to his own survival, and to help others understand the price of nationhood.

As Christian aged, his efforts on behalf of the memory of fallen soldiers caused him to reevaluate his own service and status as a veteran. Consequently, he again applied for a pension in July of 1891, sixteen years after his failed first request. Christian possibly felt that receiving a pension, so many years after the government had rejected his initial inquiry, would vindicate his self-identification as a veteran of the Civil War. He submitted his second application after the passage of a new pension law on June 27, 1890. This law promised pensions for all soldiers who had served at least ninety days in the military, were honorably discharged, and had a permanent disability not caused by their own habits. While the law still left the definition of "disability" somewhat amorphous, this time around, the U.S. adjutant general's records validated Christian's service and his disability. As vindication, he received $12 a month retroactively for missed benefits from the end of the war up to December 4, 1891. The Pension Board also granted him $10 a month for the rest of his life.[19]

While Christian might have felt that the decision to grant him a pension had settled the question of his worthiness as a veteran, the pension's validity came into question in February of 1895. The Bureau of Pensions notified Christian that it planned to discontinue his stipend because his hearing loss had not kept him out of the workforce. The notice stated that Christian had thirty days to dispute the decision. Christian received the forwarded notice in Florida, where he had sought relief from chronic illness, and he sent a desperate letter to the bureau asking for more time to consult with his doctors and send evidence of his disability. He eventually submitted affidavits from his family physician, Dr. A. Rhee, affirming his continuing infirmities, which kept him from performing manual labor—a core requirement for eligibility under the 1890 pension law. While technically true, the paperwork declined to mention that Christian made his living primarily as a businessman and not through manual labor. Nevertheless, the pension board must have found his case sufficiently compelling to restore his pension, which they did on July 12, 1895.[20]

Christian's 1895 pension fight revealed a previously veiled condition that he attributed to his Civil War service. Newspaper articles in the *Marion Daily Star* confirmed that Christian suffered from an extended illness that began in late October of 1886 and extended through mid-December. A November 12, 1886, notice in the paper proclaimed that his health had reached a critical condition during the previous week. Christian's 1895 paperwork identified his 1886 malady as nervous prostration. Physicians had identified nervous prostration, or neurasthenia, as a blanket term for a variety of psychological and physical conditions for which they found no medical cause. They posited that nervous prostration occurred when a person used too much of the body's finite nervous energy. They felt that the mental tasks and stress required of white-collar workers, manufacturers, and businessmen in the industrial age rapidly depleted their nervous energy. Christian's doctor had diagnosed his prolonged illness of 1886 as one caused by such a depletion.[21]

Although it is impossible to accurately identify the true cause of Christian's ailment or of his periodic poor health, historians have identified some modern conditions labeled as nervous maladies in the nineteenth century. Most clinical depression, anxiety disorders, forms of exhaustion, and stress-relation conditions fell under the large tent of neurasthenia. In addition, doctors sometimes diagnosed physical symptoms such as ulcers or irritable bowel syndrome as symptoms of nervous prostration. In a world with almost no understanding of mental illness, neurasthenia served as a primordial way to explain mental health issues. Christian's lifestyle as an industrialist fit the profile of a neurasthenia victim almost perfectly. No matter which modern condition slowed Christian in 1886, his doctors probably prescribed a regimen of relaxation, rest, and leisure—standard treatments for nervous prostration at the time.[22]

The government never again questioned Christian's worth as a pensioner. Congress passed additional pension laws that periodically raised the amount of money he received. By 1918, Christian was receiving $32 a month in honor of his military service and to help pay medical expenses.[23]

George B. Christian's government pension served as one of many converging factors that helped him reevaluate his role as a soldier. While Christian may have initially felt unworthy to stand side by side with those who had faced the blind horrors of death and destruction on the important battlegrounds of the Civil War, each additional pension increase offered him the government's validation of his Civil War service. Christian's advancing age and leadership in veterans' organizations also made him feel more confident about his time in the Civil War and worthy of his peers' respect. Christian's ability to commemorate the fallen gave him a mission and purpose that he never experienced as a soldier. His advocacy for former soldiers also gave him a public identity as an exemplary veteran of the War Between the States. While Christian's service had seemed inconsequential as it happened and immediately afterward, governmental and public recognition melded with perceived responsibility to make Christian a preeminent apologist for veterans of Marion, Ohio.

By April 19, 1926, Christian's health had deteriorated substantially. His doctor reported to the pension board that Christian's "[h]eart is enlarged and he is suffering from heart weakness. . . . [H]e is suffering from an enlarged prostate and irritable bladder. . . . [H]is general health is weakened to such extent as to make it unsafe to go about unattended."[24] The doctor also confirmed Christian's continued hearing problems and added that he had placed Christian on a bland diet to deal with his acid reflux, a secondary symptom of nervous disorders. This affidavit provided evidence that Christian medically qualified under a May 1, 1920, law for a pension of $72 per month given to Civil War veterans who needed constant medical attention. Pension officials accepted Christian's application on May 3, 1926, and the government paid his new pension retroactively from December 15, 1925, when a bout with the flu had left him incapacitated. This pension increased in subsequent years to $100 per month, a rate that continued until September 15, 1930, when he passed away.[25]

The legacy of his stint in the Union army framed Christian's adult life. His tour was relatively brief, and he was very young when he enlisted with the Fifth Ohio Volunteer Cavalry. Nevertheless, Christian's understanding of his military service changed as he matured. At various times during his life he played the soldier: as a young enlistee, as a pension applicant, and as an advocate for his fellow veterans. Christian's term as a soldier propelled him into adulthood, and he remembered his service not only for its hardships and ambiguities, but also for the meaning he found in his identity as a veteran in his mature years. The Civil War transformed the United States and bound its collection of individual polities into a cohesive nation. Nevertheless, the meaning and legacy of the conflict changed as the country changed. Because of its far-reaching effects on states, communities, and families, the aftermath of the Civil War forced individuals to decide how to remember, respond, and move forward with their lives. Many, like Christian, never forgot the terrible legacy of America's bloodiest and most fratricidal conflict.

CHAPTER 3

Christian Becomes the Colonel

"'It's everything,' suggested the Colonel, 'in knowing where to invest. I've known people throw away their money because they were too consequential to take Sellers' advice. Others, again, have made their pile on taking it. I've looked over the ground; I've been studying it for twenty years. You can't put your finger on a spot in the map of Missouri that I don't know as if I'd made it. When you want to place anything,' continued the Colonel, confidently, 'just let Beriah Sellers know. That's all.'" Mark Twain and Charles Dudley Warner, *The Gilded Age: A Tale of Today* (Hartford, CT: American Publishing Company, 1880), 150.

Like many of his comrades, George B. Christian Sr. struggled with reintegration into civilian life after his military service. When his six month enlistment ended, Christian was only seventeen years old and had graduated from school less than a year before. His first activities, according to a disability pension application he filed a few years later, included "going to school and doing odd jobs," though his lingering deafness restricted him from working in any career requiring good hearing.[1] Christian struggled for a while to find his economic niche, and he entered the workforce at a time of great economic opportunity and ruin. In reaction to the uncertainty, he embarked on a variety of work, investment, and entrepreneurial paths. While Christian thought of himself primarily as a civil engineer at this time, his economic experiments were as disparate as the ownership of a stationery store and a rural lumber production facility. His many attempts to participate in the changing economy earned him his nickname, "the Colonel," and placed him on the path to eventual success in the lime and stone industry.

Historians have labeled the time period between 1865 and 1876 Reconstruction to describe the struggle to rebuild both the South and national unity after the Civil War. Although this descriptor effectively captures the central political questions of the era, it downplays the commercial and industrial modernizations occurring in places such as Marion. Before the war, Ohio and the rest of the North had already commenced the transformations that would permanently change the U.S. economy, but these alterations quickly expanded throughout the nation as it reintegrated financially. National railroad development fueled economic growth. Railroads patronized related industries such as steel and coal. They also made travel and shipping faster and easier while creating a shared sense of time and space. Marion welcomed its first railroad line in 1852, but the construction of the Atlantic and Great Western Railroad in 1865 and the Columbus, Hocking, and Toledo Railroad in 1877 offered the city a wider connection to this most important engine for development.

As the growth of transportation in Marion suggests, the economic transformations that historians have often highlighted as a central part of the Gilded Age (1876–1900) began in the era of Reconstruction (1865–1876). Christian's changing employment prospects in the years after the war proved emblematic of the larger economic rumblings of these periods. Coincidentally, the term Gilded Age and Christian's nickname "the Colonel" came from the same work of fiction, written to capture the financial realities of the 1860s and 1870s. Mark Twain and coauthor Charles Dudley Warner illustrated the impact of the speculative opportunities offered by the changing economy in their 1873 novel about American greed, *The Gilded Age: A Tale of Today*. At the time, the word gilded referred to something plated with gold but worthless on the inside. In the novel, Twain and Warner documented the adverse effects of pursuing economic gain at any cost to individuals and society, which they had observed in the years after the Civil War.[2]

One of the prominent characters in the novel whom Twain and Warner utilized for comedic effect was Colonel Beriah Sellers.[3] The fictional Colonel Sellers, a former Confederate soldier, gained a memorable place in American popular culture because of his magnetism and ineptitude. Sellers constantly financed and hoped for huge payouts from speculative investments— often to the impoverishment of his family and friends. The character, however, was so lovable that readers latched on to his bumbling exploits. Mark Twain even titled his dramatic adaptation of the novel "Colonel

Fig. 30. Illustration depicting Twain's Colonel Sellers. (Mark Twain and Charles Dudley Warner, *The Gilded Age: A Tale of Today* [Hartford, CT: American Publishing Company, 1874])

Sellers," an acknowledgement that the colonel served as the story's most memorable character. Because of this schemer's popularity, the nickname "Colonel Sellers" became shorthand for someone with potentially devastating aspirations fueled by Gilded Age growth. The development of the U.S. manufacturing economy created the opportunity for industrialists such as Andrew Carnegie and John D. Rockefeller to build their fortunes. At the same time, many aspiring captains of industry never found the right business or investment and fell by the wayside. Twain and Warner offered Colonel Sellers as a type for this kind of speculative loser.[4]

Christian's pension paperwork contains the only known reference to his post-war education. While the extent of this schooling remains a mystery, Christian never made reference to college. At age seventeen, Christian might have considered teacher training or any number of other careers. Instead, Christian chose civil engineering as his profession in the years after the war. He participated in the planning and surveying process for roads and individual property in Marion County as early as October of 1868. In the 1860s, the professionalization of engineers had not yet occurred. In fact, few colleges offered specialized engineering training other than military academies such as West Point and technical schools on the East Coast. Christian chose not to join the state society of engineers, which suggests that his training was informal. While the development of land-grant universities such as The Ohio State University in 1870 completely changed the training and professionalization of engineers, most so-called civil engineers in the Old Northwest before 1870 generally received their training through an apprenticeship on practical construction projects. Within such an apprenticeship, engineers in training learned surveying techniques, basic design, mathematics, and physics. Christian probably gained his training under qualified engineers employed by the railroads or the city of Marion.[5]

In 1866, Marion County Auditor Richard Wilson appointed Christian as his deputy, and Christian rapidly began assisting not only Wilson, but also the county recorder and county surveyor. Christian acquired the jobs at the same time that his grandfather George Busby was elected as the county's probate judge. The correspondence between the two events suggests the possibility that Busby recommended his namesake grandson for these three assistant positions. These jobs allowed Christian to employ his surveying skills. In 1867, the offices of the Marion County recorder and auditor resurveyed property lines in a significant portion of the county seat. Christian and his coworkers divided the city into lots called plats, land with recorded boundaries and identification numbers based on the date when the property was incorporated into the city of Marion. This process helped to reappraise the property values of county residents for taxation. A year later, the county asked Christian to transcribe several volumes of older deeds and mortgages into record books with more durability and archival value. In general, Christian's work ensured the viability of land ownership by surveying property lines and then formalizing that proprietorship in the county records. Christian's many duties thrust him into the center of growth and development in Marion. Even though he might have needed all three jobs to earn a living wage, he thrived in this position because of his literacy and knowledge. His work as a county employee probably provided him, and later his family, with their primary source of income in the 1860s and 1870s.[6]

Christian also became involved in more diverse economic endeavors than his day job might have suggested. In December of 1866, Christian advertised that he wished to purchase poultry, game, and dried apples at his father's office. While Marion newspapers contained no follow-ups to this strange notice, Christian probably envisioned starting a business dealing in these specialized commodities. In March of 1868, Christian bought his sisters' and father's share of a property west of Marion that his mother had bequeathed to various family members. This consolidation was Christian's first attempt to enter the Marion real estate market. In the following years, he also purchased a twelve-acre lot west of the Marion fairgrounds and city lot twenty-five from one of his sisters. He even contracted with Hazard and Reed Dry Goods in 1869 to liquidate their inventory on consignment when the store went out of business. These ventures signified Christian's willingness to try a variety of economic propositions.[7]

George B. Christian Sr. invested in these business endeavors while also performing his duties for the county. His patrons in the county commissioners' office recruited him, as deputy auditor, to explain county bridge expenditures to the public. On February 11, 1869, Christian wrote a letter to the editor of the *Marion Democratic Mirror* defending the commissioners' decision to expend much of the county's bridge fund during 1868. George Crawford, editor of the Republican-minded *Marion Independent,* had accused the county of spending too much of the bridge money, but Christian methodically pointed out how war and flooding had taken their toll on the county's infrastructure. In this first published letter, Christian argued that the $51,000 spent on bridges in 1868 represented a reasonable expense for a rapidly growing county. The explanation demonstrated his capacity for understanding the county budget. At the same time, Christian served as an apologist for policies of the Democratic majority among county commissioners. Within this letter, Christian's county position, loyalty to the Democratic Party, and love of writing came together to assure the people that Marion County stewarded its funds appropriately. In July of 1870, Christian once again wrote to the *Mirror* to defend county expenditures, this time for a local hospital built to house the chronically infirm and disabled who could not pay for their own care. County Democratic leaders used Christian as a builder and an advocate. An editorial in the *Mirror,* the local Democratic organ, described him as one of the best deputy auditors in the state and one whose presence in the office made it run with an efficiency never seen before in Marion County government.[8]

Despite the busy pace of his public duties in early 1869, Christian again proved his entrepreneurial ambition when he and his friend D. S. Jones purchased a retail establishment. According to an advertisement in the *Mirror* from March of 1869, Christian's stand sold teachers' supplies, stationery, blank books, and wrapping paper to the Marion community. A later advertisement encouraged women to view the stand's stock of wallpapers and informed the public that the shop carried Victor Hugo's latest novel (either *Les Miserables* or *Toilers of the Sea*). In October 1869, the Jones & Christian stationery store requested that customers bring in rags to sell—components for making specialized papers. Christian's interest in the shop roughly coincided with his decision to marry Lydia Morris, and she might have played a role in this particular acquisition. Christian maintained his hold in the stationery and book business until June of 1871, when he sold his stake to future mayor Calvin Gailey. While Christian's store represented a short-term

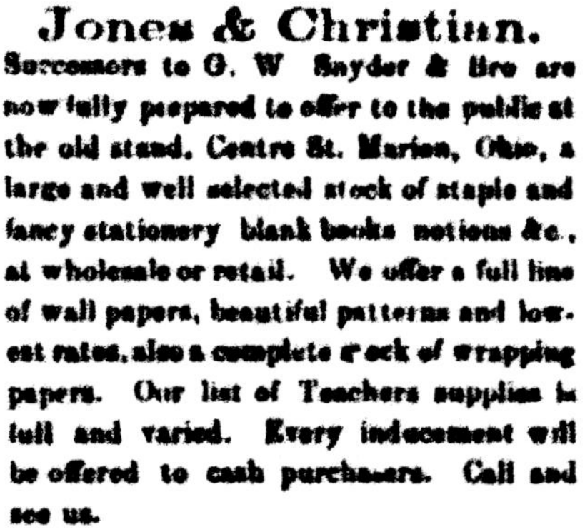

Jones & Christian.

Successors to G. W. Snyder & Bro are now fully prepared to offer to the public at the old stand. Centre St. Marion, Ohio, a large and well selected stock of staple and fancy stationery blank books notions &c., at wholesale or retail. We offer a full line of wall papers, beautiful patterns and lowest rates, also a complete stock of wrapping papers. Our list of Teachers supplies is full and varied. Every inducement will be offered to cash purchasers. Call and see us.

Fig. 31. Advertisement for Christian's stationery store. ("Jones & Christian." *Marion [OH] Democratic Mirror,* Mar. 4, 1869)

investment, he probably enjoyed the access it offered him to the good books that fueled his love of reading.[9]

In January 1871, Christian made a wise investment that ended prematurely. He and D. S. Jones partnered with Edward Huber and Lewis Gunn to form Huber, Gunn, and Company. This opportunity came when several of Huber and Gunn's previous partners left their manufacturing firm. Unfortunately, the partnership lasted only briefly—probably less than a year. Christian pulled out of the partnership well before the company began to publicly sell stock to form a corporation in 1874. The subsequent enterprise, Huber Manufacturing Company, became the largest and most prosperous business in Marion. The company gained recognition not only for its revolving hay rake, but also for its tractors and digging equipment. In addition, Edward Huber became one of the first investors in the Marion steam shovel industry. Thus, Christian just missed the opportunity to own part of one of the largest manufacturing firms in Ohio and possibly the chance to invest in one of the world's largest steam shovel companies. While Christian might still have owned stock in Huber Manufacturing Company when it incorporated in 1874, he surely regretted pulling out of the partnership.[10]

In April of 1871, Christian, who was now married, purchased 178 acres of timberland south of the village of Green Camp (sometimes called Berwick) in Pleasant Township, located southwest of Marion. This land was near Lydia Christian's parents' farm and cost the Christians $8,900 (the equivalent of $177,127 in 2016). Christian hoped to make money by extracting timber from this vast acreage, and he constructed a spur line from his property to the Columbus and Toledo Railroad to ship his lumber. Many of Christian's friends teased him about this particular endeavor, calling his spur line the "Continental Christian Railway" and giving him the nickname "Berwickian Backwoodsman." By July of 1871, Christian was advertising his ability to "furnish all grades of White Oak, Ash, Cherry, Walnut, and other native Hard Wood Lumber."[11] The *Mirror* described the operation in a boosterist editorial on January 18, 1872, as a house in the heart of a great forest with "a saw mill buzzing its power to accomplish the downfall of proud old trees; a score of sturdy woodchoppers making the forest ring with their axes; a railroad piercing the center of the woods; a scene of general activity and go-ahead-itiveness." At the same time, the *Mirror* praised Christian's "pluck, indomitable energy, and masterly financial ability" in embarking on this new endeavor.[12] Unfortunately, Christian felt compelled to divide his residence between his Pleasant Township property and the city where he worked as deputy auditor, surveyor, and recorder. This meant that none of his responsibilities received his full attention, and it soon became clear that he had to choose Marion or his country estate. In 1874, Christian began to liquidate his lumber holdings. He wrote to George Griswald, the property's mortgage holder and former owner, claiming that one of the railroads had not paid him for his work. He pleaded that he needed to sell part of the Pleasant Township property to generate enough cash to make his scheduled mortgage payment. Griswald permitted the sale, but it appears that the real reason for the request was that Christian's lumber business was not generating enough profit, especially with his divided attention. Consequently, Christian soon began divesting himself from the lumber industry. He began to alter his home in Pleasant Township into a hotel as a last-ditch effort to turn a profit on the property, but Christian eventually decided that his attention was needed elsewhere and sold the rest of his Berwick land.[13]

Christian's concurrent efforts to establish a home in Marion demonstrated that he never felt completely settled at the Berwick lumberyard. A May 9, 1872, article in the *Mirror* announced Christian's intentions to construct a house on the south side of Mount Vernon Avenue across from the future home of Warren G. Harding. Christian either disliked the home or had built it for the market, because in June of 1873 he traded it to Pauline Hummer for her house on the corner of present-day Church and State Streets. The Christian family chose not to live permanently at that location either. In January of 1874, Christian purchased lots on West Church Street in a real estate development financed by his half-uncle T. P. Wallace and Henry True. In March, he broke ground for a permanent family home on one of these lots in the Springdale neighborhood.[14]

Having a residence in the city of Marion became important in August of 1873, because Christian's fellow Democrats nominated him to run for county surveyor. Several months later he won the election by 598 votes and permanently moved his family to Marion so he could serve the people of the county from its seat. After Christian's election, his name began appearing more and more frequently in the county commissioners' journals. The commissioners often assigned Christian to design, survey, and supervise major county public works projects like roads, canals, and railroads. His notable projects included supervising the Willow Swamp Ditch and working on roads such as Radnor County Pike, Berwick and Union County Line Pike, Silver Street Free Pike, and Marion and Big Island Turnpike. Christian's efforts connected distant locations in central Ohio and made Marion County a more familiar place. In addition to these duties, Christian advertised in local newspapers to let the people of Marion know that he was available to help them with "ditch and road petitions, remonstrances, taxes, estate settlements, etc."[15] He also penned notices that heralded his availability to draw up deeds and mortgages.[16]

Beyond his work for the county, Christian also pursued his own interests. He invested in additional lots in Springdale to facilitate and profit from the growth of the neighborhood located slightly west of downtown Marion. One notable transaction involving this neighborhood occurred in

George B. Christian, County Surveyor, has opened an office in the Peter's Block, and will, we doubt not, promptly attend to all business in his line. We understand that he will, in connection with his official duties, attend to any other business that may offer— such as ditch and road petitions, remonstrances, taxes, estate settlements, etc. Will also draw deeds, mortgages, and take acknowledgements to the same. George's long experience in these matters thoroughly qualifies him for such duties.

Fig. 32. This advertisement proclaims Christian's availability as the County Surveyor, and his willingness to perform a variety of services for the people of Marion. ("George B. Christian," *Marion [OH] Democratic Mirror,* Jan. 22, 1874)

September of 1874, when Christian sold a lot to Guy Webber. While this land sale represented the first recorded contact between Christian and Webber, the two men eventually became good friends and business partners. Guy Webber had moved from Michigan to work at the *Mirror* with James Newcomer. While Christian participated in a variety of legitimate business ventures before and after his partnership with Webber, Webber became infamous as the mastermind of several fraudulent money-making schemes.[17]

Christian always seemed dissatisfied with the compensation for his work on behalf of Marion County. Consequently, he relished the chance to partner with Guy Webber on potentially lucrative ventures. Near the end of 1874, Christian and Webber announced their decision to publish an illustrated family news and literary paper called the *Western Ledger.* A subscription cost one dollar and twenty-five cents per year, which included eight handsome premium pictures. According to a story from January of 1875, the paper sold well.

Christian and Webber even contemplated distributing it on a weekly rather than monthly basis after a year of publication. No further references to the *Western Ledger* appeared in Marion papers after the January story, so the paper's demise remains a mystery.[18]

Expanded knowledge of Guy Webber's business ventures, however, throws the legitimacy of the *Western Ledger* into doubt. After his time in Marion, Webber moved to Cincinnati and became known nationally for his elaborate and fraudulent money-grabbing schemes. In 1883, he allegedly started another paper called simply *The Ledger* with a supposed national readership. To sell the paper, he offered a subscription package for one dollar that seemed almost too good to be true. Webber wanted his subscribers to feel like investors and claimed that their dollar not only gave them access to a certain number of newspaper issues, but it also increased the paper's money-making capacity. Webber told potential readers that he planned to profit from high advertising rates based on a large audience rather than the subscriptions themselves, and he offered to share some of the spoils with those who signed up. This chance to profit share motivated people to subscribe in droves. The magazine's publication ended after people sent in their dollars, and Webber made a substantial amount by ending the publication without offering any refunds. Even though Marion's established papers directed no accusations of similar corruption toward the *Western Ledger*, Christian and Webber's paper did offer artwork as an incentive for subscribers—a common tactic in some of Webber's other shady operations.[19]

Before Webber gained such national notoriety, Christian became embroiled in one of Webber's most infamous schemes, which involved the distribution of an art print named *Three Graces*.[20] This plot involved the circulation of coupons that offered a certain number of early registrants a rare fine art print for a nominal processing fee of several dollars. Subscribers were told that the print, *Three Graces*, was worth many times the fee and they were lucky to have the opportunity to sign up for it. Webber and employees George

B. Christian Sr. and Christian's half-uncle Caleb Norris must have become excellent advocates for the artwork, because orders soon overwhelmed the small Marion post office. Unfortunately, many recipients, if they even received the art, complained that the print looked like a cheap knock-off of a poor painting. Webber relocated to Cincinnati with his ill-gotten profits and formed the National Art Company to operate the same shady business model on a larger scale. Webber's art distribution efforts attracted significant complaints and buyers' remorse, but they made Webber copious profits. While the historical record doesn't indicate whether Christian knew that the prints were fraudulent, he definitely played a role in the scheme as one of the art's greatest champions.[21]

In fact, George B. Christian Sr. and Caleb Norris became so involved in the National Art Company that they accompanied Guy Webber on a trip to Europe to investigate the viability of similar coupon schemes in the Old World. The trip lasted for most of May and June of 1876 and included stops in England, France, Germany, Switzerland, Wales, and Ireland. During the trip, Christian chronicled his travels for the readers of the *Marion Democratic Mirror*. These extensive travelogues, a popular literary form of the day, foreshadowed many other travel letters written by Christian and published in Marion newspapers. In Christian's first letter from Europe, he poetically captured the beauty and loneliness involved in the ocean voyage. He described the vista for the many Marion residents who might never see the ocean:

> Sunset at sea—nothing more grand—the sun low
> down, just below the horizon; the long lines of
> swelling waves become each one capped with gold;
> not a faint glitter but a bright gleaming mass of
> molten gold, so intensely bright as to dazzle the eye.
> The horizon line becomes a band of silver. Extending
> through one-fourth of a circle, fading from silver
> into purple lines; then blue, and last, the dead grey
> and common colors. The nearer clouds rose-tipped,

crimson, gold, arrows of silvery light breaking through every opening in long, almost auroral lines. . . . And now comes quickly the changing shades and the herald of the long twilight of these Northern latitudes. The stars come out in seemingly ten times the numbers noticed on land; the Evening star, so large and bright that a long line of light is reflected in the water like as if it were another moon.[22]

(White Star Line) Steam Ship "BALTIC"

Fig. 33. Christian, Norris, and Webber sailed on the SS Baltic built in 1871. The Baltic was one of four ships that served as a predecessor on the White Star Line to the Titanic. (Reprinted with permission from www.heritage-ships.com)

Christian also bragged that he had been one of the lucky passengers who had very little trouble with seasickness. He described the feelings of hope and contentment inspired by the sight of the Irish coast and the English port of Liverpool among the weary seafarers. His writings demonstrated that even before buying a stake in the *Mirror*,

Fig. 34. Photograph of Liverpool Harbor taken in the 1870s which approximates what Christian might have seen when he arrived there in 1876. (Reprinted with permission from www.heritage-ships.com)

85

he often felt a journalistic impulse to capture places and experiences for others.[23]

Christian wrote a second letter to the *Mirror* in which he described the markets of Liverpool that sold goods from all over the world. He also narrated the train ride from Liverpool to London. Christian and his colleagues traveled in the first-class car and had to bribe the porters to allow them to smoke. Christian described the lush, green countryside in all of its beauty. He also complimented the homebuilding skills of the English. Christian felt that the English understood the value of an ancestral home much more than Americans, who easily moved from house to house and city to city. On the other hand, Christian found many reasons to criticize the English—especially when it came to the business model he wanted to promote. The National Art Company depended on newspaper advertising to market its products. Christian lamented that most local newspapers had very small circulations, and advertisements in the national papers cost too much. He also complained that neither local nor national newspapers reached residents of the English countryside. Christian and his colleagues eventually gave up on London, feeling that it provided few opportunities for expanding their business. After making this determination, the Americans became pure tourists in the city. Christian commented on London's Dickensian curiosity shops and its red-light district. He also visited museums and attended theatrical performances. Even though he acknowledged London as one of the world's most cosmopolitan cities, Christian decided that he preferred Marion because of his hometown's connectedness and congeniality.[24]

While no other accounts of Christian's European travel have survived, he and his colleagues probably met with little success selling cheap reproductions to Europeans, who generally had a much greater appreciation and understanding of fine art than their American counterparts. Later in life, Christian occasionally referred to this formative trip, which he had taken at the age of twenty-nine. For example, he wrote to Warren G. Harding in 1918 with theoretical World War I battle strategies based on his first-hand knowledge of the European landscape.[25]

Christian's affiliation with Guy Webber seems to have waned in the months and years after their European trip on account of Webber's business moving to Cincinnati. Christian also might have discovered or rejected Webber's questionable business practices and broken ties with the disreputable National Art Company. On the other hand, Webber never achieved the same infamy in Marion that he developed in Cincinnati and elsewhere. When the *Marion Star* published Webber's obituary in 1900, possibly written by Christian, it labeled Webber as an "incomparable genius."[26] Whatever the reason, Christian apparently left Webber's employment in 1876. His association with Guy Webber probably played a significant role in building his notoriety as a local Colonel Sellers. Webber's activities had a certain recklessness and duplicity, and these characteristics became a part of Christian's reputation even if he was unaware of their illicit nature. He soon entered an entirely new career when he purchased a stake in the *Marion Democratic Mirror*, where he would toil for the next eight years. Christian probably acquired at least some of the capital for his purchase of this Democratic paper, one of Marion's premier platforms, from profits he secured through Guy Webber's questionable art trade.

The years after the Civil War represent one of the least documented phases of George B. Christian Sr.'s life and career. Christian sifted through many financial opportunities in his early adulthood. From 1864 through 1876, he spent time as a soldier, county employee, contractor, surveyor, bookstore owner, real estate investor, lumberman, publisher, and art salesman. Christian often swung from opportunity to opportunity looking for an enterprise in which to build his fortune. While he never acquired great wealth from his exploits during this period, he seemingly earned enough to support his family. Christian even helped lay the groundwork for at least one of Guy Webber's money-making plots and left it before he received significant blame for its nefarious methods. Christian strove to take advantage of the developing economy in the Midwest during the age of Reconstruction. While he never found one particular economic niche in which to direct all of his efforts in these years, the scope of his search for success placed him among other struggling entrepreneurs of the time. Thus, Christian's efforts probably more closely resembled those of the fictional character of Colonel Sellers than captains of industry like Rockefeller and Carnegie. Even though he never quite found his perfect calling in these years, Christian's willingness to innovate paid off in future business ventures.

CHAPTER 4

A Trip to Summerland

"It is this 'streak of silver sea,' this glittering chain of linked
bays and coves and sunny sounds, this sun-kissed line of
sapphire waters, that makes the Indian River Country the
Riviera of America." C. Vickerstaff Hine, *On the Indian River*
(Chicago: Charles H. Sergel & Company, 1891), 58.

George B. Christian Sr. loved adventures. He also enjoyed
recounting his excursions for friends and neighbors. Storytelling gave
Christian the pleasure of reliving the exhilaration he experienced
during his travels. When he visited Europe in 1876, he wrote
letters to the *Marion Democratic Mirror* so his friends might share
his experiences in the Old World. Christian continued composing
accounts of his exploits for publication throughout his life, emulating
a long tradition of travel writing embraced by American readers in the
late nineteenth century. The expansion of railroads and prosperity in
the decades after the Civil War made travel cheaper, easier, and more
attainable for the growing middle class. With this increased mobility
came a wider demand for information about destinations far and near.

Some of Christian's most vivid writing depicted his first trip
to Florida—the state he nicknamed Summerland—in 1877. This
expedition deserves special attention, because Christian described it
in two distinct narratives: one set of contemporary letters and one
retrospective memoir. These two accounts of the journey offer the
most thorough record of any period in Christian's life. He loved
documenting his observations about the world, as well as the events
and people he encountered during his travels. By journeying with

Christian through the former Confederacy to the wild edges of the Sunshine State in 1877, readers experienced the beauty and seclusion of nineteenth-century Florida. Christian's reflections offered his readers a window into the realities and fantasies of the South near the end of Reconstruction.[1]

Christian wrote the first account of his trip in a series of letters to the *Marion Democratic Mirror* entitled "A Trip to Summerland." Although he had purchased a stake in the *Mirror* in August of 1876, he had only recently begun to share editing duties at the paper before leaving for Florida. Despite his inexperience as a newspaperman, Christian offered a journalistic and descriptive take on the locations and adventures he and his fellow travelers enjoyed. He was mindful that many of the country's greatest writers, including Mark Twain, Jack London, Washington Irving, and Bayard Taylor, wrote about their journeys for popular audiences. Historian Jeffrey Alan Melton has argued, "No other genre of American literature enjoyed a greater popularity or a more enduring prominence in the nineteenth century than travel writing."[2] It appeared in books, magazines, and newspapers throughout the country and generally served either as a guide for future travelers or an escape for those who might never enjoy the opportunity to leave their own communities.

Christian's newspaper accounts incorporated several of the themes identified by historians as central motifs of the travel-writing genre. Melton has asserted that travel writing both explicitly and implicitly promoted a sense of national community. When describing domestic travel, writers emphasized shared national traditions and identity. Even when describing the beauty of the North American continent's most isolated settings, essayists presented these locales as potential conquests for American adventurers. If they visited foreign locations, authors highlighted the "otherness" of these destinations. They also included a healthy portion of nostalgia for home as a way of maintaining their perspective when describing the grandeur of foreign art and architecture. Thus, writers not only introduced

90

readers to distant destinations, but reminded them of what it meant to be American.[3]

Christian used many of the techniques scholars have identified as a central part of the American travel-writing tradition. For example, Christian addressed his readers directly and pulled them into the narrative as travel companions and friends. In his very first letter, he invited those who wanted to experience his Summerland to "Follow me."[4] He portrayed himself as a wide-eyed spectator whose personal integrity as a tour guide was beyond reproach. He meticulously described the local history and landscapes of the locations he visited. He told humorous stories and employed highly descriptive language. Christian also reassured his readers that despite the many wonders of Florida, he could never love them more than his Marion home.[5]

Fifty-one years after his 1877 trip, Christian wrote a second narrative of his journey and placed it in *My Lost Millions*. This booklet of roughly fifty pages contained Christian's memories of his first exploration of Florida, but the story was packaged within a much different kind of endorsement for the state. He composed it during a very productive year of writing near the end of his life.[6] Having changed his political affiliation during the presidency of Woodrow Wilson (1912–1920), Christian supplemented his own lengthy reminiscences and analysis of the Sunshine State with short statements

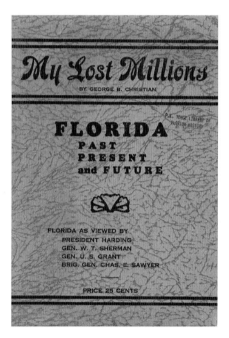

Fig. 35. Cover of Christian's *My Lost Millions*. (George B. Christian Sr., ed. *My Lost Millions: Florida Past, Present, and Future* [Marion, OH: George B. Christian, 1926])

from prominent Republicans such as Ulysses S. Grant, William T. Sherman, Charles Sawyer, and Warren G. Harding.

Christian left his reasons for publishing the booklet and his memories unstated other than to promote Florida as a wonderful place to live and vacation. In one essay, he touted Florida's salubrious weather, its potential as an adventurous destination, and the prospective profits available for land owners in the state. He explained that the title of the pamphlet expressed regret that Christian had not purchased any Florida real estate when he first began vacationing there. Many of his friends in Marion had moved to or retired in Florida. Ever the booster of business and community, Christian's writing aspired to help these friends by encouraging investment and tourism in their state.

The political atmosphere of the country in 1928 suggests another possible motive for the booklet: Christian desired to secure Florida for the Republican ticket. This political motive might explain why he quoted exclusively from prominent Republicans about their experiences in and love for the state. Such statements demonstrated their support for Florida's tourism industry. In his introduction, Christian also mentioned the impact of Florida's four disputed electoral votes in the election of Republican Rutherford B. Hayes in 1876 to emphasize the political importance of the state. The people of Florida had voted for Hayes's opponent Samuel Tilden, but a special electoral committee had ignored their wishes because Floridians had intimidated African American voters. The uncertainty caused by such racial coercion at the polls pushed the result of the election out of the hands of the people. Christian wanted members of the Republican Party both inside and outside the Sunshine State to realize that Southern states played an important role in presidential elections. He hoped that this historical reminder would keep Florida from causing similar electoral drama in the 1928 presidential race between Herbert Hoover and Al Smith.[7] Overall, *My Lost Millions* presented the Sunshine State in its most romantic, politically significant, and profitable light.

Because Christian wrote the letters which appeared in the *Mirror* and the memories in *My Lost Millions* at different times and for distinct purposes, the two accounts often focus on different aspects of the journey. When placed in proper context, however, the two accounts come together to offer a fascinating adventure story about Christian's first expedition to the Florida wilderness.

Christian's trip began on January 29 and lasted until March 1 of 1877. His companions included Thomas P. Wallace, age fifty-four; James Coffy, age sixty-four; and William Fisher, age thirty-two. Wallace was one of the wealthier men in Marion and had married Christian's aunt Jane Elizabeth Busby. After trying his hand at publishing the *Buckeye Eagle* newspaper and dabbling in the mercantile business, Wallace found his true calling when he leveraged capital from his store to enter banking. In 1854, he and several partners opened the Marion Deposit Bank, and Wallace soon became a successful financier with a hand in most of the city's prominent commercial endeavors. James Coffy was born in Ireland and immigrated to the United States at age two. He moved to Marion in 1864. Coffy initially worked as an importer of luxury goods, but he eventually turned to the shipping, breeding, and selling of fine horses. William Fisher was slightly younger than Christian, and after the trip he eventually became a partner in a company that manufactured sulkies (light-weight wagons) in Marion. While friendship was the primary commonality among the travelers, all of them, either by birth or prosperity, held or gained a place in the city's upper middle class.

As the four companions embarked on their journey, the uncertainty caused by the 1876 election dominated the national consciousness. This political context surfaced in Christian's letters to the *Mirror*, in which he argued that the Floridians he met on his trip had perceived no voter suppression. Instead, Christian opined that Florida had voted Democratic because the people hated their Reconstruction government and the federal troops still in place there. While Christian criticized Northern Reconstruction-era policies, he was also very critical, at times, of the South's culture and legacy. The vestiges of the Civil War colored Christian's view of the former Confederacy, especially in the contemporary letters he wrote for publication in Marion.

Although neither of Christian's accounts transparently stated the motivation for the trip, together they offer several clues. *My Lost Millions* makes the case that Christian, an avid outdoorsman, had been invited by his uncle, Thomas P. Wallace, to tag along. Both Christian and Wallace looked forward to the isolated hunting, fishing, and adventure offered by the southern Atlantic coast. Christian also touted the health benefits of the warm-weather state as a possible justification for the trip. Whether from mental or physical illness, Christian often struggled with his health. Consequently, he might also have felt that Florida's warm climate offered a perfect opportunity to improve his constitution.

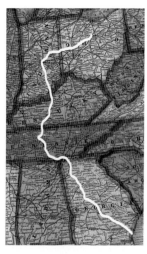

Fig. 36. This adapted map shows Christian's route from Ohio to the Georgia coast. (Map by Gaylord Watson, *Centennial American Republic and railroad map of the United States and of the Dominion of Canada*, 1876. Courtesy of the Library of Congress)

The foursome began their long adventure on January 29, 1877. The expedition first headed west from Marion by train to Indianapolis and then turned south. The travelers booked passage on the Louisville and Nashville Railroad, which took them through those two cities by way of Bowling Green, Kentucky. Along the way, a hot box (fire caused by an overheated axle) delayed their progress for three hours and caused them to miss a connection. Christian commented after this two-day jaunt to Nashville that the devil haunted the Southern railroad system.

Christian's first two letters to the *Mirror* primarily described the trip from Marion to Florida. In his accounts, he attempted to satiate readers' curiosity about the condition of former Confederate states. To Christian, the Tennessee houses that he spied from his cabin window looked old fashioned with their exterior chimneys. He concluded that the outmoded construction methods demonstrated how Southerners possessed "a seeming lack of willingness to change, to learn, a sort of slip and go-easy way of taking things easy, grafted upon them in the old slave era."[8] Such observations reflected the predominant Northern view of the South as underdeveloped, a view that persisted in newspapers and popular culture for many years after the Civil War. The conflict over slavery and the brutality of war had created significant social distance between the North and South, and Christian assimilated northern preconceptions about the southern states.

On the other hand, Christian felt a certain kinship with and empathy for many aspects of the South. For instance, he expressed genuine emotion when the party passed a cemetery. Christian hoped soldiers from both sides buried there could come to represent a spirit of reconciliation between North and South. One of the first places Christian described in detail to the people of Marion was Nashville, Tennessee, where the travelers took some time to explore. Christian praised the Nashville Public Library for displaying images of both Union and Confederate heroes in the same lobby. In many ways, Christian seemed ready to forgive the horrors of the war—though it is important to remember that he saw very little combat or danger. While in Tennessee, he also made a pilgrimage to the house of James K. Polk, the Democrat who had successfully overseen victory in the 1848 war with Mexico and the expansion of U.S. borders to the Pacific Ocean. For Christian, Polk stood as a nostalgic figure who symbolized the last time North and South fought together in common cause. Christian evaluated Nashville positively when he concluded, "On the whole, I like Nashville, a handsome place truly, an air of wealth, homes surrounded by evidences of taste and refinement, the air warm, and balmy and fragrant with magnolias, which grow in every door-yard in the city, a hospitable people, a favored location."[9] The Tennessee city that had teetered between Union and Confederate control became a symbol, to Christian, of possible regional reconciliation.

In his travelogues, Christian often expressed his prejudices and sympathies toward the South within the same letter. He, like the rest of the North, was working through feelings about the Confederacy that he and his fellow Union men had fought against more than ten years before. Such contrasting feelings persisted as his group left Nashville and took a train southeast, passing through Chattanooga, Tennessee, on their way to Atlanta. Of Georgia, Christian commented that the southern red soil looked much inferior to that of the Midwest. He also pointed out to potential readers that, despite Northern stereotypes, the Southerners there looked neither lazy nor nefarious. These characteristics were central themes of cartoonist Thomas Nast's portrayal of Southerners, which Christian blamed for much regional antagonism and prejudice. Yet after condemning such portrayals, he proceeded to racially profile both Northerners and Southerners:

> The type of race [in the South] seems to be pure American lacking in that strong infusion of foreign blood that is common with us [in the North]. And in this we may be able to account for the rather more energetic character of the Northman. We have integrated the industrious and economic habits and methods of many races who possess prominently such traits and the result is good.[10]

Thus, Christian both criticized and reaffirmed stereotypes about the North and South, demonstrating the uncertainty generated by the war and its resolution.

Developments in Atlanta impressed Christian. The city represented the possibilities for progress that existed in the South with the help of Northern capital. Christian, like many Northerners, believed that the best hope for Southern advancement required embracing the capitalist achievements of the North. Atlanta was developing into the Southern hub for processing cotton into cloth, which brought heavy Northern investments into the city. Christian wrote to his fellow Marionites that although the fall of Atlanta had represented the beginning of the end for the Confederacy, the rise of the city anew boded well for the future development of much of the South.[11]

After leaving Atlanta, the friends proceeded further south and east to the coastal city of Brunswick, Georgia, where they embarked on a short ferry ride through the Cumberland Sound to the Floridian city of Fernandina. The group then traveled south by rail to Jacksonville. Christian complained about the bumpiness of the sixty-seven-mile route that took five hours to complete. He described the rails along this stage as "two streaks of rust, and a right of way" and the rhythm of the train as "bump-it-a-bump, growling and groaning."[12] On each step of their journey, the travelers moved farther and farther to the edges of railroad development in the United States.

Fig. 37. Adapted map traces Christian's route through Florida. (Map by Gaylord Watson, *Centennial American Republic and railroad map of the United States and of the Dominion of Canada,* 1876. Courtesy of the Library of Congress)

When they arrived at Jacksonville, Christian found much to recommend about the city. In his second letter he wrote of his newfound Summerland: "For fifteen years man and boy. I have dreamed of a land like this." Christian's letter sounded almost like an advertisement. He focused on the lovely weather, nice hotels, low cost of living, politeness of the people, and general pleasantness of the location. The many vacationers who thought the warm, fresh air would improve their health prospects fascinated him. He also commented on the way the city drew in the extremely wealthy—pointing out that William B. Astor Jr., the son of the New York real estate titan, had docked his yacht in the city.[13]

In Jacksonville, the four men gathered supplies for their more adventurous expedition into the south-central Atlantic coast of the state. The Prohibition Era context of *My Lost Millions* inspired Christian to include some interesting facts about the supplying process. He joked about how he, as the only

ON THE ST. JOHNS.

Fig. 38. Depiction of the St. Johns River (circa 1875) (Sidney Lanier, *Florida: Its Scenery, Climate, and History* [Philadelphia: J.B. Lippincott & Co., 1875])

Democrat and explicit non-believer in temperance among his fellow travelers at the time, was tasked to buy whiskey for the trip. Believing his Prohibition audience might judge their alcoholic consumption askance, Christian joked that they only planned to drink the whiskey in case of snakebite. The cohort took passage on a steamboat traveling south on the northward-flowing St. Johns River, which winds through an extensive series of lakes along a slow path to the ocean. One memorable moment during the trip occurred because the steamboat captain brought his new bride, and she became upset when she thought he was being too polite to another female passenger. Christian, his colleagues, and the crew had a good laugh when the angry bride locked her husband momentarily out of their shared cabin. Seventy-five miles down the river they docked in the small community of Palatka, which Christian described as an invalid resort with a population of one thousand. After this short stop, the travelers continued south until they reached the city of Mellonville on Lake George.[14]

Mellonville's citrus cultivation impressed Christian and his friends. Jesuits had originally settled the city, and the Sicilian lemon trees growing there revealed the Old World influence the clergy had brought with them. In Mellonville, the brave adventurers hired another boat to carry them all the way down the St. Johns to Salt Lake, near the river's source. This boat had a crew of two and barely enough space for the four other travelers. They first navigated to the city of Enterprise on the shores of Lake Monroe. This branch of the St. Johns River slowly dwindled into Snake Creek, a small stream that derived its name from its meandering path.[15]

Christian commented extensively on the scenery found along the St. Johns. He recorded seeing a "mass of forest and semi vegetation as yet undisturbed" along the river's edge. "It seemed that every few rods of the slimy banks was the habitat of an enormous alligator." In fact, Christian and his companions

Fig. 39. Illustration of an alligator hunting expedition on the St. Johns River. (Courtesy of the Library of Congress.)

unsuccessfully attempted to hunt some of the reptiles. Another descriptive passage claimed that "no pen could describe the bird life that filled the air and covered the waters with myriads of beautifully plumaged birds and acres of wild life." Christian observed parakeets, flamingos, and many other exotic birds in this southern paradise. Along with his description of the parakeets, he mentioned their possible danger to local citrus harvests. Christian wanted his readers to picture the beauty of the Florida wilderness and the perilous nature of human civilization on its edges.[16]

Throughout the state, the travelers continued to encounter settlements of those who had moved to Florida because of ill health. Although he bemoaned the terrible loss and suffering experienced by those fighting consumption, a disease now generally known to have been tuberculosis, Christian noted that he would convalesce himself to death in such a community, surrounded by illness and despair. The dynamic of shared anguish embraced in such hotels and resorts seemed to trouble him.[17]

While paddling up the marshes of Snake Creek, Christian and his companions endured the rain and wind of a tropical storm that caused them to doubt their vessel's seaworthiness. Christian later described how the storm initiated a chorus of bull alligators whose bellowing was so discordant and loud that it kept all the travelers awake throughout the storm. Luckily, they arrived at their destination, Salt Lake, shortly after the tempest had passed. According to Christian, the lake was a brackish body of water spanning only two by three miles.

After landing on the shores of Salt Lake, the group fell in with a two-mule caravan headed for Titusville. Christian wrote, "We made the drive in three hours over a road where our wheels sank deep into the ever present sand, passing through, mile after mile, of open pine woods, as entirely devoid of life as I imagine the moon to be." In Titusville, they met the city's eccentric namesake, General Henry T. Titus, whose nephew had led their caravan. General Titus had served as the adjutant

Fig. 40. Henry Titus, founder of Titusville. (Courtesy of the Florida Historical Society Portrait Collection)

general of the Pennsylvania militia in his younger days. He had also supported the proslavery forces in bleeding Kansas and accompanied filibusterer William Walker on his expedition to Nicaragua before serving in the Florida militia during the Civil War.[18] Titus had settled in Florida for his health and built a hotel in the settlement that would become Titusville—so designated because he ran the post office and was thus empowered to name the town. He supposedly sat for hours each day on his front porch with a loaded gun, hoping his enemies would pass by. Christian and his companions found him personable enough, but they soon located a ship and captain to take them farther along their journey by way of the Indian River.[19]

Fig. 41. This early photograph depicts an Indian River landing in the 1870s, near the time when Christian visited the Florida Coast. (Courtesy of Florida Memory, State Archives of Florida)

The Indian River enthralled Christian and his companions. The 200-mile river runs between Florida's Atlantic coast and a parallel series of long, narrow barrier islands.[20] Beyond its natural beauty, the river also hosted a certain level of historical intrigue. As Christian pointed out in *My Lost Millions*, the Indian River served as the route that John Breckinridge, Confederate secretary of war, took to escape from the United States en route to Cuba at the end of the Civil War.[21]

Fig. 42. The Indian River at Cocoa Beach, Florida. (Courtesy of the Library of Congress.)

The company embarked on their voyage down the river aboard a boat skippered by Charley Carlin, who was, according to Christian, one of the region's most famous riverboat captains. Carlin served as guide as well as captain, and under his direction the explorers first attempted to camp on the beach. While Christian wrote of the party's apprehension at sleeping so near the forest and the dangerous reptiles within its dark reaches, the travelers slept well within their tent amid the night cries of birds and animals. They soon began to feel comfortable camping, and they often awoke to find that deer had passed near their tents in the middle of the night.[22]

In his February 15 letter to the *Mirror*, Christian described the night he awoke to a sniffling noise and saw a shadowy figure outside the party's tent. A few moments later, a shaggy head and indefinable form crept through the entrance of the shelter. Christian rapidly searched for his gun, but then remembered that it was on the boat. He drew his hands into fists to protect himself when he finally realized that the dangerous intruder was his companion James Coffy. All of the party had a good laugh at Christian's expense and then went back to sleep.[23]

While most of their trip along the Indian River cut through vast swaths of unsettled coastline, Christian and his friends occasionally came into contact with the vestiges of civilization. At one landing, they saw a prospective site for a land-grant agricultural college proposed by the Reconstruction government

Fig. 43. The Indian River near Pelican Island. (Courtesy of the Library of Congress.)

and later abandoned—Christian criticized carpet-bagging regimes for such wasteful projects. The group also ran into an alcoholic former journalist who had left his job in New York City and moved to the Florida coast. The man, a Mr. Bickley, lived a solitary life in a cabin on the river, and his wild, educated ways provided an interesting distraction for the company as well as a metaphor for the inability of technology and civilization to conquer the wild landscape.[24]

Near the present-day city of Fort Pierce, the four friends embarked on their grand oceanic fishing enterprise. They first crossed over the Indian River to Hutchinson Island, one of the many barrier islands that ran parallel to the coast. Captain Carlin, as the group's fishing instructor, caught a large number of mullet fish to use as bait.

Fig. 44. Photograph of the Indian River at Turkey Creek Landing near present-day Palm Bay. (Courtesy of the Library of Congress.)

Each adventurer used waders to walk chest-high into the sea before throwing a weighted, baited hook as far out into the surf as possible. Then each fisherman turned around with his line strung over his shoulder and walked to shore, catching and dragging fish in the process. Christian estimated that they caught 5,000 pounds of fish in one hour using this method.[25]

After their fishing adventure, they visited a camp set up by turtle hunters where hundreds of the animals were confined within a pen. It seems that the travelers were as surprised by the size of the sea turtles as by anything else they encountered on their trip. It was at this camp that Christian unexpectedly found himself in peril. On a stormy day, an African American youth from the encampment shot a duck, which fell into the middle of the river. Christian and the shooter pushed out in a small boat to recover the animal—hoping to augment their boring diet of fish and fruit. In the midst of this culinary scavenge, Christian rapidly found himself in need of his own rescue. Swirling winds had pushed his vessel into a dangerous eddy. While the boy jumped from the boat to swim to shore, Christian feared the threatening water too much to risk swimming. The crashing waves soon overturned his boat and he found himself treading water. Carlin, the boat captain, witnessed the incident and quickly rescued the floundering Christian. Once on shore, Christian recovered with the help of some whiskey and enthusiastically thanked the captain for his heroics. After their fishing, turtling, and swimming adventures, the companions set off for home, with a giant pelican skeleton as a souvenir in tow, and arrived in Marion a week later.[26]

Christian's 1877 trip to Florida introduced him to a state that he revisited many times as he grew older, especially in times of ill health. Fourteen years after this initial trip, Christian returned to many of the same sites. On this later occasion, he traveled with future president Warren G. Harding, and their party was able to ride the railroads to all of the distant locations that had required such boldness and toil to reach less than two decades earlier. Christian wrote a series of travelogues about his 1891 trip for the *Marion Star*. While the stories of his earlier trip focused primarily on the excitement, isolation, and wild romanticism of Florida, his 1891 evaluations centered on the state's subsequent development. Christian offered a lengthy discussion of the budding tourism infrastructure both for health and leisure. He also explored the development of citrus agriculture and railroads. By 1891, Florida hosted a significant population of Ohio expatriates, and Christian enjoyed interacting with those who had relocated to his so-called Summerland. But despite his many return visits, Christian never again experienced the same pristine wilderness he encountered in 1877.

During his first trip, Christian perceived the Florida wilderness almost as a mythical destination—outside the realms of history and civilization. At the time, the region seemed almost impenetrable to the forces of modernity. In Christian's heart, these unspoiled wilds could not exist in the same state as the violent suppression of African American voters which led to the controversies of the 1876 presidential election. For Christian, Florida was his summerland—a place of recuperation and adventure, of fruit and fauna, of life outside the concerns of the everyday world. At the same time, he recognized the land's great value to capitalists and developers. This is why he bemoaned his "lost millions."[27] Perhaps Christian's romantic view of Florida overwhelmed his entrepreneurial spirit until it was too late.

Nevertheless, his health and sense of adventure guaranteed continued travels to the state and its mild winter climate. Christian's 1877 trip represented only the beginning of his complex and enthusiastic relationship with the southern peninsular state which culminated in his manuscript, *My Lost Millions*.

CHAPTER 5

The *Mirror* Man

"The country editor by having his personality 'known and read of all men,' must not only shoulder the responsibility of all he writes, but of all he publishes; and this, too, amid a thousand perplexities and discouragements, of which the public have little conception, and award no indulgence. He must read all his exchanges, write articles on any and every topic, rend proof, oversee and frequently work in his office, keep books, collect his dues and pay his debts, talk to all who call, and is expected to be at the editorial table, every exhibition, auction, fire, fight or show, and gets censured if remiss in any of the multifarious duties which the reading public thus place upon him." Marcus H. Rogers, cited in "The Country Editor's Work," *Decatur (IL) Republican*, Sep. 17, 1868.

George B. Christian Sr.'s work as a small-town newspaper editor represented a relatively short period of his life, but his editorial efforts inspired his community to view him as a political and intellectual leader. He purchased a stake in the *Marion Democratic Mirror* in August of 1876, at the age of thirty, and sold it in September of 1882. At first glance, his time at the paper seems atypical when compared with his longer career's focus on manufacturing and infrastructure. Nonetheless, Christian had always demonstrated an interest in the written word, and his editorial stint personified his entrepreneurial spirit, affinity for public service, and desire to chronicle and commemorate his life, community, and changing world. During this period of his life, his associates knew him as the *Mirror* Man. The *Marion Democratic Mirror* became an extension of Christian's personality and beliefs. Since almost every issue of the *Mirror* from his tenure has been preserved on microfilm, the newspaper holds the largest surviving repository of Christian's ideas, friendships, rivalries, and political beliefs.

Because the source material in the *Marion Democratic Mirror* and its rival, the *Marion Independent*, is so vast, discerning which daily arguments, insults, and issues were most significant requires carefully sifting. This chapter focuses on three aspects of Christian's time in the newspaper business: its impact on the narrative of his life, how it reflected his personality and perspectives, and how he used it to promote improvements in the city he loved. The story of Christian's time with the *Mirror* is a tale about the purchase of a publishing business and the attempt to make it successful. Christian felt drawn to a career path that offered him influence and fulfillment, but because he had a young family of five to support, he also looked at the *Mirror* as a business venture.

In the late nineteenth century, printing country newspapers was a tedious occupation. The *Mirror* was printed on the city's first cylinder press powered by steam. Each week, editors wrote, compiled, and edited handwritten copy for the paper. They then helped set the type in frames on the press's large rotating cylinder. Typesetting required careful measurement and placement; editors arranged the metal letters backwards into headlines, articles, and advertisements. Each edition of the newspaper generally contained four pages. Newspaper workers first printed

PATENT SINGLE LARGE CYLINDER PRINTING MACHINE.

Fig. 45. Illustration of a Hoe Printing Press from an advertisement; it was similar in design to the printing press used by the *Marion Democratic Mirror.* (Courtesy of the Library of Congress)

pages one and four by manually loading the newsprint into the press. While the ink dried on this first set of pages, they reset the type and proofed pages two and three. Laborers then printed those pages on the backs of the previous ones. After completing the printing, workers folded the papers before sending them out for delivery. Because of the steam, printing was hot, sweaty work, especially in the summer. The ink was petroleum based, which meant that the fumes could cause irritation and illness. While Christian and his partners hired people to help with this process, their work as editors was hands on and not a purely intellectual endeavor. Because the *Mirror* editors also owned the printing press from which the newspaper came, they supplemented their subscription income with printing jobs for the local government and surrounding community. They also managed the newspaper's finances and sold advertisements. In truth, the editor-owners of Marion newspapers played a role in almost every aspect of their businesses.[1]

The *Mirror* was a country weekly, a classification that referred to its focus and the frequency of its publication. Under the masthead, the front page generally offered a mix of poetry, fiction, advertisements, and general news pulled from larger dailies. The *Mirror's* masthead consisted of the paper's name in big block type with the year of its founding underneath along with the volume and issue numbers. To the right appeared the names of the editors and the paper's advertising and subscription rates. Editorial

Fig. 45. A representative front page of the *Marion Democratic Mirror* during the time when Christian served as one of its editors. (*Marion [OH] Democratic Mirror,* Mar. 15, 1877)

comments on local, state, and national stories of interest dominated the second page. Page two also served as the forum for the nastiest disputes and meanest personal attacks between papers and their editors. The third page most often consisted of advertisements and personal notices. Here, a reader could peruse the births, deaths, and weddings in the community and also determine who recently had celebrated a birthday or visited nearby towns. Advertisements and notices typically covered the final page, as well as one to three columns of general interest information.

Small-town newspapers served their communities best by making the news relevant to their homegrown population. As the *Mirror* editors once pointed out, "The strong point of a country weekly is local news. . . .When a person sees his own name in print, no matter how small the item, it suddenly becomes quite important—that is, both item and newspaper."[2] The *Mirror* mixed local commentary, stories, and news with content pulled off the telegraph wires from all over the country and the world. The first job of the editor involved deciding which content merited inclusion. Overall, editors succeeded by connecting politically, socially, and culturally with local readers.[3]

Such personal relationships helped the newspaper business weather financial troubles better than industries dependent on outside markets. The Panic of 1873 had ended the post–Civil War economic boom in the North. The panic had begun in September of that year, when Jay Cooke and Company, a prominent banking firm, collapsed after struggling to liquidate bonds issued by the Union Pacific Railroad Company, one of the corporations involved in the construction of the transcontinental railroad.[4] The firm's demise showed other investors that the economic prosperity driven, in some measure, by the speculative over-financing of railroad expansion had ended. When account holders feared for their banks' viability, they panicked and converged quickly to withdraw their money. Often, these bank runs forced the institutions to close, vastly decreasing the capital available for infrastructural development. Railroads, and the industries that provided the materials for their expansion, contracted quickly. For five years, the economy declined, causing widespread unemployment and labor unrest. Like it had elsewhere, the downturn halted construction in Marion, reducing the demand for Christian's skills as a civil engineer. The printing business, while not massively profitable, offered Christian a chance to make a living outside the boom and bust cycles of the construction industry. He initially invested in the *Mirror* as a silent partner, but soon found that he wanted to play a role in Marion's political discussion.[5]

The *Mirror* offered Christian a platform to try to influence and comment on local and national politics in the Reconstruction era, which historians have identified as the beginning of the Third Party System.[6] In these years, political parties became almost tribal in nature as party affiliation aligned with religious and ethnic backgrounds. Such loyalties played a tangible role in the lives of everyday Americans, and more than seventy percent of eligible voters commonly turned out for elections. Historian Michael E. McGerr has described party loyalty during this time by arguing, "For mid-nineteenth-century Northerners, party became a natural lens through which to view the world. . . . Party encouraged an intense, dogmatic cast of mind. Men made little distinction between fact and opinion: one's beliefs, Northerners assumed, rightly conditioned one's perception."[7] According to McGerr, the press and political parties formed symbiotic relationships, as editors worked to secure partisan support in return for governmental patronage in the form of printing, advertising, and even lucrative appointments to the postal service. Thus, papers encouraged their readers to see the world through partisan glasses at every level of government and policy at a time when partisanship was divorced from ideology.[8]

Partisanship created an audience and revenue source for local newspapers throughout most of the nineteenth century, and this economic stake drove political backbiting. Readers looked to newspapers as much for entertainment as for information, and heated party rhetoric whetted their competitive spirit and loyalty. Christian and his partners, as the editors of the town's Democratic newspaper, often attacked and counterattacked his Republican

Fig. 47. George Crawford was Christian's and Harding's great editorial rival who owned and operated the *Marion (OH) Independent* (Leggett, Conaway & Co. *The History of Marion County, Ohio: Containing a History of the County* [Chicago: Leggett, Conaway & Co., 1883])

rival, George Crawford of the *Marion Independent*. Crawford was a former lawyer and soldier who had run the *Independent* for fourteen years when Christian purchased a stake in the *Mirror*. During Christian's tenure, the two men fought political battles over many candidates and issues—both national and local. Readers loved when the editors' political disagreements degenerated into the realm of personal insults, and subscribers expected strong and entertaining advocacy as one of the signs of local political leadership. For five years, Christian and Crawford clashed in a war of words that occasionally tumbled into the realm of the ridiculous, but always demonstrated both sides' love of party and political warfare.

The politics of Reconstruction provided fertile fodder for the bickering editors. Scandal had rocked the later years of Ulysses S. Grant's presidency (1868–1876). His administration, and the government over which it presided, had been accused of cronyism and corruption. Many Northerners had tired of radical Republicans' efforts to fundamentally change the tense racial environment of the South through occupation and harsh policies restricting these states' re-entry into the Union. President Grant, never a stalwart antiracist himself, had seemed to wane in his commitment to these policies. Christian invested in the *Mirror* knowing it offered him the opportunity to support the Marion paper which was making the case for the Democratic Party in the 1876 election. This contest was perceived as a referendum about how to mend a divided nation ten years after the surrender of Lee to Grant. For the first time since the war, Democrats felt they held a legitimate opportunity to win the presidency. Christian also cared deeply about the fate of local Democrats. Large-scale political involvement among Marionites created contentious city and county elections. Marion County was firmly Democratic, but Ohio as a whole tended to vote for Republicans. Competitive elections in Marion created the perception among its newspapers and their subscribers that Ohio could swing for either presidential candidate in 1876.[9]

Christian was a silent partner in the editorial battle over the disputed election between Republican Rutherford B. Hayes and Democrat Samuel Tilden in 1876. The tenured editor of the *Mirror*, James Newcomer, initially rejoiced over what he thought was a close Democratic presidential victory—Tilden had apparently won a majority in both the Electoral College and popular vote. Disputed election results in Southern states where whites had violently suppressed the votes of African Americans, however, led to a large degree of uncertainty about which votes should stand. Marion newspaper editors charged

Fig. 48. The politician the *Mirror* dubbed his Fraudulency, Rutherford B. Hayes. (Courtesy of the Library of Congress.)

into this vacuum of indecision with strongly partisan opinions and coverage. In the *Independent,* George Crawford argued that the president of the Senate was constitutionally empowered to cast a deciding vote about which disputed local election results to certify. Under such a scenario, the Senate president could have invalidated the election results from Southern states. On the other hand, the *Mirror* supported Ohio Senator Allan G. Thurman's contention that an electoral commission should be convened with members from the House, Senate, and Supreme Court to sort out the difficult situation. The *Mirror's* editors hoped the commission would find that the election fraud produced through intimidation

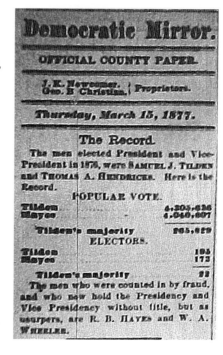

Fig. 49. The *Mirror* printed the vote totals from the presidential election of 1876 to remind the people of Marion about what Democrats believed was a fraudulent Republican victory. The notice claimed a 265,629 vote popular majority for Tilden which should have resulted in a twenty-two vote electoral college victory. (*Marion [OH] Democratic Mirror,* Feb. 15, 1877)

of African American voters in the South mirrored nefarious voting results created by political machines in the North. If one form of fraud neutralized the other, the popular will of the people could be accepted. Ultimately, the *Mirror* regretted its support of the commission when this body declared victory for Rutherford B. Hayes. The *Mirror* never considered Hayes a legitimate president and printed the "true" electoral vote totals in every edition for almost nine months in protest of the candidate it dubbed "His Fraudulency" and "Usurper."[10]

Although Christian initially signed on to the paper only as an investor, he decided to become its coeditor in January of 1877. The paper carried no reason for this change, but it meant that he became intricately involved in the work and mission of the small-town newspaper. During his first few months as coeditor, Christian wrote five letters about his trip to Florida. Upon his return to Marion in March, he started writing editorial copy for the newspaper. Christian quickly caught the attention of George Crawford, who observed:

> We supposed that for pure, unadulterated meanness
> and audacity the Senior editor of the *Mirror*, long ago,
> had reached the lowest depths, but it was reserved for
> the Junior editor of that sheet, at one attempt, "to bring
> up mud" from "a lower deep." If he enjoys the wallow
> we have no objection to such enjoyment being his.[11]

Something Christian had written had clearly antagonized the *Independent* newspaperman—beginning a rivalry that played out on a weekly basis in coming years.[12]

Local disputes in Marion often received as much coverage as national issues. For example, an editorial argument erupted between the *Mirror* and the *Independent* in early 1877. The affair began when Christian allegedly insulted Irishman John O'Ragan on the eve of the 1876 election. Christian supposedly called O'Ragan a "yellow dog," which referred to "a person or thing of no account or of a low type."[13] Christian allegedly made the comment when slightly inebriated and the exchange had attracted little public attention at the time it was made. This changed in March and April, when George Crawford printed an account of the incident. The editors of the *Mirror* and *Independent* soon clashed in a war of words regarding what had been said and to whom. Such duels took time to mellow because editors had to wait a week before they could respond to an insult. In the pages of the *Mirror*, Christian claimed that Crawford had questioned his honor and threatened to sue the *Independent* for libel. Crawford, for his part, kept referring to witnesses willing to testify about Christian's derogatory statements. Although the posturing between the two papers often felt forced, the stakes of this argument loomed over both ends of Marion's political spectrum. Irish immigrants made up one of the core constituencies of the Democratic Party, while Republicans often struggled to fight claims of xenophobia because of their anti-immigrant policies. Crawford, in accusing Christian of anti-Irish feelings, was attempting to break up the political marriage between the Irish and Democrats in Marion by discrediting an influential Democratic leader.[14]

Personal attacks related to the yellow dog incident had quieted by that summer when the Great Railroad Strike of 1877 confronted the country. This tumultuous event occurred as railroad companies, facing lower revenues in the aftermath of the 1873 financial panic, slashed railroad workers' wages. The resulting discontent coalesced with national workers' fears about unemployment and distrust of employers, creating an explosive state of affairs. In the summer of 1877, workers on the Baltimore & Ohio Railroad struck and vowed to keep all railroad routes bottled up until their bosses returned wages to pre-panic levels. The strike soon spread north from Baltimore to Pittsburgh and Philadelphia before migrating west to Saint Louis and Chicago. The movement became the largest work stoppage the country had ever experienced. The situation eventually required the intervention and violence of federal troops deployed by President Rutherford B. Hayes to end the strike.

While the *Mirror*'s editors, James Newcomer and George B. Christian Sr., took great pains to decry the tremendous violence and perceived political radicalism associated with the strike, they also claimed that "causes naturally produce effect"; namely, that the "destruction of property and mob violence," while "in no way excusable," were the direct result of legislation that "favor[ed] capital at the sacrifice of labor." The *Mirror*'s attempts to understand the strikers contrasted significantly with those of the *Independent*, which

Fig. 50. Chaotic images of Pittsburgh during the Railroad Strike of 1877 offer a sense of chaos and fear associated with the action. (Courtesy of the Library of Congress)

came out staunchly against the strike. The rival paper printed that the strike was predictable because "the communistic element was so strong in some of the larger cities that . . . trouble was certain." The Republican paper also criticized Democratic reluctance to call for federal troops to put down the strike. Clearly, each paper used its own partisan lens to identify the villains in the conflict.[15]

Although the *Mirror* and *Independent* spent significant time arguing over political issues, they often found common ground when it came to promoting business in their city. For example, both papers supported the construction of a third railroad through Marion when it was proposed in early 1878; Marion hoped to become a stop on a line that traversed Chicago and Atlanta. Such advocacy personified the booster ethos that historians have identified as a key component in the work of nineteenth-century newspapermen. According to historian Sally Forman Griffeth, "Economic growth . . . was the nineteenth-century town's reason for being, and the booster ethos assumed that the interests of local businesses were identical with those of the community as a whole."[16] Thus, most editors driven by this understanding encouraged the development of local business as a public good. This attitude extended to the local captains of industry, whom the newspapers framed as natural community leaders. The booster ethos assumed that civic and business leaders followed moral principles to guide financial and community development. Consequently, editors pushed for city improvement because they felt it would advance the overall moral foundation of the community. The spirit of boosterism in Marion was generally non-partisan—though the *Mirror* and *Independent* sometimes disagreed about which projects the community should prioritize.[17]

Christian and Newcomer felt that expansion and development were also essential for the growth and health of their newspaper. In April of 1878, the *Mirror* moved its offices into Marion's newly constructed Masonic building across from the courthouse on Center Street which provided room for expanding their workspace. The move helped support the local Masonic brotherhood to which the editors both belonged. Along with the change of office, the following months saw Newcomer make a decision to leave the paper. In August, Christian and Newcomer advertised heavily in the *Mirror* to encourage subscribers to settle their debts—citing a considerable need for money at the time. Although they chose not to comment on the nature of that need, Newcomer's impending exit from the paper might have played an important role in such an appeal; additional cash in hand would allow the partners to equally divide the paper's assets. This exit occurred on October 31, 1878, accompanied by a sentimental editorial from Newcomer. He did not explain why he left, but an 1883 history of Marion County attributed his departure to illness. In turning the editorial reins over to Christian, Newcomer outlined that "Mr. Christian assumes sole management, and we retire, with a reluctance equally shared. The tone, liberality, and political adherence heretofore pursued by the *Mirror* will be continued under the exclusive new management."[18] From November 1878 until December 1880, Christian edited and owned the *Mirror* alone. In a rare humanitarian gesture, Crawford mentioned the change of ownership and said kind things about both proprietors—wishing them good luck in everything but politics. On November 14, 1878, the *Mirror* published a series of comments from newspapers in surrounding counties about the paper's editorial shift. The statements read like pep talks, expressing admiration for the departing Newcomer and confidence in Christian and the *Mirror*'s future success. Christian wanted to assure his readers and advertisers about his capacity and drive for editing the *Mirror* in hopes of securing their future patronage.[19]

One of the first community development projects that George B. Christian Sr. supported as sole editor of the *Marion Democratic Mirror* was the construction of an opera house. Near the end of 1878, the *Mirror* printed a petition signed by a number of prominent Marionites—among them Christian, Newcomer, and George Crawford—calling for a public meeting to discuss the possibility of constructing such a facility. The committee formed at this meeting began planning the facility's construction. Although the papers reported that a series of meetings had taken place, the project seemed to fizzle out with the coming of the New Year. Even though the community boosters failed to secure their goal at the time, the publicity they brought to the project opened the door for future success. Once again, Christian and Crawford spoke out in mutual support of a project that benefitted the city they loved.[20]

Grief graced the pages of the *Mirror* on January 30, 1879, when it reported the death of a prominent Marionite. Eliza Busby was the second wife of George H. Busby, Christian's namesake and grandfather. While Eliza was not Christian's biological grandmother, she was the only one he had ever known. He framed her death as the passing of one of the last remaining pioneers of Marion County. Her death sparked a discussion of her and her husband's legacy as well as that of Marion's other early white settlers. Remembrances of early Marion persisted in the *Mirror* for several weeks. Christian often wrote about Marion's past because his roots among the county's founders gave him authority and confidence greater than his thirty-three years might have normally inspired.[21]

Newspapermen wielded political leadership in their communities, and the burdens of this leadership sometimes necessitated forceful advocacy and other times required bipartisanship. Christian and Crawford were true believers in their own political tribes. Consequently, both men demonstrated their partisan leadership through their most bitter insults and rants. Readers expected the papers to rile up political fervor, and editors often competed in explosive debates. But despite the animosity and rivalry expressed in copy between the *Mirror* and *Independent,* propriety often required that political enemies work together for the good of the community. For example, in May of 1879, Christian and Crawford served together on the planning committee for Marion's Independence Day celebration. Such interpersonal cooperation inspires skepticism about the real zeal behind their partisan writing. While the two never considered each other friends, Christian and Crawford probably never felt the same level of personal hostility that they expressed in their weeklies.[22]

Both men's editorials emotionalized political issues and loyalties to motivate their parties' bases. One emotional exchange occurred in the summer and fall of 1879 when Crawford questioned Christian's hygiene, maturity, and honesty in an editorial that initially interrogated Christian's political beliefs. Christian responded by playing off Crawford's insult about his youth and inexperience; he joked that even a boy could refute the pointless accusations published in the *Independent*. Christian then turned his own venom toward Crawford and made fun of his weight, stature, and temperament. Both sets of personal insults served as larger characterizations of the parties that each editor represented. Crawford felt that the Democrats had not matured from their pre-war foibles, and Christian thought of the Republican Party as bloated and mercurial.[23]

One especially ugly disagreement in 1880 focused on the temperance movement, because it was a politically undetermined issue. At the time, both parties in Ohio had to acknowledge the popularity of the movement, which sought to limit the sale of alcohol by passing restrictions at every level of government on its manufacture and distribution. Commitments to temperance transcended political partisanship and inspired fervent support—often because of religious convictions or economic realities. For example, John M. Christian, George Christian's father and a life-long Democrat, supported the temperance cause as an early member of the Murphys. This organization was named for temperance leader Francis Murphy, and its members signed pledges to abstain from alcohol. In contrast, George B Christian Sr.'s writing on temperance changed based on political expediency. He spoke glowingly of Democratic candidate for county sheriff J. V. Harrison's temperance credentials in one editorial, but he criticized legislation meant to benefit the movement's cause in another. Christian wanted to avoid offending Democrats who supported temperance, but he seemingly lacked moral convictions about the evils of alcohol. The conflict began when an editorial in the *Independent* criticized advertisements for alcohol in the *Mirror*. The *Mirror* responded that the *Independent's* editor simply envied the *Mirror's* monopoly over such ads and had no deep temperance convictions. Crawford replied with an unequivocal stand against the evils of drink.[24]

Christian tried to distract his readers from the temperance issue in his next editorial, which claimed that the *Independent's* moral stand would hold greater weight if it refused to advertise certain feminine drugs. The *Independent* printed advertisements for an abortion pill, which Christian argued was more morally objectionable than alcohol. Beginning in the 1850s, the American Medical Association had organized a campaign against abortions not performed by doctors as a way of protecting their unique role when it came to women. Before this campaign, many Americans felt that viable pregnancies began with the quickening phase—when the mother started to feel the movement of the fetus. Over time, physicians turned the tide of public opinion toward the idea of life at conception, and by the end of the 1860s, the opinions of journalists, politicians, and religious leaders had begun to shift toward universal restrictions on abortion. The Ohio legislature banned all abortions not conducted by trained physicians in 1867. The *Mirror's* comments about the *Independent's* abortion pill advertisements illustrated this growing stigma toward voluntary termination of pregnancies. Even though the advertisement used a variety of euphemisms to hide the purpose of the medication, Christian's editorial demonstrated that most readers understood what such advertisements were peddling.[25]

Crawford's follow-up editorial deflected the accusations about abortion pill ads by turning the talk about pills back toward Christian. He claimed that Christian needed to take some "gumption pills"— implying that Christian needed to find a way to show more strength and ability. The war of words petered out when Crawford declared that Christian's lies regarding his rival's beliefs about abortion had made him irrelevant; thus, Crawford vowed to ignore him. At the same time, the *Independent* pulled its advertisements for abortion pills, causing Christian to declare a temporary victory in the skirmish.[26]

Both papers resumed the argument six months later when Christian sarcastically noted the death of the *Independent's* temperance principles since it had run an advertisement for Speer's medicinal wines and brandies. Crawford responded by stating that the products were fundamentally different from evil forms of alcohol because:

> They are designed for legitimate purposes and are
> not nor will they ever be found in drinking saloons
> of the country. A part of these liquors are designed
> to overcome weakness, but not moral weakness nor
> weakness of the brain. Notice they are not at all suited
> to the peculiar ailments of the editor of the *Mirror*.[27]

This statement revealed some of the temperance movement's core tenets, which declared alcohol a source of moral weakness and demonized saloons as places of temptation that enabled such deviancy. Christian answered Crawford's reasonable explanation with an editorial jesting that thirsty Republicans feigned illness so that they could take Speer's medicinal liquors. Opinion content in both newspapers often focused on the hypocrisies of political opponents, and moral issues such as the intersection between advertisements and issues such as temperance and abortion offered fertile ground for such criticism.[28]

All advertisement revenue was critical because of the difficulties of the newspaper business model. Christian and Crawford often commented on the factors that squeezed their profit margins. For example, Christian wrote an editorial opposing a bill in the state legislature that proposed to cut the rates newspapers could charge for printing legal notices. He claimed that publishing costs had risen forty percent at the same time the government wanted to restrict newspaper revenue. He also believed that county property taxes were often too high, because property assessments typically exceeded actual selling prices, an opinion that would change when he became an assessor himself. In an article also written in 1880, Crawford called for subscription payments, because paper prices had risen substantially in the previous six months. The consequences of rising costs could also be seen in April of 1881, when the *Mirror* apologized for the quality of its newsprint and made the excuse that a Chicago firm had tricked it into purchasing $200 of bad paper. The newspaper asked for its readers' patience as it worked through the run of bad paper and sought to fix the situation. Perhaps Christian had tried to save money on paper and paid a sore price for the cost-cutting measure.[29]

Christian planned occasional vacations to provide relief from the stress of the newspaper business, and the trips also gave him the opportunity to write about the places he visited. In May of 1880, Christian traveled with several other prominent Marionites to the islands of Lake Erie in search of black bass. When announcing his imminent departure in the community pages of the *Mirror*, he justified the trip by claiming that "fish is good for the brain."[30] He later joked, "Some of us are old in the sin of fishing; disciples of Isaac Walton who love the placid pools where the finny tribe meat do congregate, and others are fresh fish, greenhorns at the business. Their, the latters', mishaps and miscatches will afford us the fun."[31] In April of 1880, Christian wrote of a bird-hunting expedition where he and his colleagues bagged almost one hundred birds. Christian apparently undertook at least one major hunting or fishing trip every year. He loved a good fish story, and his tales offered the occasional personal portrait in a medium in which an editor's personality generally appeared only in opinion pieces.[32]

Although Christian depended on profits from the *Mirror* to pay the bills, he also ran a printing business on the side to help make ends meet. The city and county commissioned most of the outside printing jobs that Christian and his staff undertook. Christian, however, had greater publishing ambitions. In August of 1880, he proposed compiling and editing a history of Marion County—a daunting undertaking for a man primarily trained as an engineer. A notice in the *Mirror* claimed that, in his final years, Judge John Bartram had tried to organize a project to celebrate the centennial of white settlement in Marion County in 1881. Christian expressed a desire to complete the deceased judge's project because old age might soon claim many of the county's first settlers. By tackling this mammoth work, Christian committed himself firmly to the literary world for the next few years, making occasional comments in the *Mirror* about the state of his research. He believed that such a history would easily find an audience among the citizenry of the county and yield excellent profits. He worked on this history until March of 1883, when he turned his materials over to the firm of Leggett, Conaway, & Company in Chicago. Christian's efforts had moved slowly, and the firm offered fulltime resources to the project, which Christian could not match.[33]

By July of 1880, Marion newspapers began focusing on the upcoming presidential election. President Rutherford B. Hayes, understanding the precarious nature of his election, had promised to step aside after one term, which left a wide-open race for the White House and led to one of the most competitive presidential races in history. Christian and the *Mirror* initially supported Senator Allan G. Thurman of Ohio for the Democratic nomination, but they also

Fig. 51. President James A. Garfield. (Courtesy of the Library of Congress.)

seemed amenable to Samuel Tilden, who Democrats felt should have won the 1876 election against Hayes. As for the opposing party, Christian categorically rejected the possibility of Republican Ulysses S. Grant securing a nomination for a third, nonconsecutive term, believing it would be a step toward semi-monarchical government. In the end, the Democrats chose a Civil War general and hero of Gettysburg, Winfield Scott Hancock, as their candidate. With this choice, they sought to counteract the rhetoric of "waving the bloody shirt" employed by Republicans in every election after the war. While both former president Grant and the machine politician from Maine, James Blaine, came to the Republican Convention hoping to secure the nomination, it was a dark-horse candidate, Senator James Garfield, who emerged as the nominee. Beginning in July of 1880, both the *Mirror* and *Independent* engaged in a bitter surrogate battle for Marion voters on behalf of Hancock and Garfield.[34]

This election involved two decorated and devoted Civil War generals who had served side by side. Nevertheless, the campaign also delved into the politics of Reconstruction. Over the course of the campaign, the *Mirror* painted Garfield as a participant in the rampant corruption of Grant's second presidential term. It accused the candidate of voting for congressional pay raises and claimed that numerous Republican voters planned to leave the party in order to vote for Hancock, the war hero. Christian made the extreme claim, based on his personal wartime observations, that most former soldiers identified with the Democrats. He attacked Garfield's bravery by asking why he was never shot in battle. All Democratic voters, he urged, should demonstrate their patriotism by flooding the polls. Christian tried to create a sense of momentum leading up to the November 1880 election, but it soon became apparent that his candidate was losing the contest. In a spirit of desperation, he printed the Morey letter, in which Garfield supposedly noted his support for Chinese immigration, as a way to scare whites into voting for Hancock.[35]

In contrast, the *Independent* argued that James Garfield had little connection to the scandals of Grant's presidency. Crawford defended Garfield's bravery and war record. Despite Hancock's service in the Union army, Crawford continued to wave the bloody shirt, reminding readers about the Democrats' connection to the South and the defeated Confederacy. He argued that Hancock had gained his military accolades by shooting Democrats and claimed that the candidate had showed disdain toward common soldiers during his service. In general, Crawford argued that the South was in ruins and that any Democratic victory would occur through an abundance of corruption. He claimed that Hancock, though honorable, would be advised by stooges in his party. The Democrats had prevailed in many local races in October of 1880, but Crawford remained convinced that Marionites needed to vote for a Republican in the national election.[36]

Ultimately, Garfield triumphed in one of the closest popular elections in American history. Although Hancock actually prevailed slightly in the popular vote, he lost convincingly in the Electoral College. A devastated Christian wrote in the aftermath of the election that "all is lost, save honor" as he dug in his heels for four more years of opposition to presidential leadership.[37] In this vein, Christian complained mightily at the news that some Garfield supporters had burned Hancock in effigy as his defeat became imminent. Such actions, he argued, manifested the true character of Republicans and grossly disrespected an American military hero. Crawford claimed that the *Mirror's* decision to publish the Morey letter on Chinese immigration, subsequently proven as a forgery, represented poor editorial judgment and an equal lack of good character. Consequently, Crawford asked Christian to recant editorials that used the letter to claim that Garfield supported Chinese immigration. Christian stubbornly responded that he had published the letter because it mirrored Garfield's stated policy and, consequently, represented the president-elect's beliefs even if he didn't write it himself. Both editors found it difficult to, as Crawford stated, "settle down to the everyday business of life" after such a contentious presidential election.[38]

On December 2, 1880, Christian announced a partnership with James Vaughan, who had edited a variety of papers in the region. Although Christian offered no immediate reason for giving up his editorial autonomy, his pleas for subscribers to pay their debts and his recent proposal to write a county history suggested that he was struggling to meet his financial obligations. Christian spun the merger as an opportunity to bring in another editor with vast newspaper experience.

Fig. 52. James Vaughan joined Christian at the *Marion (OH) Democratic Mirror* in December of 1880. (Leggett, Conaway & Co. *The History of Marion County, Ohio*)

He promised subscribers would see the wisdom of the partnership through the improving quality of the paper. Crawford, in a notice about the new *Mirror* coeditor, declared his hope that a new colleague might moderate Christian's attacks on everything Republican and help heal the supposed voids created in the local Democratic Party by Christian's harsh rhetoric. Each editor often played with the fiction that his rival's pointed insults placed the other editor at odds with the majority of his partisans, while claiming his own consistent morality would offer him a high ground from which to make his critiques.[39]

Crawford soon tried to foster animosity between Christian and Vaughan by commenting, "Balaam's Ass for some years tried to run the *Mirror*, but failed. The animal now has a driver and shows a marked improvement in braying capably. Good for the driver."[40] The *Logan County Index,* a Democratic paper, offered a much more supportive take on the new partnership by labeling Vaughan as a "spicy local writer and a first-class workman" who "will be a valuable addition to that paper."[41] Thus, support as well as analysis often fell along partisan lines as newspapers worked to posture politically after this personnel change.[42]

128

Despite Crawford's best efforts, the addition of Vaughan initially made little difference in the vitriol expressed weekly between the *Mirror* and *Independent*. In fact, after a few weeks, inter-paper personal attacks reached a new level of venom and creativity. Crawford had started referring to Christian as "Gall Bladder"—a nickname that played on Christian's initials. In December of 1880, Crawford composed an editorial personally using the pejorative to provoke Christian on the tariff question. The national decision about whether to raise tariffs served as a wedge issue between Republicans and Democrats at a time when they often supported similar policies on other questions.[43] At the end of his editorial, Crawford wrote, "Your party is the party of blunderers, with their 'water elm' headed editors and leaders continually fiz, fiz, fiz, fizzling in all they undertake."[44] The water elm was a very small tree, so the metaphor sought to paint the Democrats as lacking brainpower. This line of satire led to one of Christian's most acerbic responses when, in January of 1881, he wrote:

> Crawford is the worst egotistical ass that was ever
> run out of a neighboring county and inflicted upon
> the unoffending people of Marion. Lacking decency,
> not knowing the rules that govern the conduct of
> gentlemen; a hypocritical abortion, he uses the
> opportunity of a little correspondence relative to the
> tariff question that appeared in the *Mirror* to spew
> forth bile at everything in reach and at the same time
> bore his readers with his ignoramus opinions.[45]

Crawford reciprocated with a series of articles that questioned both Christian's intelligence and his behavior as a gentleman. Once again, Christian responded with a series of furious insults:

> Colder than a clam; meaner than a skunk; a snake
> in the grass; a key hole listener; a dead man defamer;
> this despised weakling is foisted upon the decent
> Republicans of Marion [C]ounty and they are unable

to rid themselves of the burden, simply because [of]
the egotistical conceit of the female pill purveyor.
Society don't [sic] recognize him, or rather does not
wink to his level; his party associates despise him, but
still he clings to the editorial place with the energy
of a drowning man, for he knows free well this is the
only place where he can be maintained. Once out here
he goes down forever.[46]

Even though it appears that such arguments had little relation
to actual policy, they demonstrated the fungibility of political
and personal concerns in nineteenth-century newspapers. With
presidential elections over, both papers returned to the politics
of personal destruction as a means to rally and entertain party
constituencies and keep partisan disagreements at the forefront of
the public conversation. Such meanness allowed both Christian and
Crawford to rally their audiences to buy their papers when national
issues failed to interest the public.[47]

These rhetorical battles must have proved beneficial for
circulation because the personal insults continued in February of
1881. While Crawford often tried to paint Christian as immature and
ignorant because of his youth and lack of formal education, Christian
increasingly moved toward insulting Crawford's masculinity.
He referred to the *Independent* editor as Nancy Crawford and
recommended him to readers as an expert on feminine problems.
Such insults carried particular weight in an era when men's traditional
roles were changing. While the language of gender has often
appeared in insults throughout American history, the characteristics
perceived as masculine or feminine have changed drastically over
time. Antebellum concepts of manliness focused on independence
and agriculture. Men ideally demonstrated restraint and principled
decision making in their land ownership and patriarchy in early
America.[48] The industrialization of the United States and the
relatively long peace that occurred after the Civil War caused a crisis

in American manliness. Historian Gail Bederman has argued that the uncertainty created by new patterns of industrial work and social interaction caused white men to feel a sense of helplessness as their strength and independence became divorced from their everyday tasks of employment. This feeling of powerlessness within their labor led many men to change their conception of manhood's prized attributes from stewardship and restraint to hostility and dominance. At the end of the nineteenth century, forceful behavior became a key component in the developing ideal conception of maleness Bederman labels masculinity. The growth of male aggression played a prominent role in the rise of organized sports, enthusiasm for the pastimes of hunting and fishing, and racial animosity in the form of lynching. The language of masculinity even invaded talk of foreign affairs by the nations' leaders to justify military action in the Spanish American War. While party loyalties and entertainment value were the principal drivers of inter-paper animosity, the confrontational tone taken by the two editors also allowed them to affirm their own masculinity. Christian's feminized portrayal of Crawford infuriated Crawford in a very real way, and he responded by threatening violence. He stated that since he had already defeated the *Mirror*'s editor on the written page, he would be happy to confront him in person. Violence, or threats thereof, offered Crawford a way to reestablish his masculine credibility. That both men worked so hard to either establish or diminish masculinity offers a window for understanding the way that changing perceptions of gender played a role in nineteenth-century America.[49]

Even though George B. Christian Sr. shared ownership and editorship of the *Mirror,* beyond his travelogues he rarely wrote about himself or his family. His default voice was the collective we, meant to represent the Democrats of Marion County. Nevertheless, every edition of the *Mirror* contained a local section. This part of the paper served as a message board for the social activities of the community, with a bias toward Christian's peer group. Any details about Christian or his family generally appeared as short statements of their comings and goings and interactions within the community, but such references were infrequent and generally observational. For example, in the first half of 1881, the newspaper printed three notices about Christian. First, it observed that he had sprained his wrist while ice skating in January. In March, when Christian's term on the school board was about to expire, the *Mirror* called on concerned Democrats to consider running to replace him. And in May, the paper printed its senior editor's intentions to go squirrel hunting. Christian dispassionately included only a few of the mundane details of his life, a practice that contrasted strongly with his continuous efforts to advocate for his political agenda.[50]

When James Vaughan became Christian's partner, the paper seemed to ramp up its boosterism for Marion community projects. In 1881, the *Mirror* championed the construction of a waterworks and sewer system to bring running water and waste disposal to the small town. The editors also pushed to build a new county courthouse and to finally fulfill the community's ambition to build an opera house. Christian and Vaughan explained their backing for public infrastructure in an editorial that defined what they felt good local government should do: "The true interests of the public require always the lowest rates of taxation consistent with the proper and necessary service of the public in the matter of such things as are for the general public good. . . . Let us reason together and do something."[51] Although Crawford often accused the *Mirror* of supporting such projects out of self-interest, Christian believed that one of his jobs was to push for municipal improvement.[52]

Christian traveled to the Upper Peninsula of Michigan, where he hoped to find respite from health problems, during late June and early July of 1881. During this trip, Vaughan assumed full editorial duties for the first time. To address the slight differences in style and philosophy, Vaughan published a notice that in Christian's absence the newspaper would publish more original material written by the younger editor. Vaughan seemed to revel in the opportunity to let his own voice shine through. When Christian returned, he published a series of travelogues titled "A Visit to North Land," which served as an interesting contrast to his previous accounts about his trips to Florida, which he had dubbed "Summerland." In several long articles, Christian commented on the quality of the fishing, the climate, and the landscape of the Upper Peninsula. He recommended it to those who suffered from infirmities such as asthma and hay fever. He also outlined how inexpensively one might live there. In one of his more interesting pieces, Christian described the continued trek of immigrants to parts farther west, which he observed on his train ride to Michigan. Once again, Christian envisioned his travels as not only a personal adventure, but as an imaginative excursion for his readers.[53]

Fig. 53. Artist's depiction of would-be assassin Charles Guiteau shooting President James A. Garfield. (Courtesy of the Library of Congress)

Upon Christian's return to Marion, tragedy struck the nation. A disgruntled and mentally unstable Garfield supporter, Charles Guiteau, shot the president at Washington, DC's Union Station. Guiteau, a failed preacher from New York, felt that he deserved a place in the U.S. diplomatic corps because of his support for Garfield in the recent election. When government officials refused his repeated requests for a job or an interview with the president, he spent months stalking Garfield, finally shooting him on July 2, 1881. Afterward, the would-be assassin proclaimed his support for the Stalwart faction of the Republican Party, of which Vice President Chester A. Arthur was a member.[54] Garfield hovered between life and death for several months. Both the *Mirror* and *Independent* ran weekly reports of the president's condition as well as long explanations of the tragic event and what it meant. As Garfield lay on his deathbed, he automatically became a national hero, which caused both Crawford and Christian to attempt to prove their superior patriotism and love for the president. For example, the *Mirror's* account of the shooting ended by stating that Republicans now felt ashamed about the intraparty fight over Garfield's cabinet nominees. The *Mirror* editors also observed that Democrats seemed to feel much sorrier about the tragedy than their divided Republican counterparts. In contrast, Crawford criticized the *Mirror's* implied characterization of the assassin Guiteau being created out of Republican infighting. In Crawford's view, any political use of the assassination was beyond the pale. As late as that August, the *Mirror* expressed hopes that the president would recover, and it proclaimed that the most loyal action to the wounded leader that Democrats could take would be to engage politically against the Republicans' policies. If tragedy changed the course of everyday life, the logic went, then the assassin would win.[55]

Garfield's death on September 19 brought a variety of tributes both national and local. The president had hung on to life for quite some time, but doctors' efforts to extract one of the bullets from his body in this era before sterilization led to infections, which weakened him to the point of death. In a rare moment of political harmony, Marionites of all political persuasions held a memorial to honor the death of the president. As secretary of the event, Christian penned the resolution expressing the city's great sorrow. Nevertheless, such an era of shared grief lasted only briefly. Christian claimed that

Ohio Democrats had initially offered to cease campaigning for state offices in the aftermath of the president's death, but resumed their politicking when Republicans refused this moratorium. Just as the paper had argued when Garfield hung on to life by a thread, the *Mirror* argued that showing their strength and support of the democratic process at the polls was their patriotic duty. However, Republican victories in local elections left Christian and the *Mirror* making excuses.[56]

George B. Christian Sr. and James Vaughan planned on expanding their printing business in the fall of 1881. Their lease on the Masonic building was ending, and they planned to purchase their own offices. To finance the project, they encouraged readers to pay their balances. In November, the editors purchased a building on Center Street that cost more than $1,200. At the same time that the business was moving, the *Mirror* reported that Christian had been confined to his home for a long spell with an eye problem. This was the first mention of such an extended and incapacitating infirmity during his time at the newspaper. Christian's partnership with Vaughan proved essential to keeping the paper in print.[57]

One event that forced Christian to write about personal matters was the death of his father. In May of 1882, the *Mirror* published a notice that John M. Christian had fallen ill and was confined to his house. For the next few months, the paper periodically commented on his condition. Sadly, John Christian passed away on June 29, 1882. The *Mirror* ran several tributes in the weeks after his death, while the *Independent* published the rather lengthy sermon given at his funeral. In print, John Christian's friends remembered his dedication to the Democratic Party and his childhood in the South. They also celebrated his spirit of public service and religious devotion. Christian composed a firsthand account of his father's fight with skin cancer. Although the family had known John Christian's illness was severe, Christian wrote that the rapidity with which his father had passed away had shocked his family and left them with great sorrow.

At that moment, the *Mirror* provided Christian with a medium to express his grief and to help others in the community ponder their own feelings about the fallen Marion doctor.[58]

After the passing of his father, Christian embarked on a professional trajectory that led him away from the newspaper business. Although he did not say so directly in the *Mirror*, Christian later claimed that he left the paper because of illness. His father's death assuredly made Christian consider his own mortality and health. A combination of grief and sickness probably led Christian to the drastic step of selling his half of the *Mirror* in late September 1882 to two editors of the *Upper Sandusky Union*. Christian chose not to publish a long explanation of his actions. Instead, the *Mirror* carried an appeal to its readers to pay up their accounts so an equitable split of the paper's assets could occur. On September 7, 1882, the *Mirror* published an article expressing renewed commitment to the community and the Democratic Party. As a mild jab to both Christian and Crawford, the editorial staff pledged:

> We shall not descend to the methods adopted by
> so many of the journals when engaged in a political
> warfare, by indulging in a spirit of vituperation against
> those who are at the antipodes with us on the questions
> dividing the parties. We shall occupy a higher plane
> than this, and try by the persuasiveness of argument,
> instead of personal abuse, to sustain the grand
> principles that have made the Democratic Party what it
> is, and cause them to triumph in the near future.[59]

Generally, Vaughan and company kept their word and the debate between the *Mirror* and *Independent* rarely reached the same level of antagonism and entertaining banter that had developed during the Christian years. This occurred, in part, because Vaughan was a newcomer to Marion. As an outsider, he probably felt less personal connection to the longstanding local political battles. On the other hand, the Democrats continued to look to Christian for leadership even after he left the newspaper. His fervent advocacy had gained their respect. Christian's stint as the *Mirror* Man had ended, and he left the publishing business for the industrial economy.

George B. Christian Sr.'s time as an editor of the *Marion Democratic Mirror* earned him credibility as a political and civic leader in his community. While he entered the newspaper business for political and economic reasons, he found meaning as an interpreter of local, national, and world events. Making a living as an editor required a powerful dedication to the journalistic craft, and Christian and his partners constantly worked to interpret the news for their weekly readers. Through his words, Christian became a partisan warrior, battling with rival George Crawford over the proper meaning of their changing world. Such battles helped readers connect with one another and the events occurring around them. Newspapers also gave editors a forum to push for expansion and development within their communities. Both the *Mirror* and *Independent* encouraged subscribers to embrace the progress and modernization that drove the American economy in the years after the Civil War. In many ways, Christian's tenure at the *Mirror* offered him a perfect outlet for his intellectual and public aspirations. Nevertheless, the business proved detrimental to his health and could never provide the standard of living he aspired to give his family. While Christian's editorship lasted for only a short moment in his adult life, it helped him develop his perception of the world. True economic success, however, had proved elusive and came only after Christian left the *Mirror* and became a partner in the lime and stone business.

CHAPTER 6

The Rise and Fall
of a Limestone Tycoon

"Life lies before us, as a huge quarry lies before the architect:
he deserves not the name of architect, except when, out
of this fortuitous mass, he can combine, with the greatest
economy, and fitness, and durability, some form, the pattern
of which originated in his spirit." Johann Wolfgang von
Goethe, *Wilhelm Meister's Apprenticeship and Travels* (London:
Chapman and Hall, 1842), 2:145.

By the fall of 1882, when George B. Christian Sr. sold his stake
in the *Marion Democratic Mirror*, he had gained a reputation for
economic aspiration fueled by the various business schemes upon
which he had embarked. And through his newspaper he had become
an advocate for industrial progress. Christian's promotion of the
developing manufacturing sector in Marion was not coincidental. The
late nineteenth century witnessed the explosion of the industrialist
and the national corporation. While some admiringly referred to the
beneficiaries of this trend as "captains of industry," others resentfully
dubbed them "robber barons." Most of these capitalists had achieved
success by riding the wave of industrial growth fueled by the mass
expansion of railroads; the railroads became the major mode of
transporting people and goods throughout the nation. Of the many
men who made their fortune in these years, none exemplified the
spirit of the times more than Andrew Carnegie, who came to the
United States as a poor Scottish immigrant and eventually built an
economic empire around the production of steel—a key component
in the rise of the railroads. Perhaps the most innovative developments

of this period were the growth of large-scale corporations and trusts. Though the captains/barons label emphasized the individualistic achievement of company protagonists, the process of incorporation is what allowed entrepreneurs to effectively raise capital and cut costs.[1] Companies also brought in engineers and managers to improve modes of production. During his time at the *Marion Democratic Mirror*, Christian had glowingly encouraged such trends in Marion's public and private economic expansion. After leaving the *Mirror*, Christian formed a limestone quarrying company to participate in this growth.

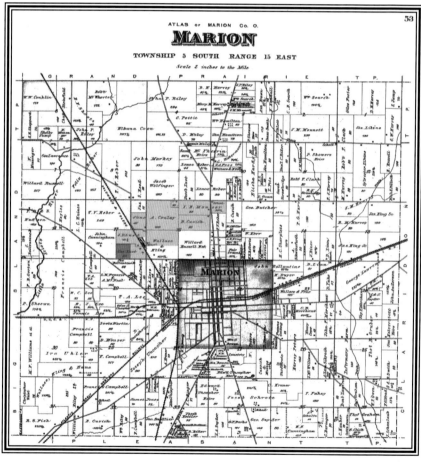

Fig. 54. This 1878 adapted map of Marion Township marks the location of the Norris and Christian quarries. Quarry land is represented by the gray area northwest of town. (Map by H.G. Howland, from *Atlas of Marion County Ohio From Records and Original Surveys* [Philadelphia: Harrison, Sutton, and Hare, 1878])

Christian achieved lucrative and significant success in the quarrying business. His achievements in lime and stone production earned him a place as a demi-captain of industry, at least in the limited universe of Marion, Ohio. Nevertheless, the forty-year rise and fall of his quarrying interests closely mirrored the ebbs and flows of national economic growth and policy. Christian's businesses ultimately failed because he invested in too many different enterprises and fell behind in the war of development during his later years. When the government nationalized the railroads during World War I, its decision to define lime and stone products as nonessential to the war effort crippled his operation. Christian's career in the lime and stone industry complicates the popular caricature of the towering industrialist who made his fortune through hard work, risk taking, and innovation. Christian incorporated all of these attributes into his economic efforts and rose to great prominence for many years, but the uncertainties of the market and wartime regulations left him, at the time of his retirement, with a shadow of his former fortune.

While Christian left no direct account stating his reasons for leaving the editorship and management of the *Mirror* in late September of 1882, several indirect sources suggest that he gave up the hot and hectic work of the print shop for the sake of his health and to take advantage of changing economic realities. In the years after he left the *Mirror,* Christian added nervous prostration to the list of maladies he reported on his pension applications. This suggests that he developed this condition while working in the newspaper business. In an interview with a rock and stone industry trade publication, Christian also specified that he had entered the quarrying business in search of open-air restoration. Christian's father had recently passed away, which might have caused him to ponder his own mortality. It also probably offered him some capital for new investment. Christian had contemplated entering the stone business since at least 1880, when he had published an article in the *Mirror* which examined the economic potential of the lime and stone industry in Marion. When the New York, Pennsylvania, and Ohio Railroad decided to pass through the city, the expanded shipping potential offered by a three-railroad town caused Christian to take the entrepreneurial leap and enter the quarrying business.[2]

Christian and his relation, Caleb Norris, purchased Jacob Lust's 160-acre farm for $7,500 in the fall of 1882. Bonded by their family ties and friendship, Norris and Christian had formed a partnership in the spring of that year. While Norris was technically Christian's uncle, his mother's half-brother, Norris was actually younger than Christian. After training as a lawyer, Norris had established a reputation for public service, Democratic partisanship, and legal know-how. Both he and Christian had

CIRCUIT JUDGE CALEB H. NORRIS.

Fig. 55. Caleb H. Norris was Christian's uncle through marriage and his partner in the quarry business. (*Marion [OH] Daily Star,* Jan. 14, 1909.)

worked for Guy Webber's fraudulent National Art Company and had traveled to Europe to try to establish a foothold for the business there. On a more legitimate note, Norris had served as Marion's prosecuting attorney and later as a county judge. He had also run unsuccessfully on the Democratic ticket for Congress in 1880.[3]

Jacob Lust's farm was located northwest of town near other known limestone deposits owned by John Evans. The site also benefited from ready access to the Columbus, Hocking Valley, and Toledo Railroad. Railroad access played a major role in the lime and stone industry because these commodities required sturdy, accessible transportation to turn a profit. While the $7,500 (equivalent to $177,035 in 2016) paid for the site represented a significant financial investment, it was not an unusual amount of capital for starting

142

this type of business. The partners obtained $5,000 of the capital through a mortgage on the property. While Norris was not exactly a silent partner, his busy legal and judicial career forced him to defer to Christian as the brains and management of the operation. Christian's civil engineering experience had given him some basic tools for developing the infrastructure the operation required.[4]

Newspapers from the time did not mention whether the quarry on the Lust property predated the sale, but they reported that the buyers' interest focused primarily on the land's limestone deposits.[5] Very little information about the property's initial development has survived, but the *Mirror* observed that Norris and Christian began their partnership with a plan for creating a company to extract, process, and sell products made from limestone. Winter delayed construction and excavation on the property in the early months after their purchase, but the cold months allowed the new partners to plan how to open the operation in the spring of 1883.

To understand Norris and Christian's endeavor, a short explanation about the nature of limestone and its utility is critical. The Columbus limestone in Marion County quarries was formed in large bodies of water during the Devonian geologic time period, which occurred 360 to 420 million years ago. The slow formation of the rock from various organic materials created distinct strata manifesting a range of chemical compositions—though the principal ingredient of all limestone is calcium carbonate. As Norris and Christian built their business, they found that the assorted layers of stone held the potential to create three categories of marketable products. Limestone that contained a high purity of calcium carbonate, typically found in the top layers, could be crushed and sold as fluxing stone or for road pavement and railroad ballast.[6] The middle layers of the stone, with an average purity, could be cut into blocks used in the construction of stone buildings. Finally, the lower layers of the limestone, which contained a significant amount of magnesium carbonate, could be burned to create lime for construction and chemical processes. Over time, the business developed ways to monetize these three varieties of limestone found in its quarries.[7]

Initially, Norris and Christian focused on the production of lime using the lower layers of stone on their land because it was the easiest product for the company to transport. Their quarry was developed in an area where geologic processes had exposed a limestone bed on the side of a hill. The partners hired workers to dig around the limestone

Fig. 56. Photograph of the first plant constructed by the Norris and Christian Lime and Stone Company. It eventually included five kilns and a stone crusher. (Photograph taken by Terry Eng, from *Marion [OH] Daily Mirror,* Jun. 15, 1895)

bed and start extracting the valuable stone in the spring of 1883. Christian and Norris also made plans to construct two large kilns to fire the limestone. F. W. Court served as the contractor for the first kiln, which the *Star* reported was built fifteen feet by fifteen feet square and twenty-five feet tall. Workers fired up the large kiln in June of 1883 and began turning out lime as quickly as possible.[8]

Lime is the residue left after burning limestone. Calcium oxide is its principal ingredient. When created from limestone with a high percentage of magnesium carbonate, such as the deposits extracted from the lower layers of stone at the Norris and Christian quarries, it is often called white lime or dolomite lime. White lime is more stable and was less dangerous to transport than lime produced from stone with a purer calcium carbonate content. It is a primary component of mortar and plaster, which were important materials for the construction of brick houses and for plastering interior walls during the nineteenth century. Lime was also used to fertilize soil and to conduct various chemical processes developed for U.S. manufacturing after the Civil War.[9]

Christian and Norris experienced early success in their lime production and soon decided to build the second kiln that had appeared in their original development plans. F. W. Court was again the contractor, and construction began in September of 1883. By that October, less than a year after purchasing the Lust farm, Christian and Norris had created a lime production plant that consisted of two kilns and a giant steam-powered tram to carry stone from the quarry to the kilns. After the burning process, workers packed the lime into barrels produced on site and loaded the material onto trains. The Norris and Christian quarry, in combination with the other limestone processing facilities in Marion, was in a part of the county known collectively as Wales—probably referencing John Evans' Welsh heritage and the mining proclivities of the Welsh people.[10]

Christian had his own ideas and decided to name his and Norris's rapidly expanding production facilities Oak Hill. By June of 1885, the partners had constructed two more kilns and employed twenty permanent workers. Eight of these men kept the kilns producing lime day and night, while others worked in the quarry and cooper shop. Later that year, Norris and Christian purchased additional land to the east of their quarries, this time from John Owens, in order to acquire more direct access to the Columbus, Hocking Valley, and Toledo Railroad. In a joint venture, the railroad worked with the company to build six hundred feet of new side track across Norris and Christian's land to the Oak Hill facility. Both the railroad and the quarry stood to benefit by increasing the ease and volume of shipments on this side track. One article in the *Marion Daily Star* boasted that after the railroad expansion the quarries produced 1,100 bushels of lime per day for shipment. Another reporter relayed that the site had shipped ninety-four railroad cars full of lime in July 1886 alone. The quarry's proximity to the railroad and the junction of so many railroad lines in Marion allowed Norris and Christian to market their lime nationwide. Nevertheless, the weight of the product meant that it was most cost effective to market it to Ohio and surrounding states first.[11]

Early prosperity bred discontent at the quarry. Norris and Christian's burners, who stoked the lime kilns, struck in June of 1887, because they felt their pay inadequately reflected the danger inherent to their jobs and the growth experienced by the company. Christian, as the company manager, had asked that the workers give notice of their intention to strike as a prerequisite for negotiations. The workers rejected this request and simply walked off the job—receiving their final pay as they left. The *Star* reported that Christian regretted the incident, having never had any previous trouble with his workers. He also claimed to have always paid employees on time and in cash. Christian hired new burners, and those who had walked out lost their jobs, victims of Christian's hostility towards those who questioned his authority.

While Christian attempted to portray the incident as an isolated event, the strike created commotion among Marion businesses when the *Independent* suggested that the strikers belonged to the Knights of Labor. The Knights had gained notoriety in the mid-1880s for their railroad strikes. They were not a national labor union because they had no central leadership that bargained on behalf of their workers, but rather an organized coalition of local groups of laborers who sometimes banded together to achieve their goals of higher wages and shorter working hours. They had begun as a fraternal organization in 1869—keeping their members' names a secret from hostile employers. Under Terence Powderly in the 1880s, however, the group began to receive national recognition. Members of the Knights of Labor had played a significant role in an 1884 strike against the Union Pacific Railroad. They united again during the Wabash Railroad Strike in 1885, where they fought against railroad mogul Jay Gould. By 1886, membership in the organization had peaked at 700,000. However, the Knights failed dramatically in the 1886 Great Southwest Railroad Strike and were involved in the unfortunate violence of the Chicago Haymarket Riot later that year. By 1887, their membership and reputation had declined drastically. Because the organization had attained such a toxic reputation, Norris and Christian fervently attempted to assure the people of Marion that their labor dispute genuinely had nothing to do with the Knights.[12]

Workers at Oak Hill had grown frustrated because the firm continually updated the technologies employed at the quarry instead of increasing their wages. Christian championed innovations during his time at the *Mirror*, and, like all successful industrialists of the era, he continually integrated such machinery into the manufacturing process. In May of 1888, for instance, the company replaced one of its kiln's wood burners with a new oil burner. Christian pushed to install this device because he realized that the Ohio forests would not always support the consumption of firewood at the pace that his and the other Marion quarries needed. The oil burner, developed by the Druecker Brothers of Druecker, Wisconsin, also promised greater efficiency than those fueled by wood. While Norris and Christian continued to use wood-burning technology for some time, they seemed to believe that oil was the fuel of the future.[13]

A month later, in June of 1888, Norris and Christian welcomed Dave Kelly as a partner in their firm. The partnership, which lasted for a little less than a year, was given as compensation for Kelly's role in helping them build a steam-powered stone crusher, a machine that enabled the firm to process and sell crushed limestone. Demand for this commodity grew quickly, and by July 5, 1888, the quarries had orders for nine hundred carloads of crushed stone. Success which allowed the two original partners to buy Kelly out. Much of this demand came from the iron foundries of the industrial Midwest, which utilized the stone to remove impurities from processed metal. Ever-expanding rail routes also required large amounts of macadam for ballast. In addition, the stone served as a paving surface for solidifying roads against wear and tear. In future years, concrete buildings would also require this material for their foundations.

Quarries throughout Marion County found the demand for their crushed stone so great that they banded together to hire a sales agent in Columbus to broker their transactions.[14]

The success of the crushed stone operation led Norris and Christian to drastically expand their land holdings. In February of 1889, the partners purchased the 195-acre farm of Edward and Jane Conley situated to the north and northeast of their older quarry. The firm paid $35,000 for the Conley farm. This exorbitant price reflected the success of the lime and stone business in the seven years since Christian and Norris had formed their partnership. Over that period, the price that the partners paid for land with good limestone prospects had almost doubled from $97 per acre for the Lust farm to $181 per acre for the Conley farm. The land purchase represented an additional large capital investment (equivalent to almost $935,000 in 2016) and reflected the confidence Christian and his partners had gained based on the flourishing lime and stone markets. A new partnership with James S. Reed of the Marion County Bank, who invested enough money to claim a third of the business, enabled the purchase of this land and its eventual development. Reed rapidly became the company's treasurer and served as one of Christian's most important financial advisors.[15]

In April of 1889, the company expanded by constructing a new boiler to help power its stone crusher. A story in the *Star* noted that the company had also constructed an on-site blacksmith shop to build and repair quarry tools. In addition, the facilities now included a car repair shop to keep the tram cars, used to transport crushed stone to the kilns, running smoothly. Such facilities provided support for increased production goals.[16]

While consistent sales of lime and stone products drove expansion at the Norris and Christian facilities, Christian also advocated for his business through his public service. At the end of 1889, he defeated several other prominent Democrats to become Marion Township's land appraiser.[17] He felt he had the skills to serve his community in this capacity, but he also wanted to exert some control over tax rates in the county. The appraisal process also allowed him to scope out prime properties for possible expansion. Under Ohio law, land holdings were re-appraised every ten years to determine their worth for the calculation of property taxes. Generally, the funding needs for local governments continued to grow over time, which meant that land valuations helped regulate the prices on which rising taxation rates would be assessed in future years. Specially elected surveyors such as Christian conducted these decennial appraisals and the numbers were ultimately approved by county officials.

In Marion Township, the appraisal process took approximately three months. Christian hired two assistants to aid him from March through June of 1890. He created a report that listed each lot within Marion Township, its location, its owner(s), and the state of improvement on the land. Along with this information, he assigned an overall value to each lot. Christian also kept track of liens and mortgages and reported on the indebtedness of landowners within the township.[18]

Fig. 57–58. Photograph of the cover of the Appraisers' Book compiled by George B. Christian in 1890. His signature appeared on the final page certifying the total value of mortgaged property in the township. (State Archives Series 3428. Appraisement of lands, 1837–1910. BV9841. Reprinted by permission of the Ohio History Connection)

In many ways, land appraisal was a thankless task. Those who invested in real estate wanted high valuations to drive up land prices, but the majority of county residents pushed for low valuations to keep tax burdens at a reasonable level. Appraisals of particular kinds of properties generally mirrored one another, so landholders for similar properties created interest groups, and these groups' agendas often conflicted. From the beginning of the process, Christian knew that some would be unhappy with the values he placed on their properties. Nevertheless, he generally followed the standard practice of valuing rural land much lower than its actual worth. For example, he valued the farm that his company had recently purchased from Edward and Jane Conley at $9,040, when a year earlier the company had paid $35,000 for it. Assessments for urban property with significant development, however, rose substantially from the values determined ten years earlier. Throughout the county, Christian and his assistants also found significant structural developments that landholders had not reported to the county assessor. Overall, these valuations meant that some inhabitants of Marion Township who lived closer to the city saw their property taxes increase. While people had the opportunity to complain about the appraisals to the County Board of Land Equalization if they thought Christian had made a mistake, most chose to accept his work. He received significant praise from the *Marion Star* and the *Marion Mirror*. The latter paper editorialized, "No more suitable man could have been selected for the position [appraiser] and this is proven by the fact that all parties interested are satisfied."[19] Even when people did argue that their property values had risen too much, they usually stopped complaining when Christian offered to buy their property at the assessed price.

As a business owner with vast land holdings, Christian held a vested interest in the appraisal rates of the land in all of Marion County. While he and his assistants vastly under-reported the value of all of the lands they had appraised when compared to actual sale prices, so did almost every other appraiser statewide. By assigning this task to a temporary elected official who quite often owned land within the jurisdiction, the laws had created a conflict of interest in the assessing process. Christian benefitted if he successfully kept tax burdens on his business at low levels, as did many of his friends and employees. It seems that Christian at least tried to evaluate properties based on his own perception of fairness, but the system incentivized under-valuation. In the end, Christian gained the respect of his peers for his diligent efforts to perform this difficult public service.[20]

Christian's business continued its growth, despite the time he spent appraising land throughout Marion Township. On August 11, 1890, an observer from the *Marion Daily Star* visited the Norris and Christian limestone industrial center and commented about its present and future growth. The paper reported that the Oak Hill facilities now employed sixty men—a threefold increase in just five years. The writer described the five lime kilns on site that ran twenty-four hours per day. The paper also mentioned the plant's new stone crusher, which had allowed the company to sign a contract to produce fluxing stone for the Columbus and Hocking Coal and Iron Company. In the story, the owners revealed plans for the construction of six new kilns on the land they had recently purchased from the Conleys. These new kilns would be built close to one another, with their oven doors opening into the same space in order to increase worker efficiency. This massive expansion offered the potential for creating more jobs in coming years.[21]

Fig. 59. Photograph of the six kiln plant built on land originally purchased from Edward and Jane Conley. (Photograph taken by Terry Eng, from *Marion [OH] Daily Mirror,* Jun. 15, 1895)

Recent facility improvements, in combination with continued high demand for their products, fueled Christian and Norris's decision to incorporate their company and take it public in October of 1890. This meant that the two partners opened the company to outside investors and sold shares of company stock on the open market. These actions offered the enterprise and owners a variety of advantages, such as an infusion of capital from new stockholders. The two owners also had an opportunity to cash out some of the capital they had provided for the company in years past. The new corporation paid Norris and Christian $50,000 to purchase the land on which the quarry and other facilities were located. This money allowed the men to pay their outstanding debts and expand their investment portfolios. Incorporation also freed Christian and Norris from personal liability for the company's actions. The process even allowed the partners to add several savvy investors as advisors on their corporate board. George B. Christian Sr. remained president of the company, and the original owners' names stayed attached to the enterprise as primary stockholders. One of the earliest decisions made by the company's new board involved developing a quarry geared specifically to the production of fine building stone, which allowed them to deliver a third marketable product.[22]

Christian's management as CEO of the Norris and Christian Lime and Stone Company made him one of Marion's foremost industrialists. He presided over a company that, at the time of incorporation, employed "an office force of five, ten foremen and sub foremen, twelve engineers, thirty-two lime burners, three expert drillers, two blacksmiths, three carpenters, four coopers, six farm hands, twenty-two teamsters, about fifty-five expert quarrymen, and an average of forty laborers."[23] In other words, the Oak Hill plant had come to employ almost two hundred workers.

Even though the company had adopted a corporate structure, it maintained some of the attributes of a family-run business. As mentioned previously, Norris was Christian's uncle, although they were about the same age and worked well as partners. Many other family relationships were embedded within the company's ranks as well. George B. Christian Jr. appeared as secretary on the company's roster of officers in 1898, a few years after he graduated from Chester Military College with an engineering degree. Christian Jr. played an integral role in almost all of his father's business endeavors, and the Christians' interests prospered most when father and son worked together. Albert Morris, George B Christian Sr.'s brother-in-law, served as the company's general foreman for many years and represented another trusted observer and advisor on the quarry grounds. Finally, Fred Dombaugh, Mamie's husband and Christian's son-in-law, took over some of George B Christian Jr.'s roles when he moved to Washington with Warren G. Harding. In addition to the labor they performed, many of Christian's family members invested in the company. By keeping his family involved in the everyday operations of the corporation, Christian hoped to avoid the corruption and subterfuge that often prevailed in the corporate world of the Gilded Age.[24]

Though the Norris and Christian Lime and Stone Company expanded rapidly in its first decade, it competed with similar operations in a state known for its abundant limestone deposits. Directly north of the original Norris and Christian lime and stone facilities stood the John Evans quarries and processing plant, which operated six kilns of its own. There were also three other lime and stone quarries in the immediate vicinity of Marion as well as quarries in other parts of the county. The lime and stone business depended on selling in volume to make money, so Marion-area producers often found themselves at odds as they bid on local projects in need of crushed stone. At other times, demand for construction was so great that many quarries had to work at capacity to extract the requested amount of macadam. In fact, crushed stone as a paving material became so popular that several editorials in the *Star* complained that Marion was in the pockets of the stone industry. One such editorial pointed out that connections with that industry might have kept the city from embracing better methods of road construction. "Marion streets are stoned to death in a primeval way," it argued.[25]

Despite fierce competition, the Norris and Christian Lime and Stone Company experienced success in the years leading up to the great financial panic of 1893. In January of 1892, the company purchased a small piece of land from Andrew Harriot, which offered its newer facilities access to the Columbus, Hocking Valley, and Toledo Railroad. The corporation also purchased a hundred acres from Ezra Campbell directly east of its first quarry and plant later that year. The Campbell property cost $39,000, which demonstrated that land prices for productive limestone beds had doubled in the almost

Fig. 60. Photograph of the six kiln plant developed on land purchased from Ezra Campbell. (Photograph taken by Terry Eng, from *Marion [OH] Daily Mirror,* Jun. 15, 1895)

Fig. 61. Photograph of the stone crushing facility known as the Chicago Plant. (Photograph taken by Terry Eng, from *Marion [OH] Daily Mirror,* Jun. 15, 1895)

four years since Christian and Norris had purchased the Conley farm. Capital supplied by new investors allowed the firm to make such an expensive purchase. Preparations to construct six kilns on the Campbell land began quickly, and the project soon developed into the company's third production facility (the first being on the old Lust farm and the second on the old Conley farm). In 1893, the firm also broke ground for a new and larger stone-crushing plant, which opened that August. It became known as the Chicago Plant, because it crushed stone to the specifications required by that great midwestern city. The new crusher had a capacity of six hundred tons per day and separated the crushed stone into three distinct sizes for different construction purposes.[26]

One blatant characteristic of the lime and stone business was the danger it presented to its workers. From heavy machinery to hellish kiln fires and explosive quarrying techniques, rarely a month went by without an accident at Oak Hill. Accidents ranged from small injuries to death. For example, on May 16, 1889, George Bolton fell off of a lime car and broke several ribs upon impact with the ground and rails. And on November 20, 1892, during some blasting at the quarries, one of the explosions created a shrapnel zone much larger than anticipated. Some of the stone crashed into a building where a fleeing worker had taken shelter, injuring him severely. One labor group later estimated that, in Christian's tenure at the quarries, 105 serious accidents had occurred, resulting in fourteen fatalities. While quarry accidents usually involved a measure of human error, the dangerous, physical nature of the work, in combination with the long hours expected of the employees, made accidents almost inevitable. The risky nature of industrial work made mutual aid societies an attractive option for employees. The idea of a mutual aid society was that each member agreed to assume liability for everyone else. Members paid a certain amount of money into a general aid fund and received guaranteed protection and support in the event of an injury or illness. If individual needs exceeded the funds available, the society assessed its members an additional fee to cover the shortfall.[27]

In October of 1892, the *Marion Star* reported that the Norris and Christian Stone Company Mutual Aid Society had dissolved. The workers had created the society as an embryonic form of insurance coverage, but its disbanding demonstrated how American workers had not universally embraced the concept of shared liability and the benefits such protection might provide from the perils of the industrial workplace. The workers disbanded their society at Oak Hill because typhoid fever had beset many of them. The plethora of ill employees had overwhelmed the society's resources and necessitated several extra assessments, which had irked members who remained healthy and caused them to leave the group. Regardless of the safety and security

155

the mutual aid society provided to the workers at the quarry, they had not learned to value this protection enough to pay for it.[28]

The next year brought the infamous Panic of 1893. Until the tragedy of the Great Depression, this five-year economic disaster stood as the worst and most complicated financial downturn in U.S. history. Problems began in France, Germany, and England as real estate speculation and investments in developing countries such as Australia, South Africa, and Argentina collapsed. This left European investors scrambling for security in the form of gold. Such investors tried to convert their assets to gold by selling their U.S. currency back to the United States government. At the same time, U.S. monetary legislation had forced the government to purchase, in place of its normal gold reserves, some of the excess silver brought to the market by large-scale silver discoveries such as the Comstock Lode in Nevada. The country's love affair with silver created the impression of a shortage of American gold reserves, which caused U.S. banks to call in many of their loans and mortgages. Most banks felt that any treasury shortage of gold might lead to a cancelation of specie payments resulting in widespread inflation.[29] Massive inflation meant that debtors might repay their loans with money that had become less valuable than the principal loan amount, leading to huge financial losses for the lenders. In addition, foreign economic turmoil meant that potential European capital sources for U.S. banks and companies had dried up.[30]

In the meantime, these financial factors confronted a weakened U.S. economy. Industrialization driven by the almost continuous expansion of rail lines throughout the country suffered, because overbuilding had destroyed many railroads' profitability. Bumper crops in 1892 had driven the price of commodities drastically lower. At the same time, many farmers had acquired too much debt in anticipation of excellent crop yields. As crop prices floored, farmers had insufficient funds to cover their massive debt loads. Such agricultural strain came at the same time that banks wanted to collect

156

on their loans and mortgages to combat the dearth of hard currency caused by the European demand for gold. In the end, the perceived lack of gold revealed the financing bubble propping up U.S. farmers and industrial pursuits. As depositors realized the precarious situation faced by local banks, they attempted to salvage any remaining funds. Even banks that stayed open faced drastic reductions in capital holdings. As industries lost access to banking capital, they began to downsize workers. At the panic's peak, as many as twenty percent of U.S. workers faced unemployment. Job loss hit the West and Midwest especially hard as local banks and farmers in these regions failed together.[31]

In August of 1893, the financial panic hit Christian's company. At a time when new construction normally spiked demand for both lime and stone, orders dissipated. The *Marion Daily Star* blamed the drop-off on credit restrictions that prevented municipalities from issuing bonds. Christian faced some of the labor unrest that occurred nationally in response to the wage declines and layoffs that accompanied the recession. He and his board decided to cut workers' wages by ten percent and to lay off twenty-four employees, mostly laborers. With its remaining workers, the plant continued to run close to its full capacity in September and October, while Christian tried to find a market for the company's products. He hoped to help his workers weather the financial turmoil tormenting the rest of the nation. Nevertheless, as winter approached, Christian felt compelled to cut workers' hours from as much as twelve hours per day to just eight hours. This further cut to real wages caused thirty of his workers to walk off the job. In response, Christian shut down the company's facilities on the former Conley farm—including its six kilns. He told the *Star* that profits from lime and stone sales fell below labor costs at Oak Hill in 1893, but he had continued to run the facilities in order to keep the workers employed. Although his concern was notable, the economic downturn also gave him an opportunity to stockpile products at a ten-percent discount that he planned to sell at an inflated rate when the market improved.[32]

When economic conditions had not improved significantly in the next year, Christian and Norris, along with the company's board, attempted to facilitate other business opportunities. For example, Christian and many of his associates created a real estate business. The purpose of this enterprise, the Limestone City Real Estate Company, was to develop housing on idle company land for quarry workers. The corporation came together on April 26, 1894, with an initial capital stock of $30,000. Christian's new business was one of the first to take advantage of a law recently passed in Ohio that allowed the incorporation of real estate companies. On May 18, 1894, the company's board agreed to buy forty acres of the Norris and Christian Lime and Stone Company's land directly west of its primary facilities on the old Lust Farm for $7,000. The same members served on the boards of both the Limestone City Real Estate and the Norris and Christian Lime and Stone Companies, and the former was designed to generate profit by selling off land that held no useful mineral deposits. Christian felt a certain paternal affection for his workers, and he probably hoped to assist them by offering housing close to their workplace while reaping profits from this real estate development.[33]

The financial downturn not only pushed Christian into real estate, but it also caused him to aggressively bid for local infrastructural contracts and to consider constructing a proprietary railway line. In June of 1894, the Marion County commissioners appointed Christian to supervise road improvements on the Hillman Ford Free Turnpike Road. A few months later, the Norris and Christian Lime and Stone Company won a bid to perform bridge maintenance for the county. In September, the company also won a contract to help Marion improve the city's Kensington Place neighborhood. In the following months, Christian became involved in a war of words defending his and his friends' public contracts from critics at firms that had been passed over for those contracts. These battles within the pages of the *Star* demonstrated Christian's tenacious efforts to protect his reputation as a consultant and provider of materials and labor for the community. When the controversy died down, Christian and his board looked into the viability of constructing a rail line that would run from Marion, through the quarries, to either Chicago or another port city on Lake Michigan. The company hoped to drastically lower its expensive shipping costs. On May 13, 1895, Christian, Norris, and some of their financiers formed the Marion and Northwestern Railway Company to promote the construction of such a line. Opening a new railroad was counterintuitive since railroad failures bore partial responsibility for the financial problems of the day, but the formation of this company showed that the panic had not stifled Christian's ambition for expanding his business. However, plans for the railroad ended in 1897 when demand for the company's products began to rise. Increasing profits made such developments, even if they might have offered a long-term competitive advantage, seem unnecessary and overly expensive.[34]

The *Marion Daily Star* highlighted the Norris and Christian Lime and Stone Company in its first Industrial Edition on June 15, 1895. Editor Warren G. Harding created this special edition to promote and inform about the city's most successful industrial enterprises. The article on Christian's business primarily presented a progressive narrative of growth and development and outlined the scope of the company's current production. For example, it stated that the company employed three hundred people during its busy season. It also documented the plant's maximum production capacity as six thousand bushels of lime, ten cars of building stone, and twenty-five cars of crushed stone per day. The emphasis on possibility over actual production betrayed the fact that the country still faced an uphill climb out of a massive financial panic, but it also offered a sense of optimism that the worst of the crisis had passed. The *Star* later reported that the company's confidence had led it to construct a new bathroom facility with running hot and cold water for its employees in July of 1895. For the first time in several years, Christian and Norris's business prospects appeared bright.[35]

By 1897, optimism began to look justified. In May, the Chicago and Erie Railroad doubled its previous order for crushed stone to a total of two thousand carloads. To meet this lofty demand, the company hired fifty additional laborers. In fact, need for crushed stone and lime began to increase so substantially that Christian initiated significant upgrades to the industrial plant for the first time since 1893. Christian hired George Turner of the Turner Engineering Company to design and install one of his newly invented coal-powered steam boilers as a potential

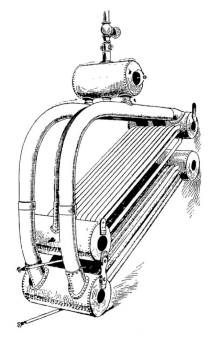

Fig. 62. Diagram of the George Turner Coal-powered Steam Boiler. (*Marion [OH] Daily Star,* Sep. 25, 1897)

power source for all of the quarry's heavy machinery. The company employed an elaborate web of steam-powered equipment to move stone to its processing and shipping facilities, and Christian and Turner hoped that the new boiler would work much more efficiently and powerfully than an equivalent wood burner. Once again, Christian demonstrated his willingness to test new and unproven technology in hopes of improving productivity. He probably also considered that a change from wood to coal might allow the plant to reduce labor costs by purchasing coal on the open market instead of employing lumberjacks.[36]

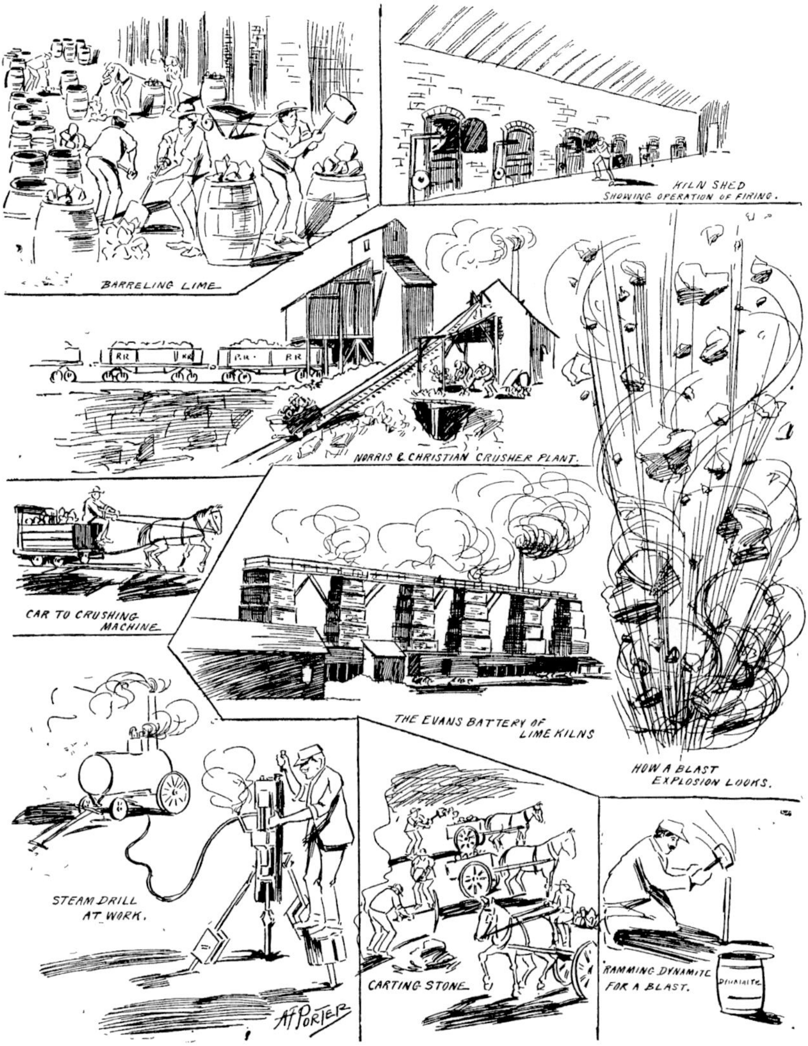
BARRELING LIME
KILN SHED
SHOWING OPERATION OF FIRING.
NORRIS & CHRISTIAN CRUSHER PLANT.
CAR TO CRUSHING MACHINE
THE EVANS BATTERY OF LIME KILNS
HOW A BLAST EXPLOSION LOOKS.
STEAM DRILL AT WORK.
CARTING STONE
RAMMING DYNAMITE FOR A BLAST.
AT PORTER

Fig. 63. Illustrations depicting various scenes at the Norris and Christian Lime and Stone Company (Illustration by Al Porter, from *Marion [OH] Daily Star,* Oct. 23, 1897)

On October 23, 1897, the *Marion Daily Star* sent a reporter and a sketch artist to Oak Hills to report on its recent improvements. From this visit emerged some of the best descriptions of the work that went on at the quarries, kilns, and stone crushers. Artist Al Porter sketched workers shoveling lime into barrels and loading wood into some of the company's many kilns. He drew the stone-crushing plant as well as workers drilling, blasting, and carting stone inside the quarries. While few contemporary photographs of the company's physical plant have survived, Porter's renderings captured the efficient but sometimes frantic work that occurred at the quarries. The drawing accompanied a newspaper story that offered a vivid description of the act of quarrying stone. The *Star*'s reporter observed:

> When it becomes necessary to war against the sides
> of the stone cliffs, the steam drills are set at work,
> generally as far back from the edge of the cliff as it is
> intended to drill deep. . . . When these holes are down
> far enough, two sticks of dynamite are placed in each.
> An electric wire is connected to the sticks. A wooden
> rammer is run down the hole and the dynamite
> rammed down. . . . On top of the dynamite is poured
> a keg of powder. The explosive force of dynamite
> is down while the force of powder is up. Thus the
> dynamite is to sever the portion of the cliff from the
> main body while the powder is to break it into pieces.
> Dry dirt is then put into the holes, and, when it has
> been tamped down, the electric battery is attached to
> the wire connecting the several mines. The whistles are
> sounded to give the alarm to the workmen to get to a
> place of safety, and the electric button is pressed. . . .
> Tons of rock fly high in the air almost simultaneously
> with a mighty explosion, which fairly shakes the hill.
> The rocks keep going up until one thinks they are
> never going to stop. . . . When the smoke is cleared
> away it is seen that many tons of rock have been
> broken from the cliff and are lying at its base.

Along with the sketches, this article, which described the quarries as Marion's own Klondike, captured the danger of the quarries and the inventiveness and ingenuity of the workers.[37]

At about the same time as this descriptive profile ran in the *Star*, Christian's obligations to the community expanded drastically. He began his failed run for the Ohio state senate in the summer of 1897 (see chapter seven) and embarked on his ill-fated association with the Ohio Centennial Celebration Committee in 1898 (see chapter 8). Despite these high-profile distractions, the Norris and Christian Lime and Stone Company continued to prosper. In August of 1898, the company won a contract to construct a road into Shelby, Ohio. The Limestone City Real Estate Company also began to sell developed properties on former company lands to limestone workers. In May of 1899, the Norris and Christian Lime and Stone Company moved its corporate offices back to downtown Marion after having spent a few lean years on site near the quarries.[38]

Success continued as the corporation entered a new century. Christian signed contracts with both the Erie and Short Line Railroads to provide ballast for future railway construction. To meet demand, the company constructed two additional stone crushers. The Norris and Christian Lime and Stone Company had gained such a prominent reputation as a good employer and successful business that many of the town's best workers aspired to jobs there. No story illustrates this better than that of the 1901 Marion High School graduating class. During the class's commencement exercises, prominent attorney William C. Cochran advised the students to enter the workforce as quickly as possible. After the ceremony ended, fourteen graduates marched directly to the foreman of the Norris and Christian quarries to apply for work. Although several factors kept the foreman from hiring the boys, this account shows the respect and confidence the community felt toward Norris and Christian's plant as a powerful economic engine and a trustworthy employer.[39]

On June 28, 1901, the Norris and Christian Lime and Stone Company purchased an additional two hundred acres, known as the Goodnow and Mouser farms, located east of some of their earlier holdings. The company's motives for acquiring these two farms were different from previous acquisitions because it harbored no plans to quarry stone there; instead, Norris and Christian wanted additional frontage near the Columbus, Shawnee, and Hocking Railroad. With this purchase, the company's total land holdings had reached almost one square mile. The scope of the purchase reaffirmed the importance that railroad access played in the quarry's success.[40]

That same summer, the company tested a coal burner that promised to drastically decrease the cost of fuel for lime production. The plant had already introduced a coal-powered boiler to run its machinery and had used at least one oil burner in its kilns since 1888. Once again, Christian embraced technological advancement for the chance to improve production and lower costs. The coal burner was so novel that many lime producers in surrounding areas came to witness the test. One of the visitors was Peter Martin, owner of the massive Western Lime Company, who was obviously impressed with the invention and the company's facilities. On August 27, 1901, the plant's supervisor declared to the *Marion Mirror* that the test of the coal burner had succeeded to such an extent that the company planned to install the devices in all of its kilns. The company also invested in the Scot-Strahel automatic wagon loader to load stone into wagons for transport to its various processing plants.[41]

The technological innovations embraced by the company changed the nature of wage work. Management avoided a strike in June of 1902 by offering workers a drastic increase in wages. Nevertheless, the contract was less of a victory for the employees than it appeared on the surface. While the new agreement increased wages for all workers, it corporatized the workplace by stratifying the interests of different groups of workers who were now paid based on their skill level. As more and more aspects of limestone extraction and processing became mechanized, the company needed fewer skilled workers. But those skilled workers who remained retained disproportionate bargaining power and received larger wage increases. Thus, the employees with the most leverage now had little reason to fight for the benefit of the mostly poor, unskilled workforce. As the company vertically integrated the many procedures involved in processing and shipping lime and stone throughout the country, the tasks of individual workers became more isolated, unique, and unskilled.[42]

In 1905, difficulties in dealing with railroad companies caused Norris and Christian to purchase their own locomotive, the famed engine named "The Colonel" in Christian's honor. The train hauled stone from various quarrying sites to the company's lime and stone processing plant. Its pulling power replaced many of the horse-drawn wagons used in previous years. This change

Fig. 64. Photograph of the locomotive nicknamed "The Colonel" utilized by the Norris and Christian Lime and Stone Company for hauling products. (Courtesy of George R. Kadelak)

represented the company's almost complete transition from manual to mechanized labor and production.[43]

Another sign of the quarries' prosperity was the labor shortage they faced in July of 1905. The shortage impeded production to such a large degree that the company offered the police department one dollar per head to bring in vagrant laborers. The company also sent recruiters to Columbus to convince workers to move to Marion. In the end, many Italian immigrants filled in the labor gaps faced because of the company's rapid expansion and success.[44]

In March of 1906, Christian's company announced plans to construct a new, modern stone-crushing plant. The *Star* reported that the plant would consist of a new stone crusher, friction hoist, 150-horsepower engine, and boiler. The company claimed that the new plant would double its stone-crushing capacity, and it contracted with the Hocking Valley Railroad to construct spur lines that led to the new crusher.[45]

The Norris and Christian Lime and Stone Company reached the apex of its financial and industrial success under the leadership of George B. Christian Sr. at the end of 1906. The company had emerged as one of Ohio's most successful production facilities of white lime, crushed stone, and building stone. The company had vast real estate holdings to the north and west of Marion, and an associated real estate venture had created a housing development for its workers. The corporation had even expanded outside of Marion County, purchasing quarries near the village of Luckey in Wood County. Christian employed so many workers that the company looked to labor sources outside of central Ohio. Constant machinery upgrades, as well as willingness to provide workspace and resources to engineers and inventors, meant that the company employed the newest and most efficient technologies available for the lime and stone production processes. Christian's effective and visionary leadership had made him an exemplar of entrepreneurship for the community. He cofounded the city's Commercial Club, a precursor to the modern Chamber of Commerce. He also lectured farmers on the benefits of lime in agriculture and temperance advocates on the blessings offered by the prohibition of alcohol for workers. Christian had attained the status of a local captain of industry with expanding business prospects and the opportunity to improve the lives of many of Marion's citizens.[46]

In 1907, the Western Lime Company out of Huntington, Indiana, made overtures to purchase many of Marion's limestone processing centers. This company was owned by Christian's friend Peter Martin. Stockholders of the Norris and Christian Lime and Stone Company, the Central Ohio Lime and Stone Company, and the John D. Owens and Son Company all deliberated the implications of accepting a buyout. The John Evans Lime and Stone Company, in contrast, refused to even consider the Indiana company's offer, preferring to keep the facility under local control. Local papers speculated that Martin might have offered as much as one million dollars to purchase the three quarries willing to negotiate. By January 30, 1907, the details of the proposed deal had changed. Despite the substantial offer, the John D. Owens and Son Company ultimately decided to remain independent, while the Norris and Christian and Central Ohio Companies sold a majority of their stock to Peter Martin's company. Martin became president of the resulting corporation, subsequently renamed the Ohio and Western Lime and Stone Company. The *Cincinnati Enquirer* reported that the purchase price for both companies had totaled more than $500,000, and the deed record held by Marion County reveals that the Norris and Christian Lime and Stone Company's property and equipment sold for $187,500, with an additional $6,000 going to pay off one of the company's debts. This payment represented a significant investment (equivalent to slightly more than five million dollars in 2016) by Martin and a significant infusion of cash for the company's stockholders.[47]

George B. Christian Sr. received sizeable stock holdings in the resulting company along with the title of assistant general manager. Because the new ownership lived a state away, he initially remained the active manager of the Marion sites under Martin's corporate direction. Nonetheless, after having served as president of his own company for such a long time, he soon tired of receiving orders. He also disagreed with many of the business decisions made by the new ownership. Consequently, Christian retired from the Ohio and Western Lime and Stone Company in October of 1907. A few months later, one hundred of his former employees held a surprise party for Christian where they presented him with a gold Swiss watch. In his acceptance of the gift, Christian invoked his most paternalistic sentiments as he recounted the shared hardships of the Panic of 1893, when he had managed to keep most of the employees on the payroll. He stated, "I believe that between us there has always existed a feeling that has been something more than the ordinary feeling between the employer and the man working for his hire. . . . It has seemed as though we were always looking for a common good."[48] He continued by explaining that even though his quarrymen were generally underpaid, they had received the great gift of health and muscle as part of their employment with him. He felt that they were some of the country's best citizens. In closing, he invoked the spirit of temperance and admonished his workers to take care of their families. Visibly moved, he thanked his former employees for their gift and shook all of their hands. While Christian had often invoked the moral high ground in dealing with employees at the quarries, this farewell speech revealed the extent to which he had embraced his self-deluded role as a benevolent benefactor. Christian, like many industrialists of the time, genuinely expressed responsibility and affection for his workers, while he systematically endangered and burdened them for his profit. At no time did the incongruity of this arrangement prove more evident than during this retirement gathering.[49]

Christian spent very little time in retirement after leaving the Ohio and Western Lime and Stone Company. Instead, he entered the quarrying business in neighboring Delaware County. In that county, directly south of Marion, Oliver Perry Bird and James Richey had opened two quarries in 1904. Their efforts found little success until Christian entered the partnership sometime in late 1907 or early 1908, and they formed the White Sulphur Stone Company, named for the White Sulphur Railroad Station immediately to the east of the quarries. In April 1908, the company expanded onto eighty-eight acres that Christian had purchased from Matthias Pound for $13,074. Christian and his partners quickly built a new stone-crushing plant, and they were ready to entertain a party of Christian's Marion friends at this new facility in June. The White Sulphur Stone Company welcomed outside investors when they incorporated that November, and Bird, Richey, and Christian sold their land holdings to the company itself. A few weeks later, Christian hosted Delaware County officials at the quarries to show them the plant's progress and smooth over a contractual inconsistency that had arisen between the company and the county. In fulfilling a construction contract, Christian had asked for reimbursement for expenses not authorized by the Delaware County commissioners. His schmoozing must have worked on this occasion, because the county chose to reimburse the disputed expenditures.[50]

Christian pushed to increase the company's holdings, and in December of 1908 the business purchased 113 acres from George C. Oliver. Expansion continued the following March with the purchase of additional land from the Pound family to gain better railroad access. The company also bought the Smith quarry, which held fifteen acres of limestone a mile east of the White Sulphur facility. That June, Christian wooed his son away from the Ohio and Western Lime and Stone Company to work for him once again, and his former superintendent John Stone joined them in November. These transfers severed Christian's last links with the Marion lime

Fig. 65. Image of drilling equipment at the White Sulphur Quarry. (Courtesy of Marie Bouic.)

Fig. 66. Image of loading facility at the White Sulphur Lime and Stone Company. (Courtesy of Marie Bouic.)

and stone industry and brought more of Christian's most trusted associates to the Delaware County quarries—at least until George B. Christian Jr. left to accompany Harding to the Senate in 1916.[51]

In late November of 1909, George B. Christian Sr. began working with his former quarry superintendent, John Stone, an aspiring inventor who sought to design a stone crusher able to manage much larger pieces of stone than existing models. The new piece of equipment was intended to circumvent the back-breaking labor needed to break large stones into pieces small enough for most stone crushers to process. Christian became personally involved in the invention of this machine, providing capital, facilities, and his own ideas. While the machine never proved particularly successful, Christian's participation in its creation showed that his relationship with new technologies had moved from patronage to design and assembly.[52]

At about the same time, Christian was called before the Delaware City Council to answer complaints about the noise produced by blasting in his quarries. In the meeting, Christian explained that the economic viability of the quarries depended on blasting for stone. He argued that the noise represented the cost of having such a productive plant able to employ two hundred people. This argument seemed to sway the city leaders, and nothing occurred to halt the company's business.[53]

Christian hoped to recapture the same level of success and respect in Delaware County that he had achieved in Marion, but changing circumstances assured that the White Sulphur Stone Company would never gain the same level of prominence or success as the Norris and Christian Lime and Stone Company. While several newspaper articles initially examined the new company's origins and potential, they rarely commented on its growth or success. In part, slower growth might have occurred because the quarry opened at a time of national economic contraction. In 1907, corruption and liquidity issues caused a run on New York City trusts (financial institutions that accepted deposits and made investments like banks without the same protections or capital requirements). Banking giant J. P. Morgan eventually organized a bailout for some of these institutions, but the net result of this panic was the shrinking availability of capital for borrowing, which caused rising interest rates and unemployment. For much of 1907 and 1908, it was difficult to obtain financing for anything like a new limestone quarrying enterprise.[54]

Despite the new company's slower growth, Christian maintained a high profile among limestone producers. In 1911, The Ohio Stone Club, the state organization of stone operators, chose Christian as its president for the year. Through this election, Christian's peers acknowledged his significant experience in and advocacy for stone production. In his presidential address, summarized briefly in the *Marion Weekly Star*, Christian argued against the practice of utilizing convict labor in stone quarrying and processing. Convict labor gangs were widely accepted in this era, though they were most common in the South. Nevertheless, he pointed out that the technological innovations achieved in recent years made convict labor an inefficient workforce. He also felt that permitting such labor allowed states to favor certain companies, since the cheap labor pool would be finite. Christian's position on this topic offers insight about the scale of the Delaware County facilities at this time. Because of the moderate size of his operation, it would have struggled to capture the attention of the state correctional establishment as a worthy contractor for convict labor. Christian had not always objected to unfree sources of labor; he had appealed to Marion County several years before, during a labor shortage, to bring arrested vagrants to work at the Norris and Christian quarries. In this instance, however, Christian should be credited for embracing a humane position even if his primary motivation was market based. In Christian's mind, morality and profitability were never mutually exclusive.[55]

In 1912, George B. Christian Sr. and his son participated in the annual meeting of the Ohio quarrymen. The discussions at this meeting focused on factors which threatened the profits of those in the limestone business like the impact of automobiles on crushed stone roads, Ohio stone pricing policies, and railroad companies' demurrage charges.[56] At the meeting, the industrialists discussed ways to overcome downward trends in their profits. A letter from Dr. Charles E. Sawyer to Senator Warren G. Harding in March of 1916 confirmed that the White Sulphur Stone Company was facing economic difficulties. In the letter, Dr. Sawyer recounted the details of a conversation with Christian about the Colonel's financial health. Christian had stated that his company struggled under a heavy debt load and that his facilities needed improvements to function competitively. Sawyer advised Christian either to sell many of his other interests to pay off his quarry debts and invest in infrastructure, or to sell the quarries and invest his money for a secure retirement. The lime and stone business ran on notoriously small profit margins and depended on a large volume of business to survive—demand had decreased at the same time the cost of production had increased. These unfortunate circumstances stifled the company's profits and kept the enterprise from generating the kinds of capital needed to increase capacity and efficiency. In addition, Christian's company seemed to suffer from his son's absence as a financial advisor. In the Norris and Christian Lime and Stone Company, bankers had always played a prominent advisory role. Perhaps Christian lacked such guidance in his new company. He also had probably invested in too many different enterprises and lost money during the 1907 financial panic. Overall, Christian and the White Sulphur Lime Company apparently had begun to struggle, and Christian worried that the company might not have the resources to overcome its difficulties.[57]

Wartime controls on railroad freight compounded the corporation's economic adversities. For several years before World War I, the railroads, like the White Sulphur Stone Company, had seen their profits dwindle. Difficult economic times affected banks' willingness to loan money to capitalize the railroad industry, and without capital the railroads chose not to invest in improving infrastructure or to pay for expensive upgrades on cars and locomotives. This meant that the drastic increase in traffic resulting from supplying wartime allies and preparing domestically for war reduced shipping efficiency and speed. Federal law allowed governmental agencies to claim priorities for shipping, which added to the shipping delays through major cities, especially in the East. Because railroad rules allowed shippers to send priority cargo whether buyers were ready to unload it or not, delays at ports and transfer stations contributed to the system's general sluggishness. The congestion hurt the White Sulphur Stone Company's bottom line, but such delays were one of the costs of wartime mobilization and the business found itself in good company.[58]

Because of the drastic and crippling delays, President Woodrow Wilson decided in late 1917 to nationalize the railroad system. He appointed his Secretary of the Treasury, William McAdoo, to also lead the newly created United States Railroad Administration (USRA). The government mandated collective action in a way that might have threatened anti-trust laws had the industries introduced the changes themselves. McAdoo primarily appointed railroad company officials to help him institute collective governance. The president assigned the USRA to create a reasonable system

Fig. 67. This World War I propaganda poster advocated support for the United States Railroad Administration. The poster connects successful railroad reform to military success. (Courtesy of the Library of Congress.)

of shipping prioritization. It also forced different railroads to share workers, facilities, and equipment. A final purpose of such centralized leadership was to bargain collectively with railroad workers, industry wide, for reasonable wage increases while at the same time collectively raising shipping rates to pay those higher wages. While many observers considered the creation and direction of the USRA as the ultimate coordination between the government and the private sector, many of the administration's policies adversely affected shippers— especially those in industries, such as lime and stone, deemed non-essential to the war effort.[59]

Christian's political views caused him to anticipate problems with the government's efforts to nationalize various industries. In January of 1918, he wrote to Senator Warren G. Harding expressing his support of Harding's efforts to block government takeovers of the paper industry. Christian commented that the Congress was "moving us toward socialism and a very bad form of it at that." Christian hoped that Harding would stand equally firm against a congressional bill which proposed to make the wartime takeover permanent "when the debate upon the railroad matter comes up."[60] He complained about government-enforced shutdowns of industry—though such stoppages were designed to conserve coal and break up the shipping bottleneck. In general, Christian thought that government intervention in the war economy would make difficult economic conditions for the lime and stone industry even worse.

Christian probably had good reason to oppose the USRA's regulations and controls. Because lime and stone were branded as non-essential shipping commodities, Christian's shipments always took lower priority than those of weapons and supplies for the United States and its allies. Christian described the situation succinctly to his friend Harding when he stated, "In my business I am fighting the Kaiser, the Big Four R.R. Co. and government orders combined."[61] In addition, the USRA required shippers to prearrange for the unloading of their cargo before it left the production facility. Such arrangements were often difficult for the heavily weighted commodities produced in the quarries. Wage concessions to railway labor groups resulted in higher shipping fees and created wage pressure for other industries as well. All of these factors caused the White Sulphur Stone Company's profits to disappear. When Christian wrote to Harding in December of 1918, he stated,

"Never in the history of Ohio has business been so dull or the future as dark as now." He bemoaned the economic policies created by "sentimental tyros and socialistic theorists," which created "uneasiness and alarm among the central Ohio industries."[62] Christian operated at a loss during the entire war, and his Delaware County quarries teetered on the edge of solvency in the immediate aftermath of the armistice.[63]

Indeed, the wartime policies of the Wilson administration in correlation with Christian's long-time friendship with Republican Warren G. Harding pushed Christian out of the Democratic Party. Articles in the *Marion Star* observed that the plants operated at only forty percent capacity because of the government's domination of the railways. Restrictions both during and after the war caused such delays that Christian later claimed he shipped his first full carload of crushed stone two years and four months after the signing of the peace accords. Christian blamed Wilson for creating a system which killed his company's ability to deliver its products. The Christian family's close relationship with the Hardings caused them to see him and his party as political saviors.[64]

Despite the company's significant losses, Christian rejected legal action against the government as a hopeless, expensive, and never-ending endeavor. By November 22, 1921, Christian tired of his battle to keep the White Sulphur Lime and Stone Company solvent. He filed a lawsuit against it in the Delaware Court of Common Pleas to try, through bankruptcy, to salvage what he felt was his portion of the company's assets. This action forced the company's board to acknowledge it could not pay its creditors, and the court appointed Benjamin Franklin Freshwater, who had taken over the vice presidency of the company after Christian's son left for Washington, as a receiver for the company. This meant that Freshwater was legally bound to supervise the business while the legal proceedings moved forward, since Christian's lawsuit created a conflict of interest between himself and the corporation. On May 27, 1922, the court ordered

Freshwater to oversee an appraisal of the company's assets and land holdings. The appraiser valued the company's 370 acres of land, six lime kilns, stone crusher, locomotive, and heavy machinery at $135,000. Freshwater arranged to sell the property to Ralph T. Lewis, who was working as an agent for the Cleveland, Cincinnati, Chicago, and St. Louis Railroad (sometimes called the Big Four Railroad), which passed directly by the White Sulphur facilities. *Pit and Quarry Magazine,* in its August 1922 issue, reported that the railroad needed the plant to supply ballast for its new track between Galion and Columbus, Ohio.[65]

Christian's cut of this $135,000 represented a significant loss from the over $200,000 fortune he had accumulated during his time at the Norris and Christian Lime and Stone Company. He had exhibited a tireless work ethic and dedication to innovation, but he had lost his status as a captain of industry. In his forty years in the limestone business, Christian experienced the successes and failures inherent in governmentally regulated capitalism. While he never really moved from rags to riches to rags, his experiences definitely broke the mold made famous by the Carnegies and Rockefellers of the era. Christian's businesses could not function without the heavy transportation capacity of the railroads. In the years after Christian left the industry, the limestone from both the Marion and Delaware County quarries fell out of favor because the use of mortar and plaster declined in domestic and commercial construction. Most of the area's limestone contained an insufficient calcium carbonate purity to be employed in the more popular cement industry. Consequently, quarries eventually filled with water and became recreational areas. Perhaps the greatest evidence of Christian's entrepreneurial acumen is the honeycombed pits now filled with water which constitute the quarry lakes that still exist in Marion and Delaware Counties today. Furthermore, two Marion city streets, which once ran through the limestone workers' neighborhoods, bear the names of the company's great founders: Christian and Norris.

Fig. 68. This exposed rock wall at Quarry Park in Marion, Ohio, shows the remaining traces of the city's limestone quarries. (Photograph by author)

CHAPTER 7

Christian the Campaigner

"The nominee [George B. Christian Sr.] is well known here
in business circles, and his nomination seems to please all,
but it takes heroic men to lead a forlorn hope [where] the
Republican normal majority is fully 1200. But Christian
is heroic and no doubt his nomination will please Marion
Democrats." "Choose a Victim: Thirteenth District Demmies
Nominate a Candidate, Col. Geo B. Christian the Man,"
Marion (OH) Daily Star, Aug. 31, 1897.

Even though George B. Christian Sr. gave up his editor's seat
at the *Marion Democratic Mirror* to enter the limestone industry, he
retained his role as a leader in the local Democratic Party. Christian's
political involvement demonstrated his conviction that community
service was a patriotic duty. Having grown up in a politically
minded family, he probably developed this belief at a young age. His
grandfather, George H. Busby, had served the Democratic Party as
Marion's county recorder, court clerk, and probate judge, and had
even served a term in Congress. Christian's father, John M. Christian,
had led the local Democratic Party and run for mayor of Marion.
George B. Christian Sr. spent most of his adult life following the
civic examples of his father and grandfather. Even as a Union soldier
in the Civil War, Christian had supported the Democrats, who had
opposed Lincoln's Republican policies. The peak of his service to
the Democrats occurred during his run for the Ohio state senate in
1897. This election represented a turning point in Christian's political
goals. After his loss, he eschewed any future ambitions for public
office, and he became content with behind-the-scenes participation

and influence. Christian's 1897 run not only played a central role in his own political career, but his loss opened the door for his friend Warren G. Harding, which affected the national political landscape in years to come.

Upon his return to civilian life in 1864, Christian had joined his father as an active member of the Marion Democratic Party, and both men served in local elective office in the years after the war. George B. Christian Sr. served as county surveyor from 1873 to 1876 and on the local school board from 1878 to 1881. John Christian served as the county coroner from 1878 to 1882. As editor of the local party's official newspaper from 1877 to 1882, the younger Christian prodded and applauded the actions of Democratic politicians while berating and shaming the Republicans. Even after leaving the *Mirror,* Christian continued his leadership by participating in local, state, and national party conventions that chose electoral candidates and policy. He also sought to rally support for Democratic candidates through his public speaking.[1]

Christian's political role changed drastically when his party nominated him as their candidate to represent Marion and several surrounding counties in the Ohio state senate. He entered the statewide political fray in an era of game-changing elections that redefined political campaigning and ideology. In 1896, William McKinley ran against William Jennings Bryan in a volatile presidential election. Up until that contest, candidates for president had generally avoided the everyday trappings

Fig. 69. William McKinley, was the Republican candidate who won the presidency the year before Christian ran for a seat in the Ohio state senate (Courtesy of the Library of Congress)

of campaigning. They obtained their parties' nominations through backhanded deals and compromises at national conventions, and then they generally stayed home while supporters spread the message of their candidacy far and wide. In 1896, Bryan destroyed these political conventions. He ran as the presidential candidate for both the Democratic and Populist parties.[2] He supported policies that appealed to the rural and working populations, and he traveled throughout the nation using his superior oratorical skills to try to convince people to vote for him. McKinley, in contrast, conducted a traditional campaign from his front porch in

Fig. 70. McKinley's opponent in the 1896 election, William Jennings Bryan. Bryan ran one of the first modern presidential campaigns traveling throughout the nation to plead his case before the American people. (Courtesy of the Library of Congress)

Ohio. McKinley was the most recent in a long line of Ohio presidents and candidates. The state's success in placing politicians in the country's highest office resulted from its growing population and mix of agricultural and industrial success.[3]

In the 1896 election, candidates perceived Ohio as a swing state. While the state had voted for Republicans in every presidential election since 1860, Democratic hopefuls often ran competitively within the state. Democrats had won statewide elections—sometimes even splitting tickets with the Republican presidential candidates who garnered Ohio's electoral votes. In 1896, this volatility meant that the state had the potential to drastically affect the outcome of the election.[4]

Despite McKinley's efforts to place Americans' focus on protectionism and tariffs, Bryan electrified the country with his rhetoric in support of the free coinage of silver. Following Great Britain's example, the United States had moved to the gold standard in 1879 as it sought to discontinue the unsecured paper greenback currency that had come into use in the Union during the Civil War. Supporters of the move hoped that the gold standard would reduce inflation and boost the value of the dollar in international trade. On the other hand, farmers and others who relied on debt to function disliked the gold standard because it created a scarcity of hard currency and deflated the prices of agricultural commodities. This was especially true in the early-to-mid-1890s, when economic turmoil, caused by the Panic of 1893, had decreased the nation's cash flow. At the same time, vast discoveries of silver had greatly increased its availability as a potential currency booster. Thus, miners and farmers pushed the government to buy silver to back a portion of the U.S. money supply. Their hope was that tying the value of the dollar to an abundance of silver would increase the country's liquid assets and enable farmers to more easily pay their debts. In a famous speech, Bryan vowed that his supporters would not allow the Republicans to hang the proponents of free silver on a cross of gold, and the 1896 platform of the Democratic Party advocated the free coinage of silver.[5]

While Bryan's candidacy and Populist appeal scared Republicans throughout the country, it especially worried national power brokers and moneyed interests, who opposed his supposedly radical views on monetary and regulatory policy. McKinley eventually emerged triumphant in the campaign of 1896—buoyed by a national network of supporters in big cities. Ohio voters supported their native son, McKinley, by a five percent majority. Nevertheless, the election results highlighted the growing divide between urban and rural voters, and galvanized support for electoral reforms. Consequently, Christian embarked on his campaign for state senator in the wake of the first modern presidential campaign when Democrats had tapped into rural hostility toward rapid industrialization and modernization.

Marion County voting results vacillated between the two major parties in the 1890s, but it was part of the Thirteenth State Senatorial District that also included Hardin, Union, and Logan Counties. Overall, this district contained a solid Republican majority. In fact, the *Marion Daily Star* reported that the Thirteenth State Senatorial District had not held a Democratic convention in twenty years. In all those years, the local party probably wanted to avoid the expense of nominating a candidate who would most likely lose. Nevertheless, the 1897 convention enjoyed a wave of enthusiasm and positivity generated by the discussion of George B. Christian Sr. as a candidate and William Jennings Bryan's tumultuous, but ultimately unsuccessful, run for president.[6]

Democratic delegates from Marion Country came to the Kenton Convention on August 31 hoping to nominate Christian for state senator, though Christian himself was not in attendance. Even though the delegation from Logan County sought to nominate a prominent farmer by the name of Kibler, Christian's popularity among the delegations from Marion, Union, and Hardin Counties made him the favorite. Marion lawyer and delegate Marcus B. Chase arose on the convention floor to nominate Christian. He praised Christian's character, war record, party loyalty, and support of free-silver principles. As the rapturous endorsement of Christian rang out among the delegates, Robert W. Thompson of Union County suggested that they make Christian's nomination unanimous, and the entire body came to their feet and voted for him by acclamation. During the proceedings, George B. Christian Jr. suggested that his father might not want to run for political office because of his business responsibilities, but his objections were quickly dismissed.[7]

After the convention disbanded, the delegates from Marion returned to their city hoping that Christian would accept their nomination despite often having expressed his opposition to becoming a candidate. They gathered a crowd of Marion Democrats and a few friendly Republicans to march to Christian's house and convince him to run. The delegates also recruited a local brass band to energize the gathering. The group quickly walked to Christian's West Church Street home, and Judge Martin J. Burke gave a speech informing Christian of his nomination.[8]

Christian, obviously flattered by the Democrats' confidence and passion, expressed hesitation but graciously accepted the nomination with a speech of his own. It was standard practice for politicians to claim they had no interest in running for office, so Christian's previous objections might have been political theater. Indeed, he might have known that the nomination was going to occur. Nevertheless, Christian thanked local Democrats for their confidence and vowed to work for the interests of all citizens should he be elected. He complimented the character of the whole region and praised farmers and workers as its greatest asset. While not commenting on any specific political questions, Christian pledged his support for the Jeffersonian, Jacksonian, and free-silver philosophies that undergirded the Democratic Party. After his short acceptance speech, the band began to play once again, and Christian shook hands with all of the successful marchers.[9]

In future weeks, local newspapers commented on Christian's nomination. For example, Bob Dumm of the *Upper Sandusky Union* opined:

> Col. Christian is one of the best stump speakers in Ohio, and straight on legislating without the consent or intervention of any other nation on earth. Politics, aside, the colonel is a grand man, and will faithfully represent the people of his district; moreover you will not hear him howling calamity while his stone and lime works, the best in Ohio, are just now over-crowded with orders. The colonel could tell a handsome little fib, if he wanted to, but he wouldn't. He is more like George Washington than any other politician, of whom, at present, we have any knowledge.[10]

To add to this high praise, Warren G. Harding, in the Republican-leaning *Marion Star*, stated:

> The Democrats have nominated the best man they
> could have selected by long odds. Col. Christian has
> the ability, the originality, the high-mindedness, the
> honesty of purpose and the knowledge of men and
> things to be a shining light in the Ohio senate. . . .
> His knowledge of Ohio affairs, his prolific ideas for
> needed reforms, his understanding of the evils that
> beset legislative bodies and his force of character
> sufficient to repel the odious lobby and act for a
> trusting constituency—these things make him
> desirable as a candidate. He would stand a fitting
> representative of the great manufacturing interests
> while he has knowledge and interest essential to care
> for agricultural needs.[11]

Republicans generally had little bad to say about candidate Christian, at least outside the *Independent*. Republicans could afford to offer kind words about Christian because he was a Democrat running for state senate in a comfortable Republican district. Even Christian's opponent, Henry J. May, complimented Christian's character in an October speech given in Marion.

Attorney Henry J. May came from one of the pioneer families of Hardin County, Ohio. At thirty-four years old, he was much younger than Christian, and he had graduated from the Ohio State Normal School (now Ohio Northern University) in 1882. May apprenticed under former Hardin County judge A. B. Johnson and became a member of the Ohio state bar in 1887. May had gained the respect of his fellow Republicans in 1896 through his tireless campaigning on behalf of William McKinley. In return, his colleagues nominated him for state senator in a district where Republican victory was almost inevitable. May chose not to pick any fights with Christian, because Republicans had won by more than 1,500 votes in the district's previous election for state senator. Despite Christian's personal popularity and likeability, Republicans felt that he had no chance of winning the seat.[12]

Christian worked hard, however, to convince voters. He and his party brought in prominent speakers to reassure voters about his support for free silver. Even the Democratic candidate for governor, Horace Chapman, came to Marion to stump for Christian. Christian's defenders formed committees in each of the four counties to campaign on his behalf. Christian also gave speeches in communities throughout the district. On September 25, 1897, he spoke at the Kenton armory to a group of laborers, farmers, and mechanics, and he reportedly won many friends with his arguments in favor of free silver and against Republican corruption. In an October 28 speech in Marion, Christian reminded the crowd of his connections to the local population. He offered bipartisan praise for Ohio's senior U.S. senator, Joseph Foraker, and advocated lowering local officials' salaries. He unsuccessfully claimed he would look out for the city's African American voters, who were always aware of the Democratic Party's racist policies in the South. While Christian's campaigning also focused on unemployment and corruption his most compelling political attribute was his ability to use humor to connect with voters. As the election loomed in a world without polling, Christian felt that he had made progress in turning the electorate in his favor.[13]

On Election Day—November 2, 1897—a vicious storm rattled across Ohio. While the storm kept workers home from their jobs, it also allowed them to vote without worrying about work obligations. The *Star* estimated that between sixty and eighty percent of Marion's voters participated in the election. In Marion, Christian polled very well, earning between three and four hundred more votes than the rest of the Democratic ticket. He won the county by 834 votes—3,790 to 2,956. He also defeated May in Hardin County by a plurality of five or six hundred votes. However, May won greater majorities in Logan and Union Counties. In the end, May squeaked

OFFICIAL ABSTRACT OF THE VOTE CAST IN MARION COUNTY NOVEMBER 2, 1897.

PRECINCTS.	Governor		Senator		Represent.		Sheriff		Treasurer		Recorder		C'missi'r.		Int. Direa.	
	Bushnell, R.	Chapman, D.	May, R.	Christian, D.	Eccles, R.	Powell, D.	Shaw, R.	Battenfeld, D.	Moore, R	Schoenlaub, D.	Williams R.	Bryant, D.	Decker, R.	Hinaman, D.	Roberts, R.	Sutton, D.
Bowling Green	74	158	71	163	73	152	106	120	93	139	74	149	75	151	84	181
Grand Prairie	53	76	55	74	54	75	66	74	65	85	54	75	59	70	51	78
Tully	73	129	71	131	72	131	70	131	75	159	72	130	71	131	72	130
Salt Rock	111	49	111	50	110	50	110	47	114	46	111	48	111	49	107	52
Montgomery, E. P.	105	109	106	107	107	106	119	94	111	100	104	109	108	105	94	115
Montgomery, W. P.	185	168	184	170	159	165	205	151	187	166	186	167	191	162	156	190
Claridon, N P.	135	178	129	179	129	181	184	176	137	173	135	177	127	183	132	178
Claridon, S. P.	89	63	87	65	88	64	103	53	99	56	88	63	97	55	86	65
Richland	42	228	42	225	42	225	63	208	52	216	48	219	80	205	46	219
Pleasant	105	160	106	161	105	161	116	151	116	148	100	157	107	159	105	160
Scott	39	90	38	90	78	90	38	91	39	89	36	92	31	99	38	90
Waldo	69	135	68	135	69	135	70	133	75	129	69	134	68	133	68	135
Prospect	226	259	217	265	226	258	241	242	244	242	225	257	225	258	223	254
Marion township	141	165	124	180	142	161	158	147	147	161	133	172	141	161	141	164
First Ward A	263	279	244	296	253	278	300	244	277	259	233	309	295	273	270	271
First Ward B.	115	123	106	120	113	122	123	122	121	118	104	138	120	118	111	127
Second Ward A.	142	192	130	199	138	190	157	179	156	175	116	218	139	188	147	183
Second Ward B.	97	103	82	118	93	105	101	101	102	98	89	113	101	100	96	102
Third Ward A.	223	208	203	232	221	213	237	207	247	190	205	226	207	225	217	215
Third Ward B.	146	171	140	173	142	147	147	167	163	160	137	175	137	173	137	174
Fourth Ward A.	207	172	186	193	203	176	224	160	208	177	195	190	195	185	206	175
Fourth Ward B.	112	102	104	114	112	105	114	106	117	112	160	112	107	173	137	105
Big Island	142	147	141	147	151	147	150	141	150	140	140	149	143	147	133	152
Green Camp.	152	146	151	147	136	142	167	131	152	146	152	146	152	146	151	147
Grand	60	57	60	57	60	57	66	51	63	55	60	51	59	58	59	57
Totals	3106	3682	2955	3790	3070	3686	3374	3429	3301	3475	2981	3779	3097	3047	3028	3608
Pluralities		556		834		596	55			174		788	550			580

The following vote was cast outside of the two leading parties, on the State ticket—Prohibition 49, People's 9, National Democratic 11, Social Labor 1, Liberty 58, Negro Protective 0. On county ticket—Prohibition 47, Liberty 51.

Fig. 71. This chart tracks the election results in Marion County in 1897. ("Official Abstract of the Vote Cast in Marion County November 2, 1897." *Marion [OH] Daily Star,* Nov. 5, 1897)

by with an overall victory of a little over four hundred votes, about two percent of votes cast. The *Marion Star* dubbed the result a "memorable scare" for Republicans. The *Upper Sandusky Union* commented on Christian's candidacy and near win by stating, "When it comes to bearing down the pressure the colonel has no peer in the state."[14] Christian seemed to take the loss in stride. He was in good spirits ten days later when he submitted his financial report for the election, which documented that he spent $264 (about $7,650 in 2016) on his campaign—mostly to pay the expenses of committees that had advocated for him in each of the counties within the district. In the days and weeks after the election, Christian retreated to his substantial work obligations.[15]

Christian's friends, however, saw his candidacy as a great victory. If he could run so close in a blatantly Republican district, they reasoned he might succeed mightily in a district without such an established Republican majority. In the summer of 1898, the Republican-leaning *Marion Star* began to float Christian's name as a possible replacement for U.S. Congressman "Doc" James Norton. The *Star* reached across party lines because of the personal friendship between its editor, Warren G. Harding, and Christian, and also because the Republicans felt that Christian represented the city's best chance for sending one of their own to Congress. Since Christian was vacationing in Michigan, where he could not refute them, such rumors of a potential candidacy spread rapidly. Soon the editors of the *Sandusky Star* also touted Christian's fitness as a congressional candidate.[16]

Whether to prevent such a candidacy or to honor Christian's commitment to public service, Republican governor Asa S. Bushnell appointed him to the bipartisan Ohio Centennial Celebration Commission on September 19, 1898. (The next chapter explores the story of Christian's participation on the commission.) Christian's decision to accept the appointment effectively ended any chance of a congressional run. In 1899, Warren G. Harding ran for the state senate seat Christian had lost two years before—Harding's first attempt at seeking political office. Although he was a Republican, Harding had offered de facto support for Christian's campaign two years earlier. Had Christian won the senate seat in 1897, it seems plausible that Harding would not have opposed him in the next election.[17]

Consequently, Christian's defeat in 1897, in part, enabled Harding's meteoric political rise. (Discussed in more detail in chapters nine and ten.) Christian turned his focus to his business and the centennial commission, a decision which guaranteed that he would remain only a local political figure without time or ambitions for state or national office. Christian was fifty-one-years-old, and he decided that his career as a political candidate was over.

CHAPTER 8

Exposition Lost

"Said commission believes it is practically the universal wish and desire of the people of the State of Ohio to commemorate by an exposition of fitting magnitude the progress of Ohio in educational, industrial, and commercial lines in its century of Statehood, exhibiting the great staples of the Northwest Territory and Ohio Valley region, which contribute so largely to domestic and international commerce; that encouragement should be given to an exhibit of the arts, industries, manufactures, and products illustrative of the progress and development of Ohio and other sections of the country; that such exhibition should be international as well as national in its character, in which the people of this country, Mexico, the Central and South American governments, and other States of the world should participate." Ohio Centennial Commission, *Report of the Ohio Centennial Commission to the Seventy-Fourth General Assembly of Ohio* (Columbus: Ohio Centennial Commission, n. d.), 9.

When George B. Christian Sr. lost his bid for state senator in the 1897 election, many of his fellow Democrats actually felt his failed candidacy had qualified him for a more important political prize. While local papers in 1898 touted his prospects as a candidate for a U.S. congressional seat, Christian instead accepted a gubernatorial appointment to the Ohio Centennial Commission, a group tasked with organizing an exposition to celebrate one hundred years of Ohio statehood. To some it might have appeared that Christian had abandoned party and politics, but in fact the commission provided the perfect outlet for his boosterist commitment to progress and public service. It also offered him a venue for demonstrating his loyalty to state and country. On the other hand, the successes and failures of the Ohio Centennial Commission presented Christian with a first-hand primer on the political corruption of his era.

Expositions at the turn of the twentieth century were specially constructed public events characterized by displays of technology, art, and culture.[1] They also generated prestige and revenue for the communities and states in which they were held. Beginning in 1876 with Philadelphia's Centennial Exposition, these grand affairs occurred periodically throughout the country. The largest and most significant expositions were dubbed World's Fairs because of the international scope of their exhibits. The greatest of these events held in the United States occurred in 1893 in Chicago and in 1904 in St. Louis. Expositions not designated as World's Fairs embraced a more regional flavor. But all these occasions celebrated the advance of civilization and technology. In his 1901 speech at the Pan-American Exposition, President William McKinley stated, "Expositions are the timekeepers of progress. They record the world's advancement."[2] On a subliminal level, expositions also offered the country's scientific, political, and industrial leaders the opportunity to instruct the masses about their elite impressions of the mission, progress, and destiny of the nation.[3]

Fig. 72. Photograph of the grounds at the World's Columbian Exposition in Chicago, 1893. This was perhaps the most famous of all of the grand expositions held in the United States during this era. (Courtesy of the Library of Congress)

One famous historian has labeled the period comprised of the late eighteenth and early nineteenth centuries as "the search for order," because rapid industrialization created widespread economic inequalities and social unrest.[4] Production workers who had once controlled the pace of their labor now found themselves constrained by the requirements of standardized manufacturing. The boom and bust nature of modern capitalism caused periodic economic panics that tormented the most vulnerable members of society. Mass immigration altered the ethnic and linguistic balances of the workforce, creating competition and animosity. In contrast with these conflicts created by the corporate reconstruction of American capitalism, national and international expositions showcased technology, history, and culture to teach the masses about the supposedly ordered evolution of life and society in the United States. Displays of machinery and industrial processes assured viewers that technological innovations improved modern life. Exhibits highlighting world history and depicting "primitive" indigenous peoples served as reminders of the progressive path of Western culture. Together, these spectacles promoted pride in America and the advancement of its political and economic institutions.[5]

Ohio had already hosted one large-scale exposition in 1888. in Cincinnati to commemorate the settlement of the Ohio Valley and the Old Northwest. The state had also sponsored exhibits at the 1876 Centennial Exposition in Philadelphia and at every major exposition thereafter. Interest in organizing an exposition to celebrate one hundred years of Ohio statehood began in 1895, when Ohio delegations observed Tennessee's centennial festivities. In the media coverage of this Nashville spectacle, prominent Ohio politicians and journalists began floating the idea for a similar landmark event in their own state in 1903. In part, expositions served as a point of pride for states and communities, and Ohio leaders wanted to build the state's national profile.[6]

Popular and influential rumblings in favor of such an event caused Governor Asa S. Bushnell, a Republican, to appoint a seven-man commission to locate a site and develop a plan for the celebration. The governor acted in accordance with a legislative resolution requiring that a site and plan be in place before the end of the 1898 legislative session. This first commission met while Christian was still running for state senator. By November of 1897, the group was hosting presentations from various Ohio cities in order to recommend a centennial location to the General Assembly. This first commission had no real power except to make recommendations, and members struggled to find opportunities to meet. Cincinnati, Columbus, and Toledo had offered the most attractive exposition proposals to the commission, but its members disagreed over whether the state should even hold an event or whether a landmark might serve as a more fitting tribute to statehood.[7]

In fact, the first commission eventually recommended to the Ohio General Assembly, in April of 1898, that the state construct a memorial building to house a state library and museum rather than organize an exposition. They argued that such a gathering "could not be made worthy of the state, except at great expense, and anything less than an exposition on a scale large enough and grand enough to comport with the importance of this great state would not be worthy of the state."[8] The commission reasoned that a special library and museum would provide a smaller scale but longer lasting tribute to the state's history of growth and progress than an exposition could offer.

The General Assembly rejected the first commission's recommendation and decided to sponsor a regional event. They designated Toledo as the exposition site because of its central location in relation to the other states of the Old Northwest. The assembly allocated $500,000 to begin renovations and plans for the celebration, and it called on the governor to appoint a new group to oversee this process. On September 1, 1898, Governor Bushnell appointed a commission consisting of one member from each congressional district. The commission's mandate was bipartisan, so the governor selected eleven Republicans and ten Democrats. While Christian's reputation and political prowess played an important role in his appointment, he also had some experience participating in expositions. Several years before, the *Marion Daily Star* had reported that the Norris and Christian Lime and Stone Company's exhibit had won an award at the 1893 World's Fair in Chicago, which was also

Fig. 73. Portrait of Ohio Governor Asa Bushnell who appointed George B. Christian Sr. a member of the Ohio Centennial Commission. (Courtesy of the Library of Congress.)

known as the Columbia Exposition because it celebrated the four hundredth anniversary of Columbus's exploration of the Americas. No other reference to this prize appeared in Marion newspapers. But even if the *Star* exaggerated the success of the company's exhibit, the reference suggests that Christian's company had at least sent a display to the event. Christian, as company president, surely played a role in fashioning the presentation for such a mammoth occasion.[9]

The new centennial commission's duties included choosing a site within Toledo for the event and supervising improvements to the site. The legislature also directed the group to research the successes and

Fig. 74. This letterhead of the Ohio Centennial Commission was used in all the group's official communications. (Courtesy of the Library of Congress.)

failures of previous expositions around the country and to seek input from the state's citizens about the kind of celebration they wanted. The commission was to plan the displays that would tell the story of

Ohio and its industrial, technological, and political accomplishments. In addition, it needed to convince the federal government and other states to contribute funds. The legislature asked the commission to submit a report of its recommendations for approval before the end of the next legislative session.[10]

From the beginning, this second centennial commission served with an extremely complicated mandate. While Christian and his fellow commissioners felt empowered to gather information and create plans, their ability to set those plans into motion was much murkier. One of the most complicated and pressing questions centered on whether the group had the authority to spend the money allocated by the state legislature. The citizens of Toledo had created the Ohio Centennial Company to raise money from prominent individuals and rent display space to manufacturers and businesses. In all, the company aimed to raise $500,000 for construction and expenses. City officials offered Bayview Park on Lake Erie as the site for the event, and they issued $150,000 in bonds to help foot the cost of improvements to the grounds. The city hoped to add this money to allocations by the Ohio legislature and the U.S. Congress to ensure a successful event. Unfortunately, the Ohio Centennial Company ran behind in its fundraising efforts, and the General Assembly and governor tied up state funds in red tape, which caused the organizers to risk losing any chance at receiving federal money. The fight over funding endangered the centennial exposition at every stage of its development.[11]

Despite its money troubles, the commission embarked on its assigned tasks with determination. In conjunction with the Ohio congressional delegation and the Ohio Centennial Company, commission members lobbied Congress to appropriate money for the event. Members also pondered whether upcoming expositions in Buffalo, New York (1901), and St. Louis, Missouri (planned for 1903), should affect their plans for a 1903 event. To prevent potential conflicts, the group recommended that the state hold its gathering in 1902, between the two other major expositions. Members also wanted to create an advertising campaign to raise awareness and generate excitement for the celebration. In the end, they divided themselves into committees assigned to plan and oversee different aspects of the spectacle.[12]

Christian's appointment to the Committee on Inspection of Work and Progress, which oversaw improvements to the exposition site in Bayview Park, utilized his background in surveying and engineering. He and his fellow committee members reported that Toledo had contracted for $200,000 worth of improvements to the park and that contractors had completed $80,000 of the work by the time of their report in late 1899. Crews worked to drain and contain the water on site and grade and improve the exposition land. In its report to the Ohio General Assembly, the committee expressed satisfaction with the improvements made up to that point.[13]

Christian also belonged to the Committee on Sanitary Exhibits, which probably required much more individual research given his relative inexperience in the field. Nevertheless, his long-standing advocacy for the development of a water works in Marion gave him at least a basic background in sanitation. Christian worked with local public health experts to learn about the technologies and techniques used to prevent the spread of disease. Christian, referring to himself as the Chemical Commissioner on Sanitary Exhibits, wrote to the State Board of Health for its suggestions on the kind of exhibits that might be organized for the exposition. The board suggested focusing on the aspects of public hygiene which could improve through public action and legislation. The committee members took this advice to heart and, in their report to the Ohio General Assembly, suggested that the exposition provide educational materials dedicated to the "practical application of modern sanitative [sic] methods."[14]

The latter years of the nineteenth century had witnessed a tremendous revolution in the scientific understanding of disease and its causes. In 1881, President James A. Garfield had passed away, not from the assassin's bullet, but from the subsequent infection introduced by doctors as they probed his wounds with dirty instruments. In the years since that national tragedy, doctors in the United States had begun to embrace the work of Louis Pasteur and other European scientists who linked bacteria and other microbes to the development of disease. By the 1890s, laboratories had emerged at U.S. medical schools devoted to identifying disease-causing agents and fighting their transmission. As scientists started to identify the causes of diseases such as malaria, cholera, diphtheria, and tuberculosis, the developing field of public health began to offer solutions for combating and controlling these killers.[15]

Christian and his committee's recommendations for the sanitation exhibits reflected the highest priorities and idealism of public health officials. Doctors and sanitation engineers of the era had argued that "all disease is preventable [and] that epidemic and contagious diseases should be at once abolished." To accomplish this goal, advocates had identified, among other techniques, the importance of "a pure and abundant water supply [and] the proper disposal of sewage."[16] Christian's committee wanted to showcase the successful implementation of these theories. For example, it suggested that the exposition provide only filtered water for its guests and create a presentation highlighting the hygienic benefits of purified water. The members also sought to implement sanitary treatments for the events' sewage and teach people about the benefits of these techniques. In addition, the committee wanted to create exhibits which would teach visitors about good hygiene and antiseptic practices. Finally, the committee hoped to feature the disease-fighting efforts of doctors throughout the country in an exhibit on inoculations. Christian's participation in creating the report of the Committee on Sanitary Exhibits was only the latest of Christian's efforts to embrace technology and progress. His sanitation work for the centennial commission showed

Christian's faith—a faith common for his time—that implementing the newest and best technologies could solve the world's problems.

The recommendations of the Committee on Sanitary Exhibits were exemplary of the larger project. In their report, the commissioners argued that all "exhibits . . . showing the advancement of progress of Ohio in educational, industrial and commercial lines," and not for advertisement, "should be controlled and exhibited by the State of Ohio." They further opined that "the State should, through its commission, not only control all of the exhibits furnished by it, but should have supervisory control of all matters and things pertaining to the holding of said Exposition." Ultimately, the group suggested that the state, through its commissioners, control the narrative of progress presented during the event. The commissioners requested an allocation of one million dollars from the Ohio General Assembly for this purpose. Their recommendations for control and legislative appropriation immediately created consternation within the various factions of Ohio government.[17]

Unfortunately, the centennial commission's work began to unravel in the months after its report reached the Ohio legislature. While the fierce battles between Republicans and Democrats had dominated the national political scene, it was internal Republican factionalism that more directly affected the Ohio Centennial Commission. For many years, John Sherman had held sway over the state's Republican establishment as the party's elder statesman and U.S. senator. The roots of his power came from his diligent congressional service during the Civil War. Because of his support of the gold standard and protectionist tariffs, he gained the backing of the state's prominent business and political power broker, Mark Hanna of Cleveland, who unsuccessfully attempted to bring about Sherman's nomination for the presidency in 1884 and 1888. In the 1890s, Hanna and Sherman threw their support behind William McKinley and played an integral role in raising money for his campaigns.[18]

197

Sherman and Hanna's dominance of the party establishment frustrated many of the younger Republicans in the state. The principal spokesman for these next-generation Republicans was Joseph B. Foraker, who publicly, and hypocritically, criticized his party's bossism while aligning himself with George B. Cox, the well-known political boss of Cincinnati. The Foraker-Cox and Sherman-Hanna-McKinley factions came to represent opposing sides of the Republican Party that, at the end of the nineteenth century, vied for

Fig. 75. Joseph Foraker was a prominent Ohio Republican who served in the United States Senate. (Society of the Army of the Cumberland, *Burial of General Rosecrans, Arlington National Cemetery* [Cincinnati: Robert Clarke Co., 1902])

political influence in the state and the nation. The election of Asa S. Bushnell, the governor who appointed the centennial commission, had emerged from a compromise between these two sides in 1896. The groups agreed that William McKinley would be the Ohio Republican delegation's choice for president if Joseph Foraker received Ohio's open Senate seat and Bushnell, a Foraker supporter, was nominated for governor. Bushnell, like Foraker, argued in favor of reforming the spoils system, and by choosing members of both parties for the Ohio Centennial Commission, he demonstrated his willingness to look beyond pure power politics.[19]

However, Governor George K. Nash, who succeeded Bushnell in January of 1900, felt that such bipartisanship represented a waste of prime political appointments. Nash, a fervent Sherman-Hanna ally, immediately began to undermine the progress achieved by the commission, assembly, and governor in the previous year. One reason for his hostility to the exposition plans came from the political affiliations of some of the event's biggest boosters in Toledo. Toledo mayor Samuel M. Jones was known as a progressive and reformer who opposed Nash and Hanna's connections to big business and machine politics. Nash feared that Jones might run against him for governor in the next election and that a centennial exposition in Toledo would give the mayor a prominent stage from which to launch such a campaign. In an early address to the General Assembly, Nash argued that the commission's request for a one-

Fig. 76. Ohio Governor George K. Nash undermined the work of the Ohio Centennial Commission on which Christian served. (Painting by C.T. Webber from Daniel J. Ryan, *History of Ohio: the Rise and Progress of the American State,* Vol. 4 [New York: The Century History Company, 1912])

million-dollar appropriation, which the Ohio House had granted, was excessive. He recommended that the state senate amend the house's bill to approve only half that amount. On March 18, 1900, the *Cincinnati Enquirer* speculated that the governor's move was designed to provoke commission members into resigning over such poor funding. The paper also claimed that the real motivation behind Nash's actions was his desire to use the positions on a new commission for patronage. Nash's opposition to funding was political theater. He wanted to block funding for the project until the Ohio Generally Assembly would allow him to appoint new commissioners which he controlled. This commission would then use the money as political spoils to shore up support for the governor. Nash felt that the commission represented the first step in creating a statewide political machine which would allocate state money in support of the governor and his cronies.[20]

The governor and his friends did not limit their attacks on the exposition appropriation bill to the legislative process. On March 25, 1900, the *Cincinnati Enquirer* reported that the state auditor and attorney general had promised not to release funds to the centennial commission even if the appropriation passed the senate, because they believed the bill to be unconstitutional. The Ohio constitution barred the state from using its credit for the benefit of any private corporation, and officials who supported the governor claimed that the state would be doing just that if it turned money over to the Ohio Centennial Company. Opponents of the centennial commissioners' plans offered this objection to provide leverage for dissolving the current commission and requiring the Ohio Centennial Company to raise its full share of $500,000 before having access to any state funds.[21]

In April of 1900, the centennial exposition bill suffered the back-and-forth whims of legislative football as the governor, his allies, and his opponents maneuvered in the fight. While the Ohio house had approved the one million dollars that the commission had requested, the state senate passed an appropriations bill with $750,000 of funding to be spent by a new commission of eleven members chosen by the governor. The house, however, was not willing to let Governor Nash appoint his own people to control the exposition finances, so it initially refused to participate in a conference committee to try to reconcile the two bills. Instead it proposed a compromise: leaving the old commission intact with the authority to spend the original $500,000 appropriation. With this new proposal on the table, the representatives finally agreed to let the bill go to a conference committee. Members of the press assumed that through the bill reconciliation process the governor would eventually get what he really wanted: a one-million-dollar appropriation and the ability to appoint his own commission to spend it. The bill that came out of the conference committee , however, contained the original half-million-dollar appropriation, but it allowed the governor to appoint a new commission to spend it. The senate quickly passed the compromise, but the house once again rejected the bill and the legislation died.[22]

During all of these machinations, individual members of the centennial commission continued their advocacy for the exposition. Christian and his cohorts tried to rally popular support in their home communities and exert pressure on legislators. These efforts, however, encountered apathy among state officials. When a committee from Toledo visited the governor to ask about the fate of the exposition, Nash argued that the General Assembly had failed to act on the matter and the present commission did not have the authority to spend the $500,000 originally mandated under the Bushnell administration. By May 30, 1900, the Ohio Centennial Company began to consider canceling its efforts due to lack of funds; the massive Pan-American Exposition in Buffalo, New York, the next year and an even larger World's Fair in St. Louis three years after that already wielded operating budgets over ten million dollars. As a final desperate act, the centennial commission members sued the governor in hopes of freeing up the original funds. Despite the valiant arguments of Joseph Foraker before the Ohio Supreme Court, it decided that the commission had no authority to spend the initial $500,000 appropriation without additional legislation. Advocates of the commission's exposition plan were left with only one recourse: Governor Nash, who still had authority to call a special legislative session to solve the problem. But because he could not control the commission in the way he wished, Nash decided that the centennial exposition did not merit the trouble and expense of such a session.[23]

So died the work of Christian and his fellow commissioners, a casualty to the corrupt power politics of the Gilded Age. Toledo's Mayor Jones noted that the money lost by his city in its failed bid to secure an exposition was "a direct contribution to the venality of partisan politics. . . . Knowing no law but their own will, the political bosses are ready to tear down or destroy any structure, however sacred, to accomplish their purpose." Jones ultimately decided that "it is better that the enterprise should cease now . . . than that it should have gone through as a mere adjunct to a political machine."[24]

Consequently, even though the exposition never took place, the forces of reform won a small victory by avoiding an event wrought with the corruption of influence peddling.

Nash's actions even created a bit of political backlash. When he stood for re-election in 1901, the Democrats ran Columbus businessman James Kilbourne as his opponent. Christian threw his support behind centennial commission president Kilbourne, since both had come to know the pettiness and corruption of Governor Nash during their service. In a campaign speech given in Toledo, Kilbourne deftly proclaimed that he had left his bitterness over the centennial situation behind—leaving the opposition to the "punishment of their own thoughts and . . . the repressed condemnation of the public-spirited citizens of the state." He also snidely commented on the governor's decision that "the substance of the people should not be wasted in mere educational, scientific and humanitarian projects, such as the proposed centennial."[25] Even though Nash's poor handling of the entire centennial exposition affair gave candidate Kilbourne a political tool with which to bludgeon the governor, the people of Ohio paid little heed to the controversy. They not only re-elected Nash, but they did so by a large margin.

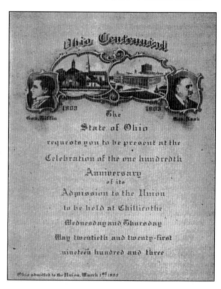

Ohio eventually held a small centennial celebration in May of 1903. The Ohio Archeological and Historical Society had begun to plan a celebration in Chillicothe, the state's first capital, during its meetings in

Fig. 77. This invitation announced the Ohio Centennial Celebration which was organized after the plans for a centennial exposition fell apart. (E. O. Randall, ed., *Ohio Centennial Anniversary Celebration* [Columbus, OH: Ohio State Archeological and Historical Society, 1902])

202

August of 1902. Instead of a grand exposition, society members built a program around the speeches of many of the state's great orators. To support the event, the Ohio legislature offered a $10,000 appropriation bill—a definite bargain compared to the potential $500,000 or $1,000,000 required for the exposition.

Christian's role on the Ohio Centennial Exposition Commission gave him a prime seat from which to observe the failure of Ohio's plans to hold an ambitious event in celebration of statehood. An exhibition would have thrust the city of Toledo, at least temporarily, into the national spotlight. Governor Nash's desire to appoint a new commission whose votes he could have influenced painfully illustrated the extent of influence peddling among Ohio politicians. If he could not have an event on his own terms, Nash decided that a two-day panel of speeches in Chillicothe would allow him to be heard without giving too large a forum to his political enemies.[26]

Christian's time on the Ohio Centennial Commission represented his last major entry into statewide politics until the rise of Warren G. Harding. He probably felt disenchanted with the entire process. He had spent four years of his life trying to serve his beloved home state and had no achievements to show for it. In the aftermath of this experience, he turned his full efforts back toward his business endeavors—leaving, at least for a time, the corrupt world of politics.

CHAPTER 9

Warren G. Harding, from Mentee to Colleague to Senator

"The writer, attempting to give you a word picture of the life and times of President Harding from the viewpoint of a neighbor and a friend, finds himself indulging at times in wonderment and asking himself, how can this be? To live beside your neighbor and meet your friend in . . . your daily walks of life; . . . then suddenly to have the curtain raised and a moving panorama of events pass rapidly before you and find these neighbors and friends [who] moved about with you in your commonplace everyday life suddenly lifted to the loftiest peak of greatness and amid the plaudits of the tremendous electorate of the American nation going to the White House, the capitol of the nation, the one as ruler of the greatest nation on earth, the other the first lady of the land." George B. Christian Sr., "Biography of Warren G. Harding" (unpublished manuscript, 1926), Warren G. Harding Papers, Box 792, Ohio Historical Society Archive/Library, Ohio Historical Society, Columbus, OH.

While George B. Christian Sr. gained prominence in his hometown and home state because of his success as a businessman and his tireless public service, any national recognition gleaned by the Christian family occurred because of their relationship with the twenty-ninth president of the United States, Warren Gamaliel Harding. As Marion became a regional manufacturing hub due to its excellent railroad access, individuals and families harnessed this economic potential to achieve financial and social distinction.

While men such as Edward Huber and George Christian found success through industry, others like T. P. Wallace and Warren G. Harding provided services such as banking and newspaper publishing to the community and its leaders. Success provided resources and time for leisure as well as social and political engagement. The community pages of Marion's newspapers followed the activities of prominent men and their families, who populated the clubs, fraternal organizations, political offices, and social circles of the town. This group of upper-middle-class residents included entrepreneurs, bankers, engineers, lawyers, doctors, managers, and other professionals. It was within this social web that George B. Christian Sr. and Warren G. Harding became friends.

Much of Harding's rise to the presidency depended on his ability to meld the popular appeal of his small-town background with the skills he had gained as a newspaper editor and entrepreneur. Harding understood the power of rhetoric and publicity; he could speak to the people of America's heartland. George B. Christian Sr. played a role in helping his friend develop this political voice. Few historians have examined the Christian-Harding friendship, preferring to focus on Harding's aspirations for and path to the presidency. The following two chapters examine how Harding's relationship with George B. Christian Sr. affected both men's lives. The changing nature of Harding and Christian's friendship offers a unique focal point from which to examine Warren G. Harding, his presidency, and his tragic death.

Christian's success as one of Marion's premier industrialists allowed him the time and the status to mentor Harding, who embarked on his career as a journalist and newspaper manager at a young age. Despite his electoral losses, Christian also demonstrated the ambition involved in making the jump from the private sector to politics at a time when creating a public persona had become an important political skill. Over time, the relationship between the two men transformed from one of mentorship to collegial friendship. When Harding successfully ran for senator in 1914, he took George

B. Christian Jr. with him to Washington, but left Christian Sr. behind. For years, Christian Sr. took pride in the fact that he had identified Harding's political potential at a young age, and he felt that Harding's success was, in part, his own.

The historical record contains only a few clues about the circumstances of George B. Christian Sr. and Warren G. Harding's first encounters and the beginnings of their acquaintance. But the evidence suggests that they probably met because of George Christian's association with Harding's father. George Tryon Harding, who generally used his middle name, was born two years before Christian in 1844. The brevity of Tryon Harding's Civil War service mirrored Christian's own—though the elder Harding came much closer to the

Fig. 78. Portrait of George Tryon Harding, father of the president. Tryon Harding and George Christian knew each other before Warren Harding and Christian became friends. (Courtesy of the Library of Congress)

principal battlefront in Virginia. Christian and Tryon Harding might have met as soldiers or as veterans trying reintegrate into civilian society in Marion County immediately after the war.[1]

After a few years, Tryon Harding moved to Cleveland and trained in homeopathic medicine—the same career as Christian's father, John Christian. Both men spent their careers working to legitimize this branch of medicine. After Harding returned to Marion County, the two men commissioned an advertisement for a Central Homeopathic Institute in Marion with John Christian as president and Tryon Harding as secretary in 1874. When Christian became incapacitated by illness in 1882, Harding moved to busy Marion from the much smaller town of Caledonia to take over the old doctor's practice.[2]

Beyond his medical practice, Tryon Harding also tried his hand at investing. He helped finance the development of a section of Caledonia, and he also bought a stake in the *Caledonia Argus* newspaper. After the *Argus* failed in 1876, Harding wrote for Christian's *Marion Democratic Mirror* as its Caledonia correspondent. In Christian's early days as sole editor of the paper, tragedy struck the Harding family. A terrible flu epidemic killed Birdie and Charlie Harding in November of 1878. The *Mirror* printed an obituary for Warren G. Harding's siblings with the sermon from their funeral, and the paper even allowed Tryon Harding space to compose an account of how and why they passed away. The public compassion Christian extended to the Harding family in their moment of grief demonstrated the goodwill that had developed between the two veterans, which would continue to grow in subsequent years.[3]

When the elder Harding moved to Marion in February of 1882, his son Warren (age seventeen) lingered at Central Ohio College in Iberia. After finishing his two years of training at this small institution, Warren G. Harding accepted a job as a teacher in a small schoolhouse near Marion. Harding hated the low pay and difficult students, so he left the profession after just one school year. He moved to Marion in 1883. Christian later claimed that he saw Harding riding a white mule into town when Harding relocated, and the story identified Christian as one of the future president's first Marion contacts. After moving to the county seat, Harding began training as a lawyer with attorney Stephen A. Court, but he soon bored of the intense study and journeyman's wages. Consequently, he signed on to work for the *Marion Democratic Mirror* as a reporter and general helper. Christian had sold his stake in the *Mirror* a year earlier, but his good friend and partner George Vaughan was still its owner and editor. While Harding generally enjoyed his job, his loyalty to the Republican presidential candidate James G. Blaine in the 1884 election drove him away from the Democratic newspaper. At about this same time, the city's small daily, the *Marion Star,* came up for sale, and Harding convinced his father and two friends to purchase it in hopes of making a career in the newspaper business. Harding (age nineteen) and his partners assumed control of the *Star* near the end of 1884 and quickly began turning it into a successful enterprise.[4]

Small towns such as Marion had found little use for daily newspapers when Harding first began publishing the *Star.* Most country newspapers published one or two editions a week. To justify the daily printing, Harding felt compelled to seek out interesting local news to engage his readers. The daily edition also tried to maintain a tone of political independence in order to appeal to all Marionites. In 1885, Harding began to publish a weekly version of the *Star* as well. Weeklies generally had higher circulations, more detail, and an intensely political tone. The *Weekly Star* was a Republican paper that sought to compete with the city's other newspapers for advertisements and legal notices. The *Weekly Star* also gave Harding a forum to develop his political voice.[5]

Sometime during Harding's early years at the *Star,* Christian began to mentor him. Christian had worked at the *Mirror* for five years and offered invaluable knowledge about the newspaper business in Marion. George B. Christian Jr. later recalled long games of Parcheesi at his family home between his father and the future president in the years after Harding took over the *Star.* In part, Christian might have advised Harding regarding how to deal with the editor of the *Marion Independent,* George Crawford, who felt threatened by and lashed out at the new Republican paper. Crawford had also bitterly jousted with Christian during their time as rival editors. Harding quickly strove to update his paper's equipment and content, and the *Star* gradually began to eat into the *Independent's* market share among Republicans—especially after Harding began publishing his weekly.[6]

Harding spent significant column space, to Christian's satisfaction, boostering local enterprises. In fact, Harding often printed laudatory accounts about the developments at the Norris and Christian Lime and Stone Company. Articles in the *Star* also revealed Harding's positive and sympathetic feelings toward Christian himself. For example, on January 20, 1886, Harding recounted that the *Independent* had referred to Christian as Marion's Colonel Sellers because of his many, often unsuccessful, entrepreneurial endeavors. In a one-sentence editorial, Harding rebutted Crawford's negativity by proclaiming, "Give us more, Col. Sellers."[7] Harding wanted to go on the record supporting Christian's risk-taking spirit. That April, the *Star* applauded Christian's role lobbying for railroad construction through Marion. Harding also published many letters to the editor that Christian had written, and he occasionally even editorialized about their quality, describing one as "moving." These examples of favorable journalistic framing illustrated a pattern of friendly coverage that Harding gave to his mentor. Christian's treatment was so positive that critics later accused him of owning the paper. During this period, Christian and Harding interacted primarily as mentor and mentee. Christian saw much of his own ambition in the young Harding and supported him affectionately as he expanded his newspaper. In fact, Christian sent seven travelogues he had written about Florida to Harding rather than his former paper, the *Mirror*.[8]

The nature of their relationship began to change in the early 1890s when Harding began to court Florence Kling, the daughter of one of Marion's most successful businessmen. Christian had become acquainted with the sensible and bright young woman when she married his cousin Susan Busby DeWolfe's troubled son, Henry. The couple soon welcomed a son, Marshall, but they were not happy. Henry drank and could not hold a job and became abusive. Thus, Florence Kling's first marriage ended quickly, and, in time, she became attracted to Harding's success and dynamic personality. After a short courtship, Kling and Harding decided to wed. Nevertheless, her father, Amos Kling, felt that Harding, like Henry DeWolfe, lacked the breeding and wealth to be a proper spouse for his daughter. Harding belonged to a newer wing of the Republican Party than Amos Kling, whose political loyalties had formed during the Civil War and Reconstruction. In addition, Harding and Kling had argued over a previous business deal. Kling's disdain for Harding was so great that he shunned the couple for many years after their marriage, cutting them off from his great wealth. In the absence of Florence Kling's father, George and Lydia Christian played an important role as supportive parental figures in the Hardings' wedding, which occurred in Warren G. Harding's home on July 8, 1891. The Christian children also took part in the ceremony: George B. Christian Jr. served as a doorman and little Mildred Christian as a flower girl.[9]

Florence Harding's head for business improved the bottom line for Harding and the *Star*, and her help freed Harding to focus on editorial work. During some of these first married years, George B. Christian Jr. might have worked at the *Star*—though there are conflicting accounts about whether he officially ever made it on the payroll. Either way, Christian Jr. spent significant time with the Hardings in his youth. Even though Christian Jr. was only eight years younger than Harding, the Hardings treated him as a surrogate son. This long-term association formed bonds of trust between the future senator/president and his future secretary.[10]

While Harding still looked to George B. Christian Sr. for advice as the *Star* grew and prospered, his marriage and success reformulated their relationship into a more collegial bond. Christian and Harding began to participate in activities as equals and friends. John J. Garberson, Christian's brother-in-law, recounted that Christian and Harding used to drive out to the Garberson farm in Caledonia on Sunday afternoons. During these visits, political debates occurred in which Christian argued for the Democrats, Garberson for the Republicans, and Harding for something in between.[11]

211

As the account from Garberson suggests, Christian and Harding had become fast friends. Their families soon began traveling together. For example, Harding and Christian, and possibly their wives, traveled to George B. Christian Jr.'s graduation at Chester Military College in Pennsylvania in June of 1894. After attending the festivities, the travelers continued on to Atlantic City before returning to Marion. The families also traveled together to Florida in January of 1895 to seek relief from their poor health. Christian and his wife even accompanied Florence Harding to the Battle Creek Sanitarium in 1903. The Michigan facility was the premier medical complex for dealing with the nervous disorders faced by so many individuals of the era. Such joint travel plans, especially under difficult circumstances, manifested the respect and esteem held between the families.[12]

Christian and Harding also belonged to some of the same fraternal organizations, such as the Elks, and they served together on the Marion Board of Trade. They both supported paving Marion's principal roads and many other developments. Despite their loyalty to opposing political parties, they often shared the same vision for their rapidly expanding city. Their agreement and friendship became clear during Christian's 1897 run for state senator in Ohio's thirteenth senatorial district. Harding not only ignored the letter from Christian's Republican opponent requesting support and information, but he also offered an endorsement of Christian, the Democratic candidate. He described Christian as a "valued friend" and praised his ability, originality, high mindedness, honesty, and judgment. He also admitted that Christian had little chance for victory in his overwhelmingly Republican district. Nevertheless, Harding still offered his highest compliments to candidate Christian and recommended his friend for an even higher office—a seat in the U.S. House of Representatives. Christian never forgot Harding's bipartisan support and often stumped for the future president in his political campaigns, including Harding's efforts to secure the same Ohio senate seat that Christian had failed to win three years earlier.[13]

After he won the election for state senator, Harding found ways to show his loyalty to Christian. As previously discussed, Christian had accepted a seat on the ill-fated Ohio Centennial Commission, which failed because of the machine politics of the era. By 1900, Harding had entered the Ohio senate and had the opportunity to vote on the commission's plan and funding. He initially supported the plan that Christian and his fellow commissioners put forward. When Governor George K. Nash sought to hold the project hostage, Harding supported a compromise that would have lowered funding for the project and decreased the number of commissioners. He made one stipulation to the arrangement—that Christian should be reappointed to the new commission. This compromise eventually failed as well, but it demonstrated that Harding, even when trying to find a middle ground, took care of his friends.[14]

One interesting view of the Christian and Harding friendship comes from a photo album compiled by Dr. Charles Sawyer, the Hardings' personal physician and friend. This collection contains a number of images candidly depicting both families around the turn of the twentieth century, and they reveal views of daily life in Marion not found in any other medium. Without any captions in the album, the full context and content of the photographs are impossible to identify, so they do not fit perfectly into a chronological narrative. Nevertheless, they offer some hints about the Christians' and Hardings' friendship. The photos prove that the families socialized with each other and in the same circles with other white-collar Marionites like Sawyer. They also suggest the nature and form of some of these interactions. While Sawyer did not date the pictures, several of them depict George B. Christian Jr.'s infant son John, born in February of 1900. Therefore, they were probably taken in the summer or fall of 1900 after Warren G. Harding won his first race for state senate. Visual clues throughout the photos hint that most of the other images likely depict a similar era.

The Sawyer pictures have neither the polish nor composition of professional photos. Amateur photography became possible when the Kodak Company began selling cameras for mass consumption in the early 1890s. In 1900, a group of amateur photographers in Marion formed a camera club with its own darkroom headquartered in the local YMCA. These advancements meant that laypeople could now capture more candid moments on film.

Sawyer's images of the Christians and Hardings can be grouped into several categories or occasions. For example, three photographs show an outing at a house that was probably George B. Christian Sr.'s West Church Street home. In one, a young Ruth Dombaugh sits on the grass in a long white dress near a house partially covered with climbing ivy—Ruth later died tragically at the age of ten from acute gastritis. Another photo depicts George B. Christian Sr., the girl's grandfather, holding little Ruth while pointing toward the camera—probably trying to make her look toward and smile at the photographer. A third image shows George and Lydia Christian sitting on the porch steps of the same ivy-covered house with their granddaughter

Fig. 79. Photograph of a young Ruth Dombaugh on a lawn which presumably belonged to Christian. (Reprinted by permission of the National First Ladies Library)

Fig. 80. Photograph of George B. Christian Sr. and his only granddaughter Ruth Dombaugh. (Reprinted by permission of the National First Ladies Library)

and two figures who appear to be Dr. Tryon Harding and his wife. The older couples seem to be admiring the child as her parents, Fred and Mamie Dombaugh, look on. Although Warren and Florence Harding do not appear in these images, the association with Warren Harding's parents shows the multigenerational friendship that the two families had formed.

Fig. 81. The Christians with Mamie, Fred, and Ruth Dombaugh as well as another couple who appear to be Tryon and Phoebe Harding. (Reprinted by permission of the National First Ladies Library)

A second set of photos reveals an occasion on which George B. Christian Sr., his son George Jr., and his grandsons John and Warren spent time with Warren and Florence Harding. These photos take place in front of the Hardings' home; the porch would later be replaced by the iconic platform used to launch Harding's presidential campaign. One photograph shows Christian Jr. and Florence Harding giving a dog—possibly the Christians' dog, Gyp—a bath near the porch. Christian Jr.'s wife, Stella, and their young son John seem to be enjoying the spectacle. There is one more woman in the picture

Fig. 82. George B. Christian Jr. and Florence Harding wash a dog while wife Stella and son John Christian observe. (Reprinted by permission of the National First Ladies Library)

Fig. 83. George B. Christian Jr. and son John sitting on the same porch steps as the previous image. (Reprinted by permission of the National First Ladies Library)

who is difficult to identify because of the hat obscuring her face. A second photograph shows Christian Jr. holding John on the porch steps that appeared in the previous image. A third picture shows Warren Christian, Christian Jr.'s oldest son who was named after Harding, dressed up in a cavalry hat, fake glasses, and overalls. His costume mimicked

Fig. 84. Warren Christian dressed as Teddy Roosevelt. (Reprinted by permission of the National First Ladies Library)

Theodore Roosevelt's iconic Rough Riders. The pictures were likely taken in the years while Roosevelt was president (1901–1908). The two families seem to enjoy the Christians' grandchildren.

A third pair of images captures the Christian and Harding families on a variety of outings. One depicts George B. Christian Jr. holding an uncooperative John or Warren Christian. George B. Christian Sr.; Christian Jr.'s wife, Stella; and the future First Lady Florence Harding also appear. The party looks to have recently finished a game of croquet because gates and mallets appear in the image. All of them seem to be enjoying their drinks, most likely beer. Christian Jr. wields a large stein—perhaps a prize—of which he appears exceptionally proud. A second picture captures George and Lydia Christian walking across the countryside with three adult companions and a baby in a carriage. Although the lack of resolution makes identifying the other subjects difficult, the unknown man pushing the baby carriage bears some resemblance to Fred Dombaugh. This might mean that the woman to the far right is his wife, Mamie, while the woman to his right resembles Florence Harding. In the picture, George B. Christian Sr. wears a straw hat with a fairly wide brim, a look that in the Victorian age signified comfort and relaxation. These images, taken together, prove that the Christians and Hardings enjoyed leisure activities and sometimes participated in such events together.

Fig. 85. George B. Christian Sr., George Christian Jr., Stella Christian, and Florence Harding in the aftermath of a game of croquet. (Reprinted by permission of the National First Ladies Library)

Fig. 86. George B. Christian and wife Lydia with Florence Harding and possibly Fred, Mamie, and Ruth Dombaugh on an excursion. (Reprinted by permission of the National First Ladies Library)

Two final photographs portray a large group of Marion travelers making their way down to Florida to enjoy the warm winter weather. One image frames George B. Christian Sr., his wife, and some of their neighbors behind a wire fence and in front of a large portico, possibly a train station. The second photo shows even more Marionites on a large boat. Christian appears in the back of the photo wearing a nautical hat and Lydia stands with some other women in front of him. Warren and Florence Harding appear arm in arm at the edge of the group. Even in the hot Florida weather, the Marionites continued to wear wool suits and long dresses with long sleeves. Victorian morality prevented them from dressing more casually in public settings. In all of the photos discussed here, Christian wore a full suit and sometimes added a vest. Such attire not only demonstrated the moral requirements that governed this class at the turn of the century, but it also separated those who wore it from the laboring classes. Overall, Sawyer's images show that the love, friendship, and comradery between the Hardings and Christians appears not only in the documentary evidence, but in photographs as well.

Warren G. Harding served in the Ohio senate from 1900 to 1904. This position required only part-time service; Harding spent

Fig. 87. A Group of Marionites at a train station on the way to Florida. (Reprinted by permission of the National First Ladies Library)

Fig. 88. Marionites, including the Christians and the Hardings, on a boat in Florida. (Reprinted by permission of the National First Ladies Library)

the first few months of the year in Columbus and usually returned to Marion sometime in April or May. When Harding was in Columbus and Christian in Marion, letters were their primary means of communication and allowed them to maintain their warm friendship. While the letters primarily conveyed expressions of amity, esteem, and good-natured humor, they also occasionally referenced politics, literature, and family. Harding referred to Christian as "the Colonel" and Christian's wife, Lydia, as "Coonie." He sometimes used the pen name Jeremiah Skates and referred to his wife as "the Duchess." Much of the correspondence revolved around Christmas as letters waxed nostalgic about the hot eggnog punch from friendly Marion gatherings. Harding often recounted imagined conversations with Santa Claus about the Christian family's excellent behavior to justify the gifts he sent them.

Harding rarely mentioned the questions he faced as a legislator, but Christian occasionally offered advice on political issues about which he felt strongly. For example, in a letter to Harding in February of 1902, Christian mentioned his opposition to a law in the Ohio General Assembly meant to regulate fraternal insurance programs. By pooling resources between the healthy and infirm, these non-profit societies behaved like insurance companies by giving their

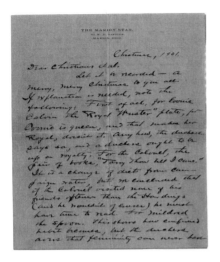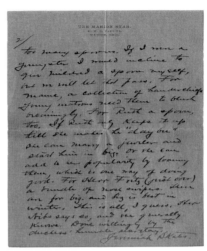

Fig. 89. Christmas letter from Warren G. Harding to the Christians. Harding signed the letter with his pseudonym, Jeremiah Skates. (Courtesy of the Roberts Family Library)

members some level of security in cases of illness or unexpected death. Christian's workers had depended on such programs to protect themselves from the omnipresent dangers of quarry life, and he wanted to secure their right to mitigate their risk. Even though the two men's friendship had started as one of mentorship, Harding no longer felt the need for Christian's help with political decisions. He never responded to Christian's concerns about the insurance bill. While he still enjoyed Christian's occasional observations and Marion perspectives, Harding's most important advisors now came from outside his hometown.[15]

Harding quickly became one of the most important members of the Ohio State Assembly by working closely with Governor George K. Nash. The early years of the twentieth century witnessed intense feuding among factions of the Ohio Republican Party. Decades-old political maneuvering between Ohio political bosses Joseph Foraker, George B. Cox, and Mark Hanna encountered the growing movement of the Progressives, which transcended traditional party boundaries and loyalties. In such divisive times, Harding gained recognition as a powerful orator with the ability to speak to all Republican factions.

His natural loyalties resided with Foraker, whose temperament, opposition to machine politics, and fiery conservatism most resembled Harding's own. On the other hand, Harding knew when to embrace Hanna's and Cox's supporters as well as the progressive members of his party. Harding's lip service to Nash, Hanna, and Republican partisanship opened the gate to his early political ambition, the Ohio governorship. Harding ran for the statehouse in 1903 but ultimately bowed out of the race in deference to the candidate from the Hanna faction, Myron T. Herrick. As compensation for this sacrifice, Harding received a nomination for lieutenant governor. Both he and Herrick won and served Ohio from 1904 to 1906. After Herrick made some political miscalculations, Harding sought to upend him in the 1906 election. When the Republican establishment stuck with Herrick, Harding retracted his name from contention for any political office and returned to Marion as the Republicans lost the governorship to the Democrats.[16]

Fig. 90. Ohio governor Myron T. Herrick served from 1904 to 1906. Warren G. Harding was his lieutenant governor. (Courtesy of the Library of Congress)

During all of these political machinations, Harding maintained contact with his friend George B. Christian Sr. A 1904 letter from Harding to the Christians contained his standard Christmas greetings but also revealed some of the Christians' recent trials. In the letter, Harding bemoaned the crippling effects of nervous prostration that had forced George and Lydia to check into a medical facility during the holiday season. He reassuringly joked that he had asked Kris Kringle to bring his friends a new set of nerves. Harding and his wife were no strangers to health difficulties; the letter also quipped that if Santa had the ability to provide relief for deficient nerves, Harding himself also needed to stand in line to receive this yuletide miracle. By Harding's tone and message, it seems that both Christians were on the mend and hoped to soon join their Marion friends. They had probably either visited Dr. Charles Sawyer's facility outside Marion or the nationally famous Battle Creek Sanitarium in Michigan. The letter contained little evidence about the length of the Christians' illness or the pace of their recovery, but it proved that both families suffered from the very middle-class disorder that at the time was named neurasthenia. Doctors described this condition as the depletion of the nerves that occurred when middle-class and white-collar workers stretched their nerves thin in order to manage the difficulties of modern life. Such mutual infirmities might have led both families to travel to Florida in January of 1906—a possible timeframe for the Florida pictures discussed earlier.[17]

In early 1907, with his political future uncertain, Harding returned to Marion with his wife. Historian Andrew Sinclair floridly observed that Harding "chose to wait at Marion, as his hero Napoleon had on Elba, until the time was ripe."[18] In actuality, Harding's defeat made him question whether to continue his political career. At about the same time, Christian and his partner Caleb Norris sold their quarry and plant holdings to the Ohio and Western Lime and Stone Company. Thus, Harding and Christian faced a moment of career transition at the same time. Harding's father-in-law, Amos Kling, had recently remarried, and Kling attempted to reconcile with his daughter and son-in-law. The Hardings and the Klings embarked on a six-week tour of Europe at Kling's expense in 1907. While on the voyage, Harding wrote to Lydia Christian, "Tell the Colonel I will greatly miss rooting with him at the ball games, and regret having to delay my ride in his Buick, but I'll think of him when I see the English bar maids and recall his Presbyterian advice when the girls kick their highest in Paris."[19]

Both Christian and Harding loved cars and America's pastime, and this letter gave a hint of Harding's sometimes-bawdy sense of humor.[20]

When Harding returned to the United States, Christian wrote to assure him that the *Star* had prospered in his absence. He also complimented Harding's stepson, Marshall, for his good conduct while his stepfather was away. Christian added that he had missed his friend. Harding's reconciliation with Kling appeared firm, since Kling, Harding, and Christian all participated in a charity event for the local YMCA in October of 1907. For Christmas, Lydia Christian received a set of Dresden candlesticks that the Hardings had purchased on their European voyage. That holiday season, for the first time in many years, both the Christians and the Hardings gathered with other Marion friends and partook of the infamous Tom and Jerry punch.[21]

In 1909, the Hardings returned to Europe, this time with friends Jim and Carrie Philips. Historians believe that Carrie Philips and Warren Harding had begun an affair in 1905 while Florence Harding had languished in a hospital. The logistics and proximity involved in this trip probably created some difficult and awkward circumstances for Harding and his mistress. When Harding wrote to Christian from Europe, the tone of his letter obscured any infidelity. In fact, no evidence indicates that Christian knew about his friend's dalliances. Christian, in fact, defended Harding's morality to the very end.

Harding wrote to Christian from onboard his ship in February of 1909 that the captain had asked him to deliver a speech commemorating Lincoln's birth—though he had found a way to avoid the assignment. Coincidentally, the people of Marion had similarly recruited Christian to speak about Lincoln and his legacy. In conjunction with this assignment, the Colonel wrote an extended piece on Lincoln's 1860 presidential nomination in Chicago for the *Star*. Both Christian and Harding had earned reputations as civic leaders and orators, and honoring one of the country's greatest presidents became one of the tasks expected from men of their status.[22]

Harding re-entered the political arena in 1910 when Republican Party officials convinced him to run for governor of Ohio against the well-liked Democratic incumbent Judson Harmon. Dissension in the Republican Party between Progressives and the party's traditional wing made him the only choice without direct ties to any of Ohio's political bosses. After securing his party's nomination, however, Harding's best efforts at campaigning could not overcome the popularity of the incumbent. In many ways, Harding's failure served as a precursor for the Republicans in the election of 1912, when former president Theodore Roosevelt ran against his chosen successor, President William H. Taft, as a candidate for the Progressive Party. Harding supported Taft in that election, and he was chosen to present Taft's nomination to the Republican Convention in 1912. Harding then watched his candidate crash and burn as Taft and Roosevelt split the Republican vote, opening the door for Democrat Woodrow Wilson to become president. Luckily, Harding avoided another run for governor in 1912 and consequently dodged a resounding defeat.[23]

In the meantime, Harding enjoyed his status as one of Marion's prominent citizens, but Senator Theodore Burton's retirement announcement in 1914 quickly threw him back into the tumultuous world of politics. The 1914 U.S. Senate election was the first in which all American men could popularly elect their senators. In his unpublished biography of the future president, Christian commented that Harding embarked on an intense study of the Constitution and the role of the Senate before throwing his hat into the ring. In this era of American politics, the office of senator held great appeal because it wielded a powerful influence over the patronage of the federal government. In addition, war broke out across Europe in 1914, and it became apparent that Congress and the president would have to make important decisions about U.S. neutrality or foreign engagement. Harding strongly supported popular isolationist sentiments and favored high tariffs to protect U.S. businesses. His desire to influence legislative decisions on these issues pushed him to enter the Senate race.[24]

Harding ran against his mentor Joseph Foraker in the Republican primary. Foraker's ties to Standard Oil and his open opposition to Theodore Roosevelt and the Progressive movement made him a poor choice to reunite a divided Ohio Republican Party. Harding played the role of unifier by refusing to attack his fellow candidates. Biographer Randolph Downes described his rhetoric as that of "sweetness and light" as he worked to avoid antagonizing the fraught coalition of Republicans and Progressives.[25] Following his primary victory, Harding proved an excellent candidate to appeal to the general electorate of the state. He avoided any direct insults toward his Democratic and Progressive opponents and instead focused his harshest criticism on the Wilson administration and its wartime policies. Harding used his oratorical abilities to great effect, and his rhetoric of positivity and patriotism led to one of the largest electoral victories in the history of the state. It also helped that his principal opponent, Timothy S. Hogan, was a practicing Catholic and roused much of the anti-Catholic vote.[26]

After his election, Harding invited his good friend George B. Christian Jr. to serve as his personal secretary. Christian Jr. had never enjoyed business as much as his father. He shared, however, his father's love for politics and had served in 1912 as the reading clerk of the Democratic National Convention because of his forceful speaking voice. As for how he became Harding's secretary, Christian Jr. later wrote:

Fig. 91. Senator Harding with his secretary George B. Christian Jr. (Courtesy of the Library of Congress)

After the election Warren Harding told me to get out
of the limestone business and come to Washington
as his secretary. We had been very close since I was a
young boy and I must admit I didn't give the idea a
second thought before accepting. It was a big job and
my political dabbling was not sufficient training, but I
was determined to do my best for him.[27]

As his secretary, Christian Jr. became Harding's most important link
to the outside world. He also stood as Harding's first line of defense
against the press. Christian screened Harding's mail and meetings,
keeping the senator abreast of relevant issues both at home and
abroad. Because of this family connection to Harding's political
work, George B. Christian Sr. always had access to the senator, and
Harding continued to show respect and affection for the entire
Christian family.[28]

Almost immediately after Harding's election to the U.S. Senate,
his friends began to suggest his name as a possible presidential
candidate. In May of 1915, George B. Christian Sr. wrote to Harding's
friend Edward Scobey in Texas and acknowledged their joint identity
as "the original unterrified out-spoken discoverers of an absolute
and certain candidate for the presidency upon the republican ticket
in 1916 in the person of the said Hon. Warren Gamaliel Harding."
After prematurely suggesting that many Americans had begun to
think of Harding as a potential candidate, Christian stated, "The
time has come when his friends, and they are legion, should take
such action as will formulate an organization to the end that he is
made the republican candidate for the presidency in 1916."[29] Scobey
replied with an action plan for Harding supporters. He posited that
Christian should begin raising money from the senator's friends
for a potential run. He also stated that supporters should work
with national pundits to write about Harding and that the senator
should give speeches throughout the country. Christian and Scobey's
presidential musings predated Harding's keynote speech at the 1916

Republican Convention and his leadership in the Senate to oppose Wilson's plans for a League of Nations, the two events that historians generally acknowledge as elevating Harding into the public discourse for the presidency. For the rest of his life, Christian took great pride in the fact that he had supported Harding's candidacy for president well before most other Republicans and the general public. After Harding joined the Senate, he became more than a simple friend for Christian; his political advancement became the Colonel's cause extraordinaire.[30]

Christian regularly insisted that Harding held no ambition for the presidency, and Harding's own words generally supported this claim. However, these assertions appear to have been mere political strategy. Feigning apathy helped Harding develop friendships and avoid criticism. Harding skillfully positioned himself as a spokesman for the Republican Party in the years leading up to the country's entry into World War I. Even though he personally favored preparing for war in 1916, he also encouraged moderation on questions such as submarine warfare and the peacetime military draft in order to maintain Republican support among the German American community. Although he endorsed isolationism in the European conflict, he promoted maintaining U.S. colonial control in the Philippines. One of Harding's principal themes was that the government should support Americanization and assimilation at home and democratization abroad, in places such as the Philippines, Panama, and Mexico.[31] He especially condemned the rise of socialism within the United States. Harding became famous for his ability to reel in progressive-minded Republicans without alienating the party's traditional base. One of the ways he accomplished this delicate triangulation was by focusing on tariffs as a key issue for U.S. prosperity. While workers and employers fundamentally disagreed about the allocation of industrial profits, both could support tariffs. These policies favored American businesses and enabled them to maintain high prices, theoretically allowing employers to pay higher wages which was an important issue for the Progressives.

Despite the support of his friends, Harding felt he had not achieved sufficient national recognition to run for president in 1916. So he supported factions in the Republican Party that wanted to reconcile its Progressive and traditional wings, leading them to nominate the well-respected and moderate Supreme Court Justice Charles Evans Hughes to challenge Wilson. Hughes questioned Wilson's actions relating to the war in Europe, in which the United States had thus far remained neutral. Hughes and his Republican supporters wanted to prepare and mobilize for what they felt was an inevitable U.S. intervention in the conflict. Harding played a significant role in Hughes's campaign. As an orator he was in great demand, giving speeches throughout the country in support of Hughes. Yet his efforts were for naught. Wilson successfully campaigned on his ability to keep the country out of war, leading to a resounding Democratic victory. Despite his party's loss, Harding won acclaim among Republicans for work in behalf of the losing candidate. This goodwill served him well in his subsequent presidential campaign. Historian Randolph Downes has argued that "the campaign of 1916 had, indeed, made Harding a 'big Republican,' big enough to be thought of seriously for the Presidency in 1920."[32]

Fig. 92. Presidential candidate and Supreme Court Justice Charles Evans Hughes. Hughes would later serve as Harding's secretary of state. (Courtesy of the Library of Congress)

Soon after Wilson's victory, relations with Germany deteriorated. In 1915, the Germans had agreed to halt their indiscriminate submarine attacks on passenger ships after sinking the Lusitania, a British ship carrying many Americans. In 1917, however, Germany risked resuming its submarine attacks on all ships bound for enemy ports, hoping this action would strangle its foes. In addition, a telegram from German foreign minister Arthur Zimmerman to Mexican officials leaked to the Americans. In it, Zimmerman offered to restore the territory their country had lost in the Mexican American War if they would ally with the Germans against the United States. Both aggressive actions helped fuel U.S. rage, and in April Congress accepted Wilson's recommendation for a declaration of war.

Both George B. Christian Sr. and Senator Warren G. Harding criticized the Wilson administration during World War I. Their complaints, however, had very different motivations. Christian's limestone business had stalled in the chaotic shipping blockages caused by the government takeover of the railroads in support of the war effort. Harding opposed the president's wartime policies primarily for his own political advancement. He rejected Wilson's goals of encouraging self-determination and making the world safe for democracy through involvement in the conflict. He felt instead that the United States should work in its own self-interest when pursuing its war aims and winning the subsequent peace. Harding criticized many of Wilson's policies as harbingers of either dictatorship or socialism—even though at times he favored some of the strategies behind the scenes. Harding held genuine concerns about the spread of Bolshevism throughout the country, and he sounded the alarm about any practices that might expand the government's role in the U.S. economy during the war.[33]

Even during these tumultuous and uncertain times in the Senate, where Harding stood at the forefront of the opposition to Wilson's policies, he maintained close contact with the Christians back in Marion. Nevertheless, Harding's term as senator amplified the uneven nature of his relationship with the Colonel. Letters demonstrate that Christian had begun to think of Harding with absolute loyalty and veneration, while Harding had begun to consider Christian's superlatives and affection with appreciative paternalism. At one point, Harding wrote to political consultant Malcolm Jennings that Christian was one of only three supporters whose motives he never questioned. However, Harding worried about his friend's financial problems and advancing age. Christian was now well into his sixties, and the lime and stone business had slowed significantly. Harding's letters to Christian and other Marion friends showed his concern for the Christian family and his desire to lend them support despite his many political responsibilities. For example, letters between Harding and his doctor, Charles Sawyer, documented Harding's worries that Christian's organization of the upcoming encampment of the Grand Army of the Republic in Marion might be too much for him. Harding asked the doctor to make sure Christian's work advanced smoothly. Sawyer also kept Harding informed about the Colonel's money troubles and debts. In December of 1916, Harding wrote to Lydia Christian, who had been crippled by a bout of nervous prostration. He expressed his sympathy by explaining that he understood the taxing despair of depression. He conveyed his hope for her complete recovery and his wish that the two families would be able to celebrate the Christmas season together with their Marion friends.[34]

Another letter from Harding to Charles Sawyer, in February of 1918, illustrated the change in the tone of his relationship with Christian. In this letter, Harding commented on a plan floating around Marion to merge the Marion National and Marion County Banks. Harding had served for years with Christian on the board of the Marion County Bank, but as he broke down the different personalities and power dynamics involved in such a merger, he told Sawyer, "Our friend Christian has practically retired from the Marion County and is no longer a factor to be considered." This statement encapsulates the complete change in the structure of Christian and Harding's relationship. Christian was no longer a factor to be considered in many of the issues confronting Harding at home and abroad.[35]

Nevertheless, Harding's success generally gave Christian much to celebrate as World War I raged on. The senator continually demonstrated his most important political talents: his ability to understand and represent the will of the majority of Americans and to take flexible positions on many of the nation's most pressing issues. Standing on the popular side of political questions helped him overcome his lack of political leadership and national name recognition. For example, Harding voted for both the Eighteenth Amendment and the Volstead Act that was designed to enforce it. Even though Harding personally held no confidence in Prohibition's viability, he argued that the passage of the amendment in Congress left the issue in the hands of the state legislatures to support or reject. In private, Harding and Christian belittled the importance of women's suffrage, but in public both offered reserved support for the Nineteenth Amendment, which gave women throughout the country the right to vote. Like Christian, Harding decried many of Wilson's efforts to control wartime prices and nationalize the country's industries as the first steps toward socialism. One proposal Harding did support was allowing President Theodore Roosevelt, the former Rough Rider, the opportunity to command a division of soldiers in World War I (although Wilson refused to send this division to Europe). This stance helped Harding make friends with Progressives in his party, a feat that had eluded most other traditional Republicans.[36]

Even though the war dominated the attention of the nation, the Hardings still found time to celebrate the marriage of the Christians' youngest daughter, Alice Mildred, to Chester C. Roberts. Mildred had a special place in their hearts because she had served as a flower girl at their wedding. The Roberts' Marion wedding took place on the afternoon of April 20, 1918 at the Christian home. Chester Roberts held a captain's commission and was stationed at Camp Taylor in Louisville, Kentucky, one of the military's largest training facilities at the time. Florence Harding wrote to Mildred Christian immediately before the wedding bemoaning the Hardings' inability to attend and inviting the couple to visit them in Washington, DC, while on their honeymoon in the East. Florence Harding joked that she had always hoped to play the role of "chief cook and bottle washer" at Mildred's wedding.[37] The bride and groom accepted the offer to visit, and Warren G. Harding later wrote to the Christians to tell them that "both she and her husband seemed to be in the very height of happiness."[38] A little more than a year later, in July of 1919, Harding wrote to Christian to congratulate him on the birth of his new Roberts grandchild. He reported his confidence in Mildred as a mother because of the quality of her character.[39]

Harding's political stock began to rise quickly as World War I came to its ambivalent conclusion. Perhaps his most nimble political maneuvering came in reaction to Wilson's proposed League of Nations, part of the Treaty of Versailles, envisioned as one of Wilson's famed fourteen points for peace. As the conflict moved toward the standstill that eventually led to the armistice, Wilson offered a vision for the world of "peace without victory." His fourteen points included ideas

Fig. 93. The big four at the Versailles Peace Conference which ended World War I. From left to right: Prime Minister David Lloyd George, Great Britain; Premier Vittorio Orlando, Italy; Premier Georges Clemenceau, France; and President Woodrow Wilson, USA. These four leaders played a principle role in setting the terms of the peace. (Courtesy of the Library of Congress)

such as assuring the protection of free trade, creating open diplomatic agreements, fostering democracy, allowing ethnic minorities to create their own states, supporting decolonization, and forming an international body to settle disputes. Given in January of 1918, the fourteen points speech became a tool of American propaganda. Germany and the Central powers eventually surrendered, in part, based on the assurances of leniency made by the U.S. president in this speech. Wilson attended the peace conference in Versailles as its U.S. representative but chose not to invite high-ranking Republicans. He fell ill at the beginning of the conference and never exercised the comprehensive leadership role he had anticipated. In addition, allies such as France and the United Kingdom felt that their greater sacrifices entitled them to reparations. Wilson focused entirely on the League of Nations as the greatest of his proposals and allowed many of the other European powers great latitude in their demands in return for supporting his pet project. In the end, the Treaty of Versailles embodied very few of the ideals from Wilson's fourteen points. Nevertheless, Wilson felt that the formation of the League of Nations would supersede all of the treaty's other deficits. The league's charter created an assembly, council, and secretariat drawn from member nations. While the league had no military of its own to enforce its policies and mandates, member states pledged to help impose its decisions. The organization's principal responsibilities involved maintaining the territorial integrity and political independence of member nations. It could establish forums for settling international disputes and create economic and military sanctions to punish any nation's bad behavior.[40]

Woodrow Wilson returned from France near the end of 1918 with hopes to push the treaty through the Senate as quickly as possible. The league, however, proved unpopular among Republicans at home. Some Americans felt the organization threatened the country's sovereignty. They also feared that membership might force the United States to wade into European disputes. Political opponents of the league, and the Treaty of Versailles more generally, split into two camps. Senators such as William Borah of Idaho and Robert La Follette of Wisconsin became the so-called irreconcilables, because they felt that the League of Nations was a destructive, unworkable mess. A larger group of opponents, led by Senate Foreign Relations Chairman Henry Cabot Lodge, were revisionists. They believed the treaty might go forward with certain amendments that guaranteed the sovereignty of member nations.[41]

Warren G. Harding appropriated ideas from both groups of critics for his denunciations of the Wilson administration. He argued that President Wilson had abandoned the country to create a secret agreement that damaged its power and potential for progress. In March of 1919, Harding joined many of his colleagues in signing a statement that they could not support the Treaty of Versailles as written. He felt that the most important result of the U.S. war effort was the unity it had inspired among the American people. Harding contended that the League of Nations and the international entanglements it might require could destroy such unanimity. The senator joined many fellow legislators in favoring a league based on moral commitments instead of legally binding covenants. More than anything, he opposed the organization as conceived by Wilson and sought to reopen the decisions made in Versailles about the league's power and place in international relations. Harding worked both in the Senate and in Ohio to help Americans understand the importance of revising the Treaty of Versailles. When Wilson embarked on an extended tour of the Midwest and West to drum up support for the league as originally constituted, Harding followed him to Columbus to refute his arguments. Harding also participated in the Senate's hearing on the league, as well as a conference between Republican senators and Wilson in which Harding suggested scrapping the components of the treaty that might obligate Americans to become involved in foreign conflicts.[42]

Republican members of the Senate Committee on Foreign Relations eventually issued a set of revisions, formulated by Senator Henry Cabot Lodge, to add to the treaty obligations created at Versailles. While Harding did not play a pivotal role in composing these revisions, the party leaders called on him to help popularize them. Harding continually emphasized the importance of not sacrificing the country's Americanism or American world leadership. The United States would happily offer moral guidance, but not at the cost of surrendering any sovereignty to the League of Nations. Harding gave the country a way to support peace and Americanism at the same time. Wilson, however, felt that the Senate's revisions neutered the agreement, and he instructed his supporters to defeat the amended treaty. Throughout the entire debate, Harding's articulate opposition made his friends seriously consider a Harding presidential run in 1920. The fight for the Republican Party's nomination was open, because Theodore Roosevelt, who had contemplated seeking another term after reconciling with the Republican Party, had passed away in January of 1919.[43]

By the end of World War I, Harding had come a long way from his time as a young, small-town newspaper editor. He had become a major voice in the League of Nations debate and spoke as a senator of some distinction. Harding's position had thrust him into the national spotlight, while Christian's concerns were personal, such as the problems that wartime government controls had caused for his business. Harding, though he saw eye-to-eye with Christian on many matters and still considered him a close friend, stopped seeking Christian's advice on issues of national import and moved forward as he considered a run for president.

CHAPTER 10

The Life and Death of a Presidential Friend

"America's present need is not heroics, but healing; not nostrums, but normalcy; not revolution, but restoration; not agitation, but adjustment; not surgery, but serenity; not the dramatic, but the dispassionate; not experiment, but equipoise; not submergence in internationality, but sustainment in triumphant nationality." Warren G. Harding, speech, Boston, MA, May 14, 1920.

Warren G. Harding's call for normalcy after the tumult of World War I brought hope and inspiration to the American people, and George B. Christian Sr., whose business had begun to unravel, took special comfort from his close relationship with the man he considered a political visionary. As Christian's prospects declined, he put all his stock into Harding's 1920 presidential run. Because he had played a role in the formation of Harding's character, Christian believed that Harding's success could redeem him. Upon Harding's untimely death and subsequent fall from grace, the Colonel stridently defended his friend, refusing to acknowledge the possibility that his mentorship of the president had been in vain. Christian's devotion to his fallen friend cast a long shadow over his family, and his children and grandchildren felt tied to Harding's legacy for good or ill.

To anyone who would listen, Christian had put forth Warren G. Harding as a potential presidential candidate as early as the 1916 election, but Republicans throughout the nation had not perceived him as a serious contender. However, Harding's role in the Senate during and after World War I (see chapter 9) thrust him into the nation's civic consciousness. Ironically, some of Harding's political antagonists sparked his presidential campaign in 1919. In order to open his Senate seat to a more Progressive candidate, some of Harding's enemies within the Republican Party disingenuously called for him to run for commander in chief. At the time, the Progressives felt he had little chance in a national election, while he had the potential to hold his Senate seat against Progressive challenges for many years. Harding ignored these calls and guarded his options to stay in the Senate or to run for the presidency, playing coy whenever others encouraged the latter. At one time, he even suggested Massachusetts governor Calvin Coolidge as a potential candidate to those who continually pestered him about the White House. Nevertheless, Harding knew that he had to decide quickly so he might convince Ohio Republicans, hungry for presidential patronage, to start working for his election. Even though he might have harbored ambitions for the presidency much earlier than he let on, his outward hesitancy allowed him to frame his decision as an answer to the call of the people and to test the waters before entering the race. One assurance he needed before deciding to run was the support of the Ohio Progressive Republicans who had initially viewed his candidacy only as a way to gain a Senate seat for their cause. Harding's reconciliation with this group occurred near the end of 1919 when he offered Toledo Progressive mayor Walter Brown a leadership role in the Ohio Republican Party. Even though Harding still viewed Progressive policies with skepticism, this promise assured them that they would share in presidential patronage should Harding win the 1920 election.[1]

Harding finally declared his candidacy on December 16, 1919, and the Christian family immediately became rampant supporters. When a Kansas journalist requested a life history as background for Harding's presidential run, Harding suggested that Christian write it. This assignment clarified the role he felt his friend might play most effectively for the campaign. Even though Christian had supported Harding for the presidency earlier than most others, the candidate now looked to Christian primarily as a spinner of the Harding story. When journalists came to Marion seeking background on the candidate, the Harding campaign counted on Christian to convey down-to-earth, witty tales about his friend's time in that city. Such stories helped to weave the Harding small-town mythology that appealed to the American heartland.[2]

Christian embraced his role as one of Harding's cheerleaders. For example, Harding gave a speech in January of 1919 at the Waldorf-Astoria Hotel in New York City in which he emphasized one of the central themes of his campaign—the importance of U.S. nationalism. He boldly stated, "In the spirit of the republic we proclaim Americanism and acclaim America."[3] When Christian read the speech, he wrote Harding an effusive letter. He stated that the speech "was grand, glorious, and to me it seemed to be the trumpet call of a leader predestined to lead a great people in the ways of truth and righteousness that our fathers taught us, the ways from which we have wandered. The stars of the whole historical host . . . all are dimmed by this new luminary. You have opened the eyes of a world."[4] Even Harding became uncomfortable with the level of hyperbole in this letter. In response, he told Christian that he felt "praised excessively" despite his general respect for Christian's opinion of such things. Christian had begun to see stars when he pictured his friend as leader of the country. His gushing compliment boosted the future president's ego but offered little in terms of strategy.[5]

Harding's principal opponents for the Republican nomination included Leonard Wood, a former Rough Rider and military commander; former Illinois governor Frank Lowden; and Senator Hiram Johnson of California, a Progressive. Of the four candidates, Harding was the most unfamiliar name for national voters, and had raised the smallest amount of money to fund his campaign. Because of these deficiencies, Harding and his advisors were forced to focus on Ohio where he enjoyed popularity as a native son.

Fig. 94. General Leonard Wood served with Theodore Roosevelt as one of the Rough Riders and later served as Army Chief of Staff and Governor General of the Philippines. He was probably the favorite to receive the Republican nomination for president in 1920. (Courtesy of the Library of Congress)

Fig. 95. Frank Lowden served as governor of Illinois from 1917 to 1921. Lowden, with Leonard Wood, was one of the principle contenders for the 1920 Republican nomination. (Courtesy of the Library of Congress)

Fig. 96. Senator Hiram Johnson of California was the third Republican candidate which ran against Harding for the 1920 presidential nomination. (Courtesy of the Library of Congress)

238

The presidential election of 1920 represented the third race in which Ohio Republicans held direct primaries. At the party's national nominating convention, almost all Ohio delegates would initially be tied to the candidate who won the primary vote in their congressional district. Four delegates, however, would be elected statewide and could vote for whichever candidate they chose. Harding submitted his campaign manager, Harry Daugherty, as a contender for one of these four prestigious open seats, even though Christian advised him against it.[6] Christian felt that Daugherty's propensity to acquire enemies made him a political liability. Harding, on the other hand, decided to support Daugherty because he felt his campaign manager could serve as a leader of the Ohio delegation. Although Harding won the Ohio state primary with a small plurality of votes, Daugherty lost his contest to serve as an open delegate to the convention. This loss soured Harding's victory because it meant that the people of Ohio had not wholly trusted his judgment. Harding's narrow victory prevented the overwhelming showing that Harding had hoped would propel his national candidacy. In this case, his decision not to trust Christian's advice about Ohio politics stifled some of the excitement associated with his presidential run.[7]

The Ohio primary results gave Harding a small victory, but he remained somewhat unknown on a national scale. When they realized he would never be a frontrunner, Harding's advisors created a brilliant strategy for securing the Republican presidential nomination. They sought to make Harding the second-choice candidate for as many convention delegates as possible. Voting results from individual states would determine most delegates' first-choice candidates. At the convention, delegates would vote for the candidate to which they were committed during a roll call vote. But if no Republican garnered a majority in the first round of voting, the delegates would be free to select any candidate in subsequent rounds until someone received a majority. Harding knew he had no chance to win the nomination on the first ballot, but he felt that when the other candidates struggled to reconcile their differences the convention might turn to him.[8]

During primary campaigning, Harding and his advisors found subtle ways to turn his opponents against one another. For example, Harding's advisors bemoaned the vast funding disparity between their candidate and Wood and Lowden, but they allowed Senator Johnson to critique the richer candidates' largesse. In fact, the two well-financed contenders spent such large sums on their primary campaigns that Congress decided to investigate their expenditures. Meanwhile, Harding ran an extremely positive campaign, and he tried to keep any bitterness toward or attacks on other Republican candidates under wraps. He made no enemies. Over time, Harding began to receive assurances that he would indeed be many delegates' second-choice candidate. His ability to avoid controversy, while his fellow Republicans fought amongst themselves, meant that he went to the convention as a legitimate dark-horse candidate.[9]

As the Republican Convention convened in the Windy City on June 8, 1920, Harding's campaign strategy was tested. Harry Daugherty assigned campaign workers, including Christian, to meet all the delegates as they came into town and ask them about their presidential preferences. Many years later, Christian recounted this exercise:

> On the second day of the convention the writer [Christian Sr.] with three young men, members of his family, related to Mr. Harding's secretary, all warm personal friends, well versed in politics, organized a little flying squadron with the intention of making a thorough investigation of affairs outside and endeavoring to find out just what the attitude of these great bodies of adherents to favorite candidates would be toward Mr. Harding in the event of a deadlock in the convention. One of our number [probably Chester Roberts], a resident of Chicago for more than twenty years, was a valuable aide in preparing formative programs for each day's action.[10]

Christian's long Democratic background probably relegated him to the role of an observer rather than a political powerbroker, but his participation demonstrated the depth of his support for Harding and the reality of his own conversion to the Republican Party.[11]

Fig. 97. This photograph depicts the 1920 Republican Convention held in the Chicago Coliseum. (Courtesy of the Library of Congress)

For the first few days, delegates quibbled over the Republican platform for the 1920 election. On June 11, however, the real drama of the convention began. Potential nominees needed to secure the votes of 493 delegates to capture the nomination. On the first few ballots, Wood, Lowden, and Johnson split the majority of the votes, with none receiving more than 315 delegates. Harding, on the other hand, received only about sixty votes. As the rounds of voting continued, it became apparent that neither Lowden nor Wood could secure enough support to win the nomination without some sort of deal or reconciliation. The convention appeared deadlocked after the first day of voting, so Harding began to work his second-choice strategy. That night, he summoned individual delegates previously pledged to other candidates to his campaign headquarters and lobbied them personally using the Harding wit and charm, a plan for which Christian claimed credit. Although journalists later theorized that a meeting of Harding's Senate colleagues swung the nomination in his direction after the first day of ballots, such stories appear divorced from the actual course of events at the convention. The real key to Harding's nomination was his ability to maintain the support of the entire Ohio delegation throughout the balloting process—especially that of Mayor John D. Galvin of Cincinnati, who vowed to continue backing Harding when many of the other Ohioans contemplated jumping ship. After the evening's lobbying, some of the New York delegation moved to Harding instead of one of the two more popular candidates. Harding began to make serious progress when the delegates cast their ninth nomination ballot on the afternoon of June 12. On that ballot, Harding received 375 votes, which exceeded Wood's 249 and Lowden's 122. This breakthrough opened a landslide of votes in Harding's favor, and he received the nomination on the tenth ballot with more than 690 delegates. George Christian Jr. stood near the convention's speaker, and, upon seeing this result, he ran downstairs and was the first to inform Senator Harding of his nomination. Candidate and secretary shared a very personal moment of triumph before Harding emerged to accept the veneration of his entire party.[12]

Several weeks later, the Democrats also nominated an Ohioan, James M. Cox, for president in their San Francisco convention. Cox had served as governor of Ohio, and he had also published a well-regarded newspaper in Dayton. Harding's advisors feared Cox's similar background and competency, so they began formulating a strategy to differentiate the two candidates. In consultation with Harding, they decided

Fig. 98. James M. Cox was the Democratic nominee for the 1920 presidential election. He was the newspaper publisher of the *Dayton Daily News* and the governor of Ohio from 1913–1915 and 1917–1921. (Courtesy of the Library of Congress)

to use a time-honored approach. Harding, having greatly admired former President William McKinley's campaign, decided to emulate McKinley's front-porch approach. McKinley had rejected campaign travel in favor of making speeches from his home in Canton, Ohio, forcing the media and supporters to come to him. This format allowed Harding to control his message and avoid possible embarrassing ad-libs, which had plagued Republican candidate Charles Evans Hughes in the 1916 election. This decision immediately made Marion the epicenter of the Republican campaign.[13]

Christian's excitement resonated in his letters to the candidate before Harding even returned to Marion. Upon congratulating his friend on his nomination, Christian claimed to lead the "I-told-you-so" bunch, and he joked about his future appointment as "hugmaster general" in the Harding administration. How Harding and Christian understood the title of "hugmaster" is a mystery, but its use proves that Harding saw Christian's role in the campaign and any subsequent administration as inconsequential. In this June letter, Christian seemed to jokingly interpret the title in the context of women voters, but it was probably meant as a tribute to his general amiability.[14]

While other Marion business leaders, such as Hoke Donithen and Daniel Crissinger, probably played a larger organizational role in Harding's Marion campaign, the Christians' contribution was much more personal. They offered their own homes for the use of the candidate and his staff. On June 14, 1920, George Christian Jr. wrote to his father asking him to prepare Harding's and Christian Jr.'s homes for the upcoming electoral operation.

Fig. 99. A powwow on George B. Christian Jr.'s front porch located next door to the Harding home. (Courtesy of the Roberts Family Library)

Even though the Harding home served as the chief stage and meeting house for the front-porch campaign, George Christian Jr.'s residence functioned as the nerve center for the candidate's support staff. Christian Jr. became the chief coordinator for the Marion workforce of twenty-four who answered letters, made travel plans, received the press, and arranged accommodations for dignitaries. In Christian Jr.'s backyard, the campaign constructed a press center to house reporters. Harding's backyard connected with George Christian Sr.'s, and the elder Christian's home became an oasis away from the constant visitors and offered Harding the luxury of privacy.[15]

George B. Christian Jr. and other campaign staff arrived in Marion on July 4, 1920. They attended church and readied everything for the Hardings' arrival the next day, when a reception of Marion neighbors and friends greeted the couple. The front-porch campaign strategy was announced publicly on July 10, and from that moment the Harding team began coordinating with city leaders to accommodate the mass of journalists and visitors soon to visit Marion.[16]

One of the first major events in Harding's general election campaign involved the traditional candidate notification ceremony. On July 22, 1920, Senator Henry Cabot Lodge visited Marion and, in front of reportedly 100,000 people or more, formally announced Harding's nomination as the Republican candidate for president of the United States. Harding accepted this nomination in a solemn, lengthy speech in which he famously proclaimed, "We stabilize and strive for normalcy."[17] The rest of the speech was heavy in platitudes and soaring rhetoric and extremely light on policy. Harding took a strong stand against the League of Nations, but he barely touched on any of the other dominant questions of the moment. One observer argued that Harding said nothing exciting, risky, or controversial. In many ways, Harding's acceptance personified much of the front-porch campaign, which featured a candidate completely under control and who only criticized the policies of the sitting president and no one else. The front porch became the setting where Harding could give his stump speech to all those who came to Marion to meet a potential president.[18]

Harding's campaign strategy emphasized his dignity and everyman qualities. It also represented a middle ground between the unseen candidates of the nineteenth century and the highly publicized spectacles of modern campaigns. Harding's operation depended on Marion boosters, who provided facilities and logistical support for the many visitors to what was still a very small town. Republican National Chairman William Hays had assumed a major role in Harding's campaign once he secured the Republican nomination, and he coordinated the party's efforts to publicize and disseminate the messages generated in Marion.[19]

One of the Harding campaign's most important innovations involved exploiting the growing power of the national media. Harding allowed William Hays to hire Albert Lasker, a well-known advertising figure, to help with branding, slogans, and advertising. Lasker brought on chewing-gum magnate William Wrigley, with whom he had worked to create advertising for Wrigley's brands. Hays also hired newspaperman Judson Welliver to handle national publicity. The local campaign functioned well because Harding had these media experts helping to spread the messages from his front porch throughout the country. Harding's profile contrasted significantly with that of the outgoing president, which made branding and publicity more effective. His Democratic opponent, James Cox, was forced to run on the Wilsonian legacy, while Harding represented a direct rejection of Wilson's wartime policies, progressive values, and internationalism.[20]

George Christian Jr. was responsible for making sure the Marion and national branches of the campaign communicated with each other. He also provided the press corps in Marion with official campaign information for their columns. In addition, Christian Jr.

maintained his duties as the candidate's personal secretary, reading and writing letters on the candidate's behalf and controlling who received access to Harding.[21]

His father, on the other hand, had no formal role. Yet Harding's national tastemakers quickly identified George Christian Sr. as someone who could help them create Harding's origin story for the press, and they utilized him to weave the mystic tale of a small town publisher whose character and abilities destined him for the White House. On July 29, 1920, the campaign asked Christian Sr. to introduce a New Jersey journalist to Marionites who might offer the authentic story of the presidential candidate. In August, Harding's advisors introduced reporter Zoe Beckley of the *Saginaw News* to the Colonel and he proceeded to share his opinion about how Harding was a true friend of the women's suffrage movement. Journalists also reported that Christian Sr. had occasionally entertained them with his Civil War stories. Harding, upon hearing this, told the reporters that his father and Christian Sr. had a long-standing argument about which of their soldierly efforts had done more to end the war.[22]

Much later, when Christian wrote his unpublished biography of Harding, he remembered the many Republican luminaries who had passed through Marion. He highlighted Elihu Root, Charles Evan Hughes, John Pershing, Leonard Wood, and Reed Smoot as visitors who had particularly impressed him. He also recounted an occasion when Harding had asked for his help with the history of indigenous peoples in Ohio in preparation for a visit from a group of Native American leaders. Christian mentioned that he "was very pleasantly located for enjoying the opportunity of meeting these notables and frequently there would be visits interchanged back and forth through the neighbor gateway that brought our home close to that of the president." Nevertheless, it seems that his function in regard to dignitaries was passive at best, since he recounted very few occasions of meaningful conversation or experience with them. Given his tendency to emphasize his relationship with Harding and his role in the campaign, Christian's limited comments about his interaction with visitors implies that he generally stayed in the background of the front-porch effort.[23]

Over 600,000 visitors passed through Marion from the end of July through the end of September. While Christian played a very minor role in dealing with these throngs, his son coordinated all of the Marion speeches and visits. The Harding campaign required potential visitors to submit information about their organization far in advance of their trip. If a spokesperson planned to address the crowds alongside the candidate, he or she had to submit remarks ahead of time to Christian Jr. Speakers then had to adhere strictly to their submitted texts. Sometimes, the campaign advisors planned themed occasions, such as a traveling salesmen's day or women's day, that allowed

Fig. 100. Throngs of suffragettes crowded around Warren G. Harding's front porch to speak with the candidate. (Courtesy of the Library of Congress)

Fig. 101. Warren G. Harding meeting players from the Chicago Cubs in Marion during a campaign-related exhibition. (Reprinted by permission of the Ohio History Connection)

Harding to reach out to demographics deemed important for his election. The Republican Party also staged events in Marion, such as the visit of the Chicago Cubs to play a local team, with Harding throwing out some of the game's first pitches. While Harding's personable, easygoing manner proved to be the campaign's greatest asset, such relaxation proved possible only because of meticulous planning. The front-porch approach worked so well because it allowed the campaign a level of control not available on the road.

Eventually, Harding's advisors felt that the front-porch strategy had fulfilled its usefulness. Cox had traveled more than 22,000 miles and visited thirty-six states. His widespread campaigning worried Harding's people, and by mid-September the Republican candidate began to make stops in some of the major battleground states—mostly in the Midwest but also in the mid-Atlantic region. Harding's choice to begin the campaign exclusively in Marion highlighted his background as a small-town newspaperman, which continued to resonate as he traveled throughout the country in the waning months before the election. Even though he discussed the important issues of the day, such as taxes, Prohibition, and the League of Nations, his treatment of these subjects was generally non-controversial and played on the vast unpopularity of the Wilson regime.[24]

The one issue with the potential to damage Harding concerned the rumor of his mixed-race heritage. Professor William Chancellor of Wooster College in Ohio leaked research that supposedly proved Harding's African American ancestry. Such rumors had dogged Harding throughout his political career, and his first inclination was to ignore the stories and let them play themselves out. Christian, in a rare moment of trying to influence the campaign, leveraged his Southern heritage to force Harding to take the allegations seriously. He attempted to show Harding the importance racial purity might play among voters in the Deep South. In his unpublished biography of the president, Christian implied that his urging caused Harding to issue a certified statement about the Anglo-Saxon origins of his white forbearers. This statement caused the story to dissipate. Nonetheless, its momentary importance illustrated the racial tensions that beset the country and the influence these issues wielded in the South. Harding ran at a time when race riots and lynching were common and when most national politicians ignored the country's vast racial injustices.[25]

In the month before the election, reports from various regional observers began to predict a resounding victory for the journalist from Marion. However, the Harding camp was skeptical. In 1920, because of the nineteenth amendment to the Constitution, women would be allowed to vote for president for the first time, so election results seemed unpredictable. Years later, Christian remembered having asked Harding if he felt nervous in the closing days of the campaign. Christian painted a picture of a potential president who had left the decision in the hands of the voters and who felt at peace with victory or defeat.

Historian Randolph Downes has argued that the election of 1920 represented a rejection of the governmental activism favored by Theodore Roosevelt and Woodrow Wilson. In addition, lingering resentment about U.S. involvement in World War I and reconciliation between the Republican Party base and its Progressive wing opened the door for the "steady, implacable, and eloquent candidate."[26] Harding invited both father and son of the Christian clan to his home to await the election results on November 2, 1920. Christian Sr., however, preferred to wait outside for the returns, because he wanted to witness the celebration that was sure to erupt in Marion when Harding's

Fig. 102. Harding awaiting election results in 1920 with George B. Christian Jr. and wife Florence. (Courtesy of the Roberts Family Library)

Fig. 103. Crowds in Marion congratulate Warren G. Harding after his presidential victory. Chester C. Roberts is at the focal point of this particular photograph. (Courtesy of the Roberts Family Library)

victory was announced. Christian was not disappointed. Harding won 404 electoral votes to Cox's 127, and he won 60.2 percent of the popular vote. Because of these landslide numbers, Harding knew that evening that he had won, and he stepped out to his front porch to acknowledge the festivities taking place in his honor. Chester C. Roberts had helped plan the massive parade for the people of Marion to celebrate Harding's victory. Christian later described the joy of the crowds outside the Harding home as "unconfined" in the aftermath of Harding's victory speech.[27]

Immediately after the celebrations ended, Harding left Marion to see his friend Edward Scobey in Texas and relax. He then embarked on a trip to Panama, where he enjoyed the sunshine and the opportunity to confer with military leaders in the Canal Zone. He returned to Washington, DC, early in December to take his leave from the Senate and then returned to Marion to put together his cabinet. In the time between Harding's reappearance in Marion and his inauguration, he organized a "listening post" where he heard opinions from various party leaders about whom he should appoint as part of his administration. According to Christian, Harding also consulted his friends about these important decisions. The Colonel later recalled at least two occasions on which he queried the president-elect about potential cabinet members and the leading politicians of the day.

On Christmas Day, Harding wrote the Christians a letter reaffirming his friendship despite the chaos of the previous year's campaign. He waxed eloquent when he observed:

> But all that distraction and engrossment and attending weariness is gone now, and when we look ourselves in the faces and pinch ourselves to make sure we are not dreaming, we are still the same old neighbors and friends, valuing friendship more highly when it is proven, and loving our neighbors not merely as we love ourselves, but better than ourselves.[28]

Harding referred to Christian's appointment as "hugmaster general" and joked that the prospect of this position had reinvigorated his old friend. Harding and his wife spent New Year's Day at the Christians' house with twenty-eight members of the Christian family, having fun and avoiding the topic of the presidency. Christian recalled this holiday celebration as "our parting with them" It was the culmination of "a close personal friendship for a third of a century. They would go from among us and it seemed to us we would not be able to greet them again after the same manner and form that had marked our previous association."[29] Harding never returned to live in Marion despite his great desire to do so after his time as president. He left his home, however, under the caretaking eye of Chester and Mildred Roberts, who also looked after George B. Christian Jr.'s home, after it suffered an unfortunate fire near the end of January in 1921.[30]

In the next few months, Harding worked to secure his cabinet in time for his March inauguration. His choices included men of great stature, such as Herbert Hoover, secretary of commerce; Charles Evan Hughes, secretary of state; and Andrew Mellon, secretary of the Treasury. Some of his appointments later garnered notoriety, including Albert Fall, secretary of the Interior; attorney general Harry Daugherty (Harding's former campaign manager); and Charles Forbes, director of the Veterans Bureau. Harding's most important appointment, as far as the

Fig. 104. Portrait of George B. Christian Jr., presidential secretary. (Courtesy of the Roberts Family Library)

Christians were concerned, was George B. Christian Jr. as his personal secretary. Christian Jr. had become one of Harding's most loyal friends and protectors as the former journalist rose through the political ranks, and his service as Harding's senatorial secretary demonstrated his ability to succeed in the White House. Harding waited to announce Christian Jr.'s appointment until the inaugural train ride from Marion to Washington, DC. In the interim, George B. Christian Sr. had become worried about the delay and had learned that some Republicans had pushed for an alternate spoils-system candidate with long-held loyalty to the Republican establishment. In the end, Harding appointed the secretary he trusted the most.[31]

For this and many other reasons, Senator Harding had invited George and Lydia Christian and their son to accompany him on the train to his March 3, 1921, inauguration. As they prepared to leave, a crowd of Marion friends appeared at the railway station to shake their hands. After the train embarked, according to Christian Sr.'s biography, Harding brought

Fig. 105. Harding takes his leave of Marion en route to his presidential inauguration. (Courtesy of the Library of Congress)

him a copy of his self-authored inaugural address. Harding delivered the speech to his old friend, who held a regional reputation for oratorical skills, in private for his evaluation. While no other evidence corroborates this meeting, fabricating such an impressive moment would have been out of character for Christian. When Harding asked for his opinion of the speech, Christian replied, "I am personally too much affected by my regard for you to be an unbiased critic." He then offered his sincere opinion that the speech was perfect and that the president-elect should not change a single word.[32]

The end of World War I had dragged the United States into an economic recession, and such woes, in combination with President Woodrow Wilson's ill health, made Harding accept the Republican National Committee's recommendations to limit the scope of the inaugural celebration. While Harding and President Wilson still passed hundreds of thousands of spectators as they drove to the inauguration ceremony, the many associated formal balls were cut to a single gathering. Chief Justice Edward D. White gave Harding the oath of office on the steps of the Capitol, and then the new leader gave a thirty-seven minute address to general acclaim. After delivering this first presidential

Fig. 106. Warren G. Harding and Woodrow Wilson rode together on the way to Harding's inauguration. (Courtesy of the Library of Congress)

Fig. 107. Warren and Florence Harding with George B. Christian Jr. on Harding's inauguration day. (Courtesy of the Roberts Family Library)

discourse, Harding retired to a private luncheon with his close family members, followed by a reception for the Marion friends who had accompanied him. A little later, Harding and his wife appeared at the lone inaugural ball and danced late into the night. Shortly after the proceedings concluded, George and Lydia returned to Marion, leaving their oldest son to serve the president they loved.[33]

While Harding enacted a fair amount of policy during his short time in the White House, he wrote to George B. Christian Sr. about a very small number of the political issues he faced as president. Nevertheless, the length and breadth of their letters on other topics hinted at the lasting nature of their affection as well as Harding's

Fig. 108. Harding giving his inaugural address. (Courtesy of the Library of Congress)

increasing longing for a simpler Marion lifestyle. Generally, their communications focused on the everyday news from Marion, their families, and their shared memories. Only occasionally did they refer to national affairs. Christian wrote about politics or world affairs when he had an opinion to share, and Harding described the difficulties of his job only in passing. Whether the two men spoke over the telephone is difficult to know, but in his biography of the president, Christian sometimes wrote of conversations that do not appear in the documentary record.

One matter of national significance that the two men did discuss in their letters involved Harding's opposition to a bonus bill for soldiers who had served on foreign shores. On July 13, 1921, Christian wrote to Harding and applauded his courageous stance against the bill, which garnered support from both Republicans and Democrats. Harding threatened to veto the bill, citing its expense.

After all, he had entered office promising to cut the size of government from its World War I mobilization. While the American Legion and other soldiers' groups deeply criticized the president's position as a rejection of returning soldiers, Christian supported his fiscal responsibility despite its unpopularity. Harding faced similar criticism two years later when he vetoed the Bursum Pension Bill, which would have provided pensions for Mexican and Civil War soldiers' widows no matter how long couples had been married. Harding feared that younger women might marry much older soldiers for the simple chance of obtaining a pension, and he felt that the proposal was unsustainably expensive. Whether or not Christian might have initially supported this measure, designed to assist veterans of his era and their wives, he assured the president that he respected his real commitment to forcing the nation live within its means.[34]

The president mentioned another political issue in a December 27, 1921, letter to Christian. He briefly noted that "the Conference is going along with a fair degree of satisfaction."[35] This description referred to the Washington Disarmament Conference, which had begun on November 12 with the secretary of state, Charles Evans Hughes, serving as one of the chief delegates. The meeting demonstrated Harding's disavowal of his predecessor's soaring internationalism. Harding had rejected the League of Nations' power to threaten the country's sovereignty. Instead, he

Fig. 109. Image of delegates to the Washington Naval Conference held in 1921–1922 where agreements were made to limit the build-up of naval armaments and tension in the Pacific. This photograph shows representatives of the nine countries which participated. The Japanese were ultimately dissatisfied with the terms of the agreements and would reject their renewal in the years leading up to World War II. (Courtesy of the Library of Congress)

felt that individual nations should come together to create mutually beneficial agreements in order to maintain stability and peace throughout the world. Harding wanted governments to be able to act in their own self-interest to keep peace rather than embracing the compulsory enforcement required by the League. The rapid expansion of many nations' naval capacities and the colonial implications of such mobile weaponry had helped trigger the Great War. Thus, at the disarmament conference, Harding and his advisors negotiated an agreement between the U.S., Great Britain, France, Italy, and Japan to limit their new construction of naval ships. The U.S. also signed a treaty with Great Britain, France, and Japan to respect each other's territorial possessions throughout the Pacific. Harding assisted in pushing these treaties through Congress. His support for the conference showed his desire to advocate for international peace even though he had opposed the methods of the League of Nations.[36]

The previous communications were rare moments in Christian's correspondence with the president. Nevertheless, Christian closely observed the key moments of his friend's presidency and later recorded his conclusion about them in his biography of the president. For example, Christian discussed Harding's confrontation with labor during the Railroad Shop Workers' Strike of 1922. In the recession that corresponded with the years after the armistice, the Railroad Labor Board concluded that railroad companies needed to reduce shipping rates. To help companies weather the lower profits that would follow, the board approved reduced wages. In response, the shop workers for the railroads went on strike. Initially, Harding felt little sympathy for the workers—he felt striking was a counterproductive tactic. But as he examined the situation further, he concluded that the employees had suffered due to the railroads' failure to follow the board's suggestions for safety and general working conditions. Consequently, Harding tried to mediate the dispute, pushing both sides to accept a three-part compromise. First, both parties had to comply with the decisions of the Railroad Labor Board.

Second, workers and employers had to end all legal proceedings associated with the strike. Finally, the railroads had to allow workers to return to their jobs without any punitive consequences to their seniority status. The railroads refused the last condition, and the strike raged on. Eventually, Harding allowed Attorney General Daugherty to try a more heavy-handed approach, and Daugherty filed an injunction that ended the strike. Christian believed that Harding's reputation with labor declined rapidly because of these events, even though he had initially tried to reach a fair agreement. Of the many problems Harding faced as president, Christian felt that this event weighed most heavily on his view of his own competence and diminished his desire to serve another term.[37]

One person who kept the Christians and the Hardings connected throughout Harding's presidency was George B. Christian Jr. Christian Jr. held one of the most taxing and difficult positions in Washington with a staff of only seven people. He and his employees handled all of the president's correspondence and scheduling, and they played a major role in public relations as well. Charles Hard, one of Christian Jr.'s assistants, described the division of labor among the secretaries thus: Christian Jr. handled visitors and press, Hard kept the schedule and finances, and Harding's former press guru Welliver helped the president transcribe and adapt his speeches. Christian Jr. organized and refereed press conferences and press releases by controlling the timing, distribution, and recipients of the information coming from the president's office. Harding's newspaper savvy generally made Christian's public relations duties easier, because the president had a good sense of what to share with the press and whether such information should be on or off the record. Nevertheless, Christian's responsibilities were exhaustive and gave him access to almost every facet of the presidency. During Harding's years in the Senate and White House, George B. Christian Jr. spent more time with him and knew him better than any other person. Harding felt completely confident in his neighbor's loyalty and discretion.[38]

Even after Harding's final departure from Marion to live in the White House, he and George B. Christian Sr. found occasions to meet. Harding returned to Ohio twice in 1922. He first came to Point Pleasant, located southeast of Cincinnati, to celebrate the one-hundredth anniversary of former president Ulysses S. Grant's birth. Harding also visited his beloved Marion to help the town celebrate its centennial on July 3. The festivities took place in front of the Marion First Presbyterian Church, which Christian had helped plan and construct. The celebration lasted over two hours with speeches and musical numbers accompanying the presentation of city keys to the grandson of city founder Eber Baker. The *Jersey Journal* reported that Harding ate at Christian's home while in Marion for the centennial. The article made a point, when speaking of the meal, to discuss the oft-renewed comical tension between Tryon Harding and Christian over which of their limited Civil War tours single-handedly helped the North prevail over the South.[39]

George and Lydia Christian also traveled to Washington to visit their son and the first family in the fall of 1922. In his memoir, Christian stated that they arrived after Florence Harding had recovered from the severe kidney ailment that had beset her in September. He claimed that they ate dinner with the Hardings on the first day that Florence felt sufficiently strong to eat in the dining room, which placed the time frame for the visit around Thanksgiving. During this meeting, Harding told Christian about his plan to visit Alaska the following summer in order to evaluate the territory and its natural resources. The president had recently recovered from the flu, and Christian recounted that he appeared tired and somewhat sickly—positing that Harding's health had already begun to decline. The Colonel counseled his friend to avoid exerting himself too strenuously, but Harding insisted that he planned to improve his health by eating better and traveling to Florida for part of January. This visit was the last time George B. Christian Sr. saw his friend alive.[40]

Harding returned from Florida invigorated and began planning his trip to Alaska. While many of his advisors tried to dissuade him from taking such a long and potentially dangerous journey, others felt the trip offered him a chance to jump start a 1924 reelection campaign. On his way west, Harding planned to give speeches in numerous cities and towns along his travel route.

In the period between the Christians' Thanksgiving visit to Washington, DC, and Harding's Alaska trip the following summer, Christian and Tryon Harding received invitations, as prominent members of the Ohio Grand Army of the Republic, to attend the annual encampment of the United Confederate Veterans in New Orleans. This invitation represented a notable opportunity for reconciliation between former enemies. Some newspapers joked that the Confederates might finally be able to determine whether Christian or Harding's short service more directly affected the outcome of the War Between the States. Unfortunately, Christian was forced to cut his trip to the encampment short when he heard that his half-uncle and former business partner, Caleb Norris, had passed away. Christian returned to Marion hoping to pay proper homage to his friend and uncle.[41]

During the final months before the Alaska trip, Christian and Harding exchanged one last set of letters. Christian related the comical story of a swindler, supposedly a distant cousin of the Ohio Christians, who asked the Colonel for a loan to help him make an emergency trip to a last minute destination. The man swore he would repay the loan upon returning home. Naturally, a repayment check never came. Christian joked that he belonged in the "Ancient and Honorable Order of Suckers." His letter also referred to a time when Harding had fallen victim to a similar kind of scam artist. Harding's reply recounted the event: During his time as a journalist, a man calling himself a Virginia Harding had convinced him and other prominent men in the community to give him money. Harding wrote that he had never felt too bad about the "bunkoing" he received, since the man took him for a small amount and had been pleasant company during their visit. The president returned to the story of Christian's swindler and joked that Christian had probably begun to trust the charlatan when he began complimenting the Christian and Harding families. One of Christian's weak spots, Harding felt, was the pride he took in his friends and relatives. This light-hearted subject proved to be the last one the two men discussed.[42]

Fig. 110. Harding, the First Lady, and George B. Christian Jr. ride the train during his trip through Alaska. (Courtesy of the Library of Congress)

The presidential convoy departed for America's final frontier on June 20, 1923. As he had planned, Harding stopped along the way and spoke on the topics his advisors thought might play well in each region. Although he became progressively more tired throughout the trip, he initially showed no signs of grave illness. In Tacoma, Washington, Harding boarded the boat tasked to carry him on his exploration of Alaska. The prospect of the adventure seemed to invigorate him, but the long hours of daylight and excitement impeded sufficient sleep. Harding spent two weeks in Alaska. First visiting its coastal islands, he reached the state capitol of Juneau on July 10. The convoy continued up the coast to Anchorage before embarking on a train ride of more than 300 miles inland to Fairbanks. As the party turned southward from Alaska, it became apparent that Harding had begun to suffer from severe exhaustion. He was able to stop in British Columbia for a meeting with local dignitaries, but his condition subsequently deteriorated rapidly. By the time he reached California on July 28, he felt unable to continue his scheduled visits and checked into a hospital in San Francisco. He seemed to improve slightly after four days of bed rest, which gave George B. Christian Jr. sufficient confidence to leave his side on August 2, 1923, and give a speech on the president's behalf to the Grand Commandery of Knights Templars in Hollywood. However, that evening the president's condition quickly became dire once again, and he passed away from heart failure.[43]

George B. Christian Sr. had worried about his friend's health for several days after having received anxious telegrams from his son, but the news he heard on August 2 assured him that the president appeared stronger. Christian awoke on August 3 to the sound of Marion's church bells ringing to memorialize the country's fallen leader, and his wife broke the sad news. A reporter from the *New Castle News* interviewed Christian four days later, and the Colonel emphasized Harding's honesty. He also recalled Harding's first arrival in Marion on the back of a stubborn mule and compared the fallen president to the martyred Christ who had similarly ridden a donkey into Jerusalem. In his grief, Christian beatified the leader.

President Harding's body left California by train a day after he died. The crew propped up the casket so that observers could see it through the train car windows, and many citizens gathered at the railway stations through which the body passed. The train arrived in Washington late on August 7, 1923, and President Harding's body lay in state in the Capitol building for a day. After a brief official

until a mausoleum can be built.

Vault in Marion, O cemetry Friday, Aug.10,1923 where
Pres. Harding's body was placed this date, temporarily,

Fig. 111. Photograph of Harding's funeral in Marion. (Courtesy of the Roberts Family Library)

ceremony for government officials, another train took the body to Harding's beloved Marion for burial. George B. Christian Jr. served as Florence Harding's greatest support during the solemnities of the funeral. He resigned as presidential secretary soon after Harding's death in order to help her settle the president's affairs. On August 10, 1923, the people of Marion took leave of their hometown president.[44]

After Harding's death, George B. Christian Sr. became one of the primary combatants in the struggle to define the former president's legacy. In the following months and years, scandals emerged from the ashes of Harding's administration. During his last year as president, Harding had learned that his director of the Veterans Bureau, Charles Forbes, had sold government supplies to private contractors for a pittance and had accepted bribes related to hospital contracts. As evidence mounted of Forbes's corruption, Harding dismissed him but tried to keep the scandal under wraps. The situation only escalated as Charles F. Cramer, general counsel to the Veterans Bureau, committed suicide on March 14, 1923, and left a news clipping about a potential Senate investigation of the affair on his desk. The events inspired rumormongering, but the details of the suicide did not become public knowledge until after Harding had passed away.[45]

A new scandal quickly surpassed the Forbes disgrace when Ohioan Jess Smith took his own life in May of 1923. Smith had worked for Harry Daugherty in the Department of Justice, but he held no official position. Before Harding came to the White House, Smith had served for many years as Daugherty's chief political fixer, and he continued this work when Daugherty became attorney general. Smith also fostered friendships with other Ohio transplants in the capital city, and he and this Ohio Gang notoriously peddled influence to various business and criminal elements—especially those involved in organized crime. After Harding discovered the corruption in the Veteran's Bureau, he became more suspicious of Smith's activities and forced Daugherty to remove Smith from the Alaska trip. Fearing the worst when it came to the discovery of his activities, Smith committed suicide. The combined magnitude of these two scandals led to terrible anxiety for the president at the same time that his health was already in decline.[46]

Several months after Harding's death, Senate investigations began to reveal the scope of the Veterans Bureau and Department of Justice scandals. These revelations, however, became only the first in a series of public disclosures that blackened Harding's legacy. At the beginning of 1924, Senate hearings uncovered a much larger disgrace. Albert Fall, secretary of the Interior, had always supported the development of natural resources on federal land. In May of 1921, Fall made a deal with Edwin Denby, secretary of the navy, to take control of the navy's oil reserves in Wyoming. Fall then leased the Teapot Dome reserves' oil rights to Henry Sinclair's Mammoth Oil Company in a secretive bidding arrangement. A 1924 hearing revealed that Fall had granted the oil contracts without a competitive bidding process, which made them illegal. The Senate appointed one of its members, Thomas Walsh, to conduct a more detailed investigation. Senator Walsh eventually discovered that Fall had accepted bribes in return for the secret leases. This infraction led the new president, Calvin Coolidge, to remove both Fall and Denby. The Teapot Dome scandal, when combined with the revelations about other executive malfeasance, presented a portrait of corruption and mismanagement in the Harding White House—though no evidence ever emerged that Harding himself had been involved in any corruption.[47]

While scandal after scandal emerged from congressional and journalistic investigations, the Christian family worked to counteract the shadow overtaking their fallen friend. In September of 1923, George B. Christian Jr. published an article in the magazine *Current History* promising that future historians would value Harding as one of the country's great presidents. He listed ten of the president's achievements including the Washington Disarmament Conference, retrenchment from wartime spending, and resolution of labor disputes. Such accomplishments, Christian argued, were monumental in the space of Harding's brief presidency. The former secretary also attested to Harding's good character, and attempted to combat the idea that Harding was an instigator of the corruption found in his administration.[48]

In a November speech to Marion's Boy Scouts, George B. Christian Sr. provided another defense of Harding. He testified that:

> President Harding may fittingly be called an apostle of peace. His handling of this great country when in the wake of the greatest war of all history has won for him a crown of an apostle. His gentle but firm influence brought America up and out of the pits of unchaotic rest and gave to us a new feeling of liberty and placidness. . . . I urge you to uphold the principles of good citizenship which were a part of our great friend and which forms [sic] the keynote of the Scout organization.[49]

Christian also shared the plans formulated by the community to construct a fitting memorial to the president.[50]

Christian and his children were among the prominent Marionites who formed the Harding Memorial Association to build a tomb and memorial worthy of a deceased leader. Dr. Charles Sawyer quit his job at the White House in 1924 to head up the association's efforts and to take control of the more than $900,000 that had been collected for the purpose. President Calvin

Fig. 112. President Herbert Hoover speaking at the dedication of the Harding Memorial. (Reprinted by permission of the Ohio History Connection)

Coolidge also pledged government support for the construction of the monument. Unfortunately, both Sawyer and Florence Harding passed away in late 1924, and the project was left mainly to the people of Marion to complete. Hoke Donithen and George B. Christian Sr. became the new leaders of the effort, and in 1926 they helped break ground for the structure. The memorial was completed and ready to be dedicated on July 4, 1927. But by this time, the Coolidge administration had worked hard to separate itself from the corruption of the Harding era and would have nothing to do with the event. Coolidge's successor, Herbert Hoover, also hesitated at first to dedicate the memorial. He would not come to Marion until 1931, after the Great Depression had destroyed his popularity and credibility. Thus, George B. Christian Sr. never lived to see a president dedicate the memorial for which he had worked so vehemently.[51]

Christian's efforts on behalf of the memorial represented his most visible attempt to redeem his friend's legacy, but his most vigorous defense came in his unpublished biography of the former president. Christian wrote the majority of this manuscript in 1926, after most of the scandals in the Harding administration

265

had become common knowledge. He probably wrote with some inside information from his son, who surely had some impressions about the events that Harding had tried to keep quiet. Christian Sr. wrote to try to wrest the Harding presidency's reputation from the tabloids. In the years since Harding had entered the U.S. Senate, the former Marion newspaperman had become more than a friend. To Christian, Harding represented the apotheosis of small-town values and sensibilities translated on the national stage. He embodied everything good and decent about the American dream. In his writings, Christian connected Harding's Ohio origins to Washington's early survey of the Ohio Valley, and he made sure to mention Tryon Harding's youthful audience with President Abraham Lincoln, connecting Harding's origins to the nation's mythology. Christian also emphasized his own role as one of the president's early guides along the path to the White House. The narrative is a love letter about Harding's character and integrity. According to Christian, Harding never sought office. Instead, the people called him into public service. Near the end of the biography, Christian made one of his most decisive stands against those who claimed Harding had been a corrupt and inept leader. The Colonel asserted that he would have carved the following epitaph into Harding's final resting place: "Here lies the noblest work of God—an honest man."[52]

George B. Christian Sr.'s defensive tactics became even more explicit after 1927, when Nan Britton's licentious exposé of her supposed affair and illegitimate child with Harding threw more mud on the former president's already besmirched reputation. Britton was the daughter of a Marion doctor and had attended public school with Mildred Christian. Considering Harding's earlier affair with Carrie Phillips, a dalliance with a young admirer might have garnered some credibility. Britton's book, Christian would later claim, was filled with meticulous detail that could be easily disproved when cross-checked with the public record of Harding's activities. For instance, Britton claimed to have rendezvoused with Harding at the Republican

National Convention and again several times at the White House, times when Harding's presence elsewhere had been meticulously documented. She professed to have written her tell-all to help provide for herself and her daughter. Many people embraced Britton's tawdry claims because they fit into the narrative of corruption and debauchery that had emerged out of Harding's years in office.[53]

Christian, probably with the help or support of former Harding secretary Kathleen Lawler, wrote a refutation of Britton's book in which he attacked both her character and her conclusions about the former president. To undermine her claims, he utilized his background and knowledge of Marion society. For example, he argued that Britton had gained a reputation within Marion for befriending the daughters of newly arrived families and berating them with details about her many crushes on prominent local gentlemen. Christian also claimed that the jaw-dropping details contained in the book were actually evidence of fabrication, because it would have been impossible to remember events with such clarity. Additionally, the Colonel called out specifics that contrasted with the character of the Harding he knew. He doubted that Britton's family would have so easily approved of the relationship and that Harding would have introduced her to so many members of his family and important political characters in Washington. Christian's strongest and most personal argument questioned how Britton could have carried on such an extensive relationship with the president without coming into contact with George B. Christian Jr. The majority of Christian's misguided arguments boiled down to the belief that he and his informants had a much better sense and understanding of the president than Britton exhibited within her book.[54]

Neither of George B. Christian Sr.'s manuscripts in defense of his friend ever made it into print—though Kathleen Lawler, Harding's social secretary, consulted them when she wrote her own unpublished memoirs about the Harding presidency. George B. Christian Jr. planned to write a treatise in support of the Harding administration, but his declining health and blindness caused by glaucoma made the project impossible. The public seemed to have little taste for full-throated defenses of the Harding years—especially after the Great Depression threw a cloud over all three Republican presidents and their policies during the 1920s. Even though Christian Sr.'s apologetic compositions never reached the general public, he never lost hope that someone might find value in them. He bequeathed his manuscripts, and any profits garnered by them, to his children as part of his estate.[55]

A year after George B. Christian Sr.'s death, his family was drawn into one last encounter with Nan Britton when she filed a libel suit against Charles A. Klunk. Klunk had published and distributed Joseph De Barthe's book, *The Answer to the President's Daughter* which took many of Britton's claims to task. In the subsequent trial which took place in Toledo, Klunk's defense team called Mildred Roberts as a witness about Britton's reputation. Roberts and Britton had known one another in high school, and Roberts testified briefly to the fact that Britton's name had been tarnished long before De Barthe's book emerged. The defense had tried to subpoena George B. Christian Jr. to testify, but he had refused citing hardships of distance and health—though he really wanted nothing to do with the tawdry proceedings. Because of its connection to the scandals of the Harding presidency, the case received national press attention. Even after Christian and Harding's deaths, their families were bound together.[56]

George B. Christian Sr.'s compulsion in his later years to write about Harding demonstrated the men's long-standing friendship. At the same time, his instinct to defend the former president came from his need to find meaning in his own life and family. In many ways, Christian had failed in his final years as a businessman. The fortune he had acquired through skillful leadership of the Norris and Christian Lime and Stone Company had all but disappeared by the time he retired from the White Sulphur Lime and Stone Company.

His claim to prestige within the community now stemmed from his status as one of the town's last surviving Civil War veterans, his successful family, and his intimate relationship with Warren G. Harding. For Christian, his family's close connection to the twenty-ninth president was their most important contribution to the world. He had taken great pride in his bond with the Hardings during their time in the White House. When scandal threatened, Christian took up his pen to support the fallen president. And in his defense of his Marion friend, Christian also protected his own heritage and worth.

CHAPTER 11

"A True Christian Gentleman"

"If a man be a Christian gentleman, the fact will be known by his cat, his dog, his horse, his children, his servants, and every living being that comes in his way." Edward John Hardy, *How to Be Happy Though Civil: A Book on Manners* (New York: Charles Scribner's Sons, 1910), 61.

The last decade of George B. Christian Sr.'s life took place in the period following the end of World War I and before the outbreak of the Great Depression often referred to as the Roaring Twenties. Thus, the aging Civil War veteran witnessed numerous economic, cultural, and social shifts in his final years. The huge expansion of industrial productivity in the United States, when combined with the wartime collapse of the European economy, created unprecedented American prosperity. Because of their rapid growth, many industries and companies began to seek public financing, which expanded stock market accessibility beyond the banking and speculating classes to some in the general population. Many investors leveraged their acquisitions by borrowing money in order to invest based on the assumption of perpetually rising stock prices. This tactic made many investors' fortunes, but it created an artificial sense of wealth divorced from the strengths or weaknesses of the companies that issued the stock. Corporations began to overproduce in order to justify high valuations, and eventually supplies of goods outpaced demand. When this economic bubble burst and share prices fell drastically, the Great Depression ensued.[1]

Accompanying the large expansion of paper wealth was the public growth of decadence, leisure, and consumerism. Even in small cities such as Marion, department stores offered consumer credit in hopes of encouraging people to spend their discretionary income on the newest fashions. Households purchased appliances and radios

Fig. 113. Women dressed as flappers in the 1920s. (Courtesy of the Library of Congress)

more than ever before. Henry Ford offered almost every American the opportunity to buy a reliable and affordable automobile. For the first time in the history of the country, more people lived in cities than outside them, and urban prosperity served as an alluring draw for rural youth. Many young metropolitan men and women began to challenge Victorian perceptions of morality. Young women dressed as flappers—flaunting their sexuality and independence. Jazz, an improvised fusion of African American musical traditions, gained mainstream appeal as white elites embraced its perceived earthiness and sensuality. The constitutional prohibition of alcohol made a generation of drinkers into lawbreakers. Scholars have pointed to these cultural factors to argue that the 1920s represented a challenge to the ethos of the Progressive Era. World War I had proven that humanity could not always count on a progressive societal trajectory. The inhuman brutality of trench warfare had destroyed many people's confidence in the future, so they sought fulfillment in the present. Writers of the so-called Lost Generation, such as Ernest Hemingway and F. Scott Fitzgerald, captured the connections between the era's disillusionment and hedonism in their most famous writings.[2]

Significant racial, ethnic, and class conflicts also tore at the fabric of American society. Ugly confrontations occurred between workers and their employers as labor forces sought to retain the benefits they had acquired in the wartime economy. Returning soldiers created a glut in the workforce that pushed wages downward. Segregation and violence continued to haunt African Americans. Many black soldiers had experienced more tolerant racial attitudes in Europe and returned to face the worst manifestations of Jim Crow. During and immediately after the war, an influx of southern African Americans had relocated to the North to take advantage of the jobs that had opened up when young men entered the military. This influx caused the expansion of race riots and lynching to the North as white supremacists employed force and coercion to ensure that the black population continued to understand their subordinate position in society. Legal and de facto segregation assured that African Americans would remain politically and economically separate and unequal.[3] The Klu Klux Klan re-emerged during this time as an organization of terror that enforced not only racial but also ethnic and religious boundaries. The Klan sought to reduce or ban Asian and Southern European immigration, and it intimidated those of darker hues with violence, bullying, and death. Consequently, the 1920s represented a decade in U.S. history in which wealth disparity and the politics of prejudice plagued both the poor and the rich in real and significant ways.[4]

While the turbulent decade raged on, both Christian's age and his residency in the moderately sized city of Marion kept him relatively disconnected from many of the issues afflicting urban America. In truth, the rapid changes occurring within the country seem to have pushed Christian to revisit the past and tighten his bonds with his family and community. Despite his interest in technology, in some ways Christian was profoundly conservative.

For most of his life, Christian had juggled his political, economic, and journalistic ambitions. After retirement, he finally found substantial time to record his experiences and observations for posterity. Christian contemplated writing a full-blown memoir or autobiography, but if he did, his efforts failed to survive to the present day. Nevertheless, a variety of essays, histories, and commentaries from this time period have survived. Christian was a generous observer who wrote admiringly about his heroes and friends. On the other hand, he could still be scathing toward those with whom he disagreed. In his later years, Christian also assumed a role as one of Marion's elder statesmen—using his oratorical and rhetorical skills to promote community appreciation for fallen soldiers. Most importantly, Christian found time to draw closer to his family— especially after the passing of his beloved Lydia. Instead of worrying about the Roaring Twenties, Christian's thoughts and enthusiasm turned to the legacy he wished to leave for his family, community, and the rest of humanity.[5]

To assist in his work as an amateur historian, Christian recruited Carrie Bain, his long-time secretary at the Norris and Christian Lime and Stone Company. Bain had grown up with George B. Christian Jr. and was a close family friend. To help him pay for her services, Christian submitted a pension application to the federal government in 1925 in which he claimed that the disabilities resulting from his military service required him to employ a caregiver. Bain assisted him with the pension paperwork and even served as a second witness for one of the affidavits. She continued to work as a hybrid secretary-caregiver until Christian's death in 1930. Christian felt such affection for her that he left her a small amount of money in his will. After Christian's death, Bain went on to serve as the assistant to the Marion County auditor, one of Christian's former jobs, before passing away in 1942.[6]

Bain helped Christian produce an impressive number of histories, essays, and anecdotes. Christian's most substantial surviving work told the history of President Warren G. Harding from the Colonel's perspective as a long-time supporter and friend. As described in the previous chapter, Christian found meaning and purpose in his efforts to redeem the former president's sullied reputation. While only his Harding manuscript has attracted the attention of scholars, Christian produced a variety of other texts on diverse subjects after his retirement. For example, in 1926 he wrote and self-published the previously discussed promotional tract about Florida entitled *My Lost Millions* (see chapter four). Christian displayed passion in almost everything he wrote, but he seemed particularly enamored with his Summerland and his friend Warren G. Harding.[7]

When Kathleen Lawler, Florence Harding's social secretary, wrote her own memoir about President Harding, she sought out George B. Christian Sr. as a credible source on the president's early years in Marion. She connected with Christian during his late-life period of literary productivity, and he gave her copies of several of his manuscripts, which found their way into her personal papers now held at the Ohio Historical Society. Fortunately, Lawler's papers contain some Christian retirement writings that cannot be found anywhere else.[8]

One of Christian's manuscripts, collected by Lawler, recorded the dramatic events of the 1868 Democratic Convention. Christian was inspired to write this account after reading about the 1924 Democratic Convention held at Madison Square Garden. Although he had since grown disaffected with the Democratic Party, the newspaper coverage in 1924 reminded him of an

Fig. 114. Image depicting the 1868 Democratic Convention held at Tamany Hall in New York City. This was the first national political convention which George B. Christian Sr. attended. (Courtesy of the Library of Congress)

earlier New York City convention when he had still felt excited about the party of Jefferson and Jackson. Christian had attended the Democratic Convention of 1868 at the age of 22 with his half-uncle and future business partner, Caleb Norris. He had grown up with a father who was a leader in Marion's Democratic Party,

275

but the 1868 meeting offered Christian his first opportunity to see political machinations at a national level. That year, the Democrats nominated former New York governor Horatio Seymour to run against Ulysses S. Grant for the presidency. In his account, Christian framed the convention as the beginnings of post–Civil War regional reconciliation, since delegates from the South and North had gathered to find a candidate to beat Grant and roll back congressional Reconstruction efforts in the South. Christian's short account began with the hopeless indecision which tormented the initial stages of the convention. The chaos ended when the controversial Ohio copperhead Clement Vallandigham suggested that his delegation drop its original loyalties to native son George Pendleton and switch their support to the compromise candidate and convention speaker, Horatio Seymour. Seymour appealed to both Northern and Southern Democrats, which allowed him to prevail as the party's candidate. Almost sixty years later, Christian argued that Southern discontent, when combined with Seymour's competitiveness at the polls, led to the rebirth of the post-war Democratic Party to which he had dedicated so much of his life. Christian's account exemplified themes identified by present-day historians, who have observed that most Americans focused on regional reconciliation after the war rather than sorting out the sticky quagmires of racial conflict. To Christian, the Democratic Party of 1868 prioritized the development and presentation of a united front, while he felt that the Democrats in the 1920s had lost their way.[9]

Most of Christian's manuscripts were journalistic or historical in nature, but Lawler's papers also include an interesting proposal for the plot of a motion picture. While the proposal contained no clues about where Christian wanted to submit the story or the context that led to its creation, it showed Christian's intentions to try his hand as a screen writer in his eightieth year. His proposal adapted the story—based on historical events—told by English Romantic poet Lord Byron about a soldier named Mazeppa. Byron's poem followed the man, born as a Polish squire, who fell in love with a married duchess and for his crimes was banished from the kingdom, strapped naked to a wild horse, and literally run out of Poland. After his horse collapsed from exhaustion, Mazeppa was rescued by a Ukrainian maiden and eventually became the commander of Ukraine's feared Cossack mounted soldiers. Christian's proposal expanded and deepened Byron's tale by adding a vengeful return to Poland to defeat the duke who had banished him. Christian also added the discovery of a long-lost son. At the urging of friends and family, he even suggested that Mazeppa reunite with his lost love at the end of the film.[10]

Fig. 115. Illustration depicting Lord Byron's poem about the legendary Cossack, Mazeppa. In this image, servants of a Polish duke tie Mazeppa naked to the back of a horse as punishment for a dalliance with the duke's wife. (Courtesy of the Library of Congress)

Christian's treatment of the story and his decision to write the proposal in the first place indicated that he had become captivated with the new visual medium of motion pictures. In his letters to Warren G. Harding in the White House, he had often commented on the newsreels he viewed as part of the movie-going experience. In the mid-1920s, silent films were still the norm—though the 1927 release of *The Jazz Singer* and subsequent talkies would transform the movie industry. Christian's offering of the story of Mazeppa for a film reflected his desire to share this personally beloved story with a new generation. For Christian, Mazeppa epitomized the courage and dedication lost in the hedonism of the Roaring Twenties. Because Christian had served in the cavalry during the Civil War, the tale of the mounted Cossack was also one with which he personally related. He argued in his proposal that the story "would give fine opportunity for a display of horsemanship centering about a most remarkable yet truthful tale of love and intrigue."[11] Lord Byron had written his poem in 1819, but Christian had probably become familiar with it through a popular dramatic reenactment which appeared at the end of circus shows in the 1850s and 1860s. By proposing to modernize the story through the medium of film in the 1920s, Christian hoped not only to retell an enduring story of heroism, but also to resurrect the martial memories of his youth.[12]

While little of the long-form writing by George B. Christian Sr. has survived, a letter from Fred Dombaugh to George B. Christian Jr. offered a snapshot of the Colonel's diverse musings. Dombaugh listed the following manuscripts included in Christian Sr.'s estate: "The Evangelist, a Romance of Suppression," "Andrew Jackson Morgan, His Solution to the Economic Problem of Unemployment," "Tragedies of the Courts Martial," "Some Spell-Binders and Hog-Callers of the West," "My Nephew's Story," and "V.M.I.—The Virginia Military Institute—A Confederate Tragedy of the War Between the States." Thus, Christian's retirement manuscripts touched on the political, personal, historical, comical, and dramatic. Though none of these manuscripts have been preserved, the inventory proves that he wrote many more articles than have been found. Even Christian's family members sometimes had little clue about the scope of his compositions. For example, Fred Dombaugh believed that Christian had never written about Nan Britton, the woman who claimed that Harding had fathered her illegitimate child, yet such a manuscript appears in Lawler's papers. Christian's retirement allowed him the luxury of time to write about the things for which he cared and to record his thoughts, opinions, and memories for future generations.[13]

Christian's role as a writer in his later life correlated with his role as an elder statesman in the community. His public speaking, much like his writing acumen, had been nurtured over the course of many years. Groups generally recruited Christian when looking for someone whose age and respectability would bolster celebrations of nostalgia and veneration. His energy and life experience, when coupled with his eloquence, made him a perfect figure to lead these events. The local post of the Grand Army of the Republic (GAR) recognized Christian's place in the community by designating him its patriotic instructor. This position gave Christian the latitude to define for his brothers-in-arms the meaning of good citizenship. For Christian, true patriotism involved service to family, community, and nation. He reminded members of the GAR, and the community at large, of those that paid the ultimate price in defending their ideals. Christian took his responsibility seriously and found great pride in his opportunities to pay homage to Marion's veterans.[14]

Fig. 116. Christian's official portrait from a publication sponsored by the Ohio chapter of the Grand Army of the Republic. (*Roster and Proceedings of the 55th Annual Encampment of the Department of Ohio Grand Army of the Republic* [Columbus, OH: F. J. Heer Printing Company, 1921])

Christian's patriotic leadership was on vivid display in a *Marion Star* report which summarized Christian's speech at Marion's fifth annual Armistice Day celebration in November of 1923. This holiday, commemorated today in collaboration with Veterans Day, honored the agreement that ended the hostilities of World War I. While fewer Americans died in the Great War than in the Civil War, the brutality, carnage, and fear resulting from trench warfare scarred returning veterans in a way that only Union and Confederate soldiers might have understood. In addition, Christian felt a personal connection to World War I veterans because his son-in-law Chester Roberts had served in the military during the conflict, and his grandson Warren had entered West Point soon after the armistice. Christian had never seen significant or brutal fighting in the Civil War, but he had witnessed the terrible consequences that the conflict had wrought on friends who had experienced the worst of the battlefield. Consequently, he had gained a great respect for soldiers without developing an equivalent aversion to the horrors of combat. These two characteristics pervaded his words during such solemn occasions as the anniversary of Armistice Day. In his speech, he declared, "The boys who fought the fight of the righteous on the war-torn and blood-soaked fields of France can be proud of this day. Their achievements guaranteed us our liberty. They should feel proud of the part they took in the greatest war of the world's history." Such embellishment came from Christian's love of country as well as his nostalgia for his Civil War service. He hoped to convey the terrible romance of the battlefield to future generations while honoring the service of Marion's veterans.[15]

Christian's Armistice Day speech and his dedication to preserving the memory of Warren G. Harding were just two ways that he honored his community's fallen sons. Along similar lines, Christian was chosen to eulogize popular senator Frank B. Willis in a Marion memorial held in 1928. As Christian drew close to his eightieth birthday, his longevity compelled him to take more of a leadership role in the Marion GAR as others passed away. He also continued serving as the president of Marion's Memorial Day celebrations. Moreover, Christian served on the Soldiers' Burial Committee that had been formed to help veterans' widows with the cost of funerals. His commitment to honoring the past in public forums in his later years sometimes seemed almost obsessive, but it always worked to honor the memories of the dead.[16]

George B. Christian Sr. revealed a similar devotion to family in a speech he gave to the Cooper Post of the GAR as their patriotic instructor.[17] After giving a short synopsis of his economic demise caused by the World War I policies of the Wilson administration, Christian went on a long tirade against the Progressive wing of the Republican Party and its poor treatment of his son, Warren G. Harding's former personal secretary. Christian Sr. explained that it was customary for former presidential secretaries to receive a comfortable government job upon their retirement from the White House. In accordance with this custom, Calvin Coolidge appointed George B. Christian Jr., pending Congressional approval, to the Federal Trade Commission (FTC), where he would have received a salary around $10,000 a year (the equivalent of a six-figure salary in 2016). Christian Sr. claimed that the Progressive-leaning *Chicago Tribune* ruined his son's confirmation to the FTC by questioning his qualifications and putting forward its own candidate who opposed "Pittsburgh Plus" pricing for steel, an issue that the commission was scheduled to consider.[18] In addition to the *Tribune*, the union leadership of several railroad workers' organizations opposed Christian Jr.'s appointment. This antagonism resulted from the supposedly brutal treatment of workers at the Norris and Christian quarries and Christian Jr.'s alleged stance against government support of farmers. Union disapproval soon influenced Robert La Follette, a famous Progressive politician, to hinder Christian Jr.'s confirmation, leading to an extremely contentious Senate hearing. In the hearing, a serving member of the FTC accused Christian Jr. of trying to influence a commission decision while serving as the president's secretary. Although Christian denied the accusation, it was the last straw. He decided that serving on a commission where one of the members had opposed his appointment was untenable, and he asked the president to withdraw his nomination. George Christian Sr. blamed the *Tribune*, union leaders, and Senator La Follette for opposing his son, who was a veteran and graduate of a military college. He urged his GAR post to stand against La Follette and his fellow Progressives as a way of supporting the cause of veterans everywhere. Christian's reasoning in this speech, which called on GAR members to connect the Progressives' actions against his son with anti-veteran behavior, encouraged his listeners to reject an entire body of political thought. His advocacy for his son was unmatched and raw.[19]

In April of 1924, George B. Christian Sr. entered into a business relationship with his son-in-law Chester Roberts. The venture involved a property nicknamed the McGruder Building, which Christian had purchased in 1907 from Mary Short and J. William McGruder for $26,000 (the equivalent of about $677,000 in 2016). The building was located in downtown Marion on the west side of State Street between Center and Church Streets. At least twice after purchasing the property, Christian dipped into the building's equity through mortgages in order to secure cash for one reason or another. The money for the initial investment probably came from Christian's divestment from the Norris and Christian Lime and Stone enterprises. While no deed or mortgage records illuminate why Roberts entered into this partnership with his father-in-law, the pairing probably occurred for one of several reasons. First, Christian possibly wanted to help support his daughter and new son-in-law by giving them a stake in one of his properties. Second, the Robertses might have chosen to help their father-in-law financially by investing in one of his most important and valuable developments. Third, Christian could have needed his son-in-law's help managing the building. Whatever the reason, Christian and Roberts extended their family ties into the realms of business in the later years of Christian's life—a metaphor for the love and trust that they built.[20]

On December 27, 1926, Christian celebrated his eightieth birthday with seventy-five of his friends and family at his home on East Church Street. For the occasion, his guests presented him with two birthday cakes, including one adorned with eighty candles. The *Star* noted that Christian had not only attained the rare milestone of longevity, but he still enjoyed "physical vigor" and a "youngness of heart."[21] The paper also observed that he had seen Marion grow from a small village with a population less than three hundred to a thriving city of more than 50,000, and he and his family had grown with it.[22]

Despite this celebration of his long life, Christian began to set his affairs in order a few years later. Beginning in 1928, he sought to sell his letters from Warren G. Harding. Christian had heard that similar letters had secured a high auction price, and he wanted to sell them rather than "leave them to the uncertainties of posterity."[23] He first offered them to Henry Ford, a friend of Harding's who had accumulated a large collection of Americana as he built his automobile empire. Ford was creating a museum to share his artifacts with the public. Nevertheless, he must have passed on the offer, because Christian continued to consult with his son about when and how to sell the correspondence. Christian attempted to prepare for any difficulties his estate might encounter, and he probably preferred to keep the potentially valuable letters from becoming a source of tension among family members after his death. His overtures to Ford demonstrated that he also wanted the letters to go to a collector who might preserve them for future generations. Even after selling many of the letters, Christian kept his own transcription of the correspondence as a remembrance of his friend.[24]

While the Christian family members assuredly wrote to one another in the time when work and school separated them, a majority of their surviving letters span the last years of George and Lydia Christian's lives. These letters, found primarily in the Ohio Historical Society's collection of papers connected

Fig. 117. George and Lydia Christian in their later years. (Courtesy of the Roberts Family Library)

to Warren G. Harding, paint a picture of a family struggling to keep in touch despite long distances and the realities of old age and death. George B. Christian Sr. and his wife lived well past the average life expectancy for their contemporaries. The family letters tell the story of the final years of Christian's life, politics, business, and family.

Fig. 118. Three generation photo of the Christian Family. (Courtesy of the Roberts Family Library)

Christian and his son often wrote to each other about the state of American politics. Christian Jr. shared newspaper articles and books with his father, and they both communicated their impressions of the authors' ideas. One of these books was Blair Coán's *The Red Web: An Underground Political History of the United States*, which Christian Jr. sent to his father in the summer of 1928. Coán had worked in the Department of Justice, and he undertook a full-throated defense of former Attorneys General Harry Daugherty and A. Mitchell Palmer while untangling the vast communist conspiracy that supposedly beset Washington. Coán's exposé blamed a left-wing plot, perpetrated by Progressives and Democrats, as the source of the various scandals that emerged ex post facto from the Harding administration. Christian Sr. seemed inclined to embrace the truthfulness of this narrative, while his son expressed more skepticism about the author's conclusions. Nonetheless, the book framed Harding as a bulwark who had attempted to stem the tide of communist conspiracy, and this rendering offered the two men a way to consider and create meaning out of Harding's tarnished reputation.[25]

The Christians' discussion of *The Red Web* occurred within the context of the presidential election of 1928, when Republican Herbert Hoover ran against Democrat Al Smith. The Christians supported Hoover for the presidency and Republican Myers Cooper for the governorship of Ohio. Hoover had been a part of Harding's cabinet, and Cooper had been friends with Christian Sr. for many years. Christian Sr. wrote to his son on July 31, 1928, and predicted that most of the Midwest would support Hoover—though he worried that Al Smith might manipulate the African American vote in his favor. Christian Jr. wrote back that he was pleased that his father thought Ohio would vote for Hoover, since he had confidence in Christian Sr.'s ability to read the state's political pulse. Christian Sr.'s support of gubernatorial candidate Myers Cooper soon created a stir in Marion, when former mayor C. J. Nichols claimed Christian's endorsement should deter other Republicans from voting for Cooper. Nichols argued that Christian's endorsement, coming from a former well-known Democrat, meant that Cooper might be a Republican in name only. Nichols opposed Cooper because the would-be governor had abandoned William Howard Taft in the controversial presidential election of 1912 to support Theodore Roosevelt. At age 81, Christian wrote a scathing rebuttal of Nichols and a defense of Cooper in the August 11, 1928, edition of the *Marion Star*. He reminded readers that the early members of the Republican Party were anti-slavery defectors from the Whig and Democratic Parties. Christian questioned why such a party of converts would deny him membership, and he claimed to have voted for Republican candidates in the previous four presidential elections. The Colonel sought to allay fears about Cooper's Republican credentials and reassure his fellow Marionites of his own commitment to the Republican Party.

In the end, the election proceeded in the manner he anticipated, and he bragged to his son that he won over thirty dollars betting on Republicans. Chester Roberts proved an even better gambler and won more than $150. Despite Christian's advancing age, he continued to find politics fascinating and invigorating.[26]

In 1928, George Christian Jr. relocated permanently to Washington, DC. Through all his years serving with Warren G. Harding, he had kept his Marion home near the Harding residence. For part of this period, Chester and Mildred Roberts had occupied and cared for that home. But in the fall of 1928, Christian Jr. decided to sell his property to the Harding Memorial Association, which already owned and maintained the former president's home. To push the transaction forward, he gave Chester Roberts power of attorney in the matter. The association struggled to secure financing for the purchase, so Roberts obtained a mortgage in Christian Jr.'s name and then transferred the note to the association. The foundation then paid the former presidential secretary $4,500 for his Marion residence. The sale of Christian Jr.'s home acknowledged the rapid disappearance of his family's ties to Marion.[27]

In September of 1928, Chester Roberts wrote to George B. Christian Jr. to inform him about the sale of his home as well as the condition of his mother. In the letter, written on Roberts Kelvinator Company letterhead and dated September 19, Roberts reported that the Christian matriarch was lying in bed with bladder problems and high blood pressure.[28] Lydia Christian had entered a stage of declining health from which she never fully recovered. A week or two later, another letter from Roberts notified the far-off son that his mother was still suffering from bladder trouble and felt dejected because she had not recovered quickly. Her condition had degenerated to such a point by October that Christian Jr. came for a short visit to make sure to see her one last time. Surprisingly, Lydia Christian seemed to improve somewhat in December and arose from her bed to try to celebrate Christmastime with her family. On Christmas morning, however, she tripped and fell on the way to look at her presents. Although the fall caused no apparent trauma or fractures, she never left her bed again. She died on February 3, 1929 at the age of seventy-seven. While her symptoms might have suggested a variety of conditions that led to her death, her obituary stated that she died from arteriosclerosis or heart disease. Lydia Christian's funeral was held in her home on February 5, 1929, and the local Presbyterian minister, Howard L. Olewiler, led the services. After the funeral, the family interred her in a plot within the Marion cemetery.[29]

George B. Christian Sr.'s family helped him cope with the traumatic loss of his wife. She had lived a long life of seventy-eight years but had suffered terribly in her final months, which made her passing somewhat easier to confront. Nevertheless, Christian faced freezing temperatures and illness in the month after her death

Fig. 119. George B. Christian Sr.'s East Church Street home. (Courtesy of the Roberts Family Library)

and probably would have suffered greater anguish without the love and support of his children and grandchildren. In accordance with a tradition of the day, the title of the Christians' East Church Street home had been secured in Lydia Christian's name. In her will, she split the ownership of the house between her three children: George Jr., Mamie Dombaugh, and Mildred Roberts. Of course, the children allowed their father to continue his residence there. Mildred Roberts and her husband moved in with her father to help care for him and the property. Consequently, the noise of Christian's grandchildren soon filled the home. When the Robertses moved in, they had three children: Frank, age ten; John, age eight; and Charles, age four. George Christian Jr. confirmed the new youthful energy in the house

287

when he affectionately referred to his nephews as roughnecks—an exaggerated term for the rowdy and misbehaved—after a visit to Marion. Eventually, the Roberts family bought out the other siblings' claims to the residence.[30]

The death of his beloved Lydia caused George B. Christian Sr. to ponder his own mortality. Christian enjoyed fairly good health for the last year of his life, especially for his age. Nevertheless, he rapidly made his three children the beneficiaries of his $5,000 life insurance policy. He hoped the cash would pay for his funeral expenses and any unsettled debts, so that creditors would have no lien on his half of the McGruder property—a messy prospect that might have resulted in a difficult probate court battle. Christian traveled to Washington, DC, to visit his son and grandsons one last time in the year after his wife passed. In addition, he continued working hard to sell the family's Harding letters, even considering a trip to New York to present them for appraisal to various dealers. His efforts to sell the letters demonstrated the new market for collectables that had developed in the prosperity of the early twentieth century.[31]

One interesting dynamic that appeared in letters near the end of Christian's life was his family's shared love for team sports—especially America's pastime. Christian and his posterity often discussed teams and games. Marion newspapers had recorded Christian's participation in local baseball games as far back the 1870s. Harding and the Colonel had often attended ballgames together in Marion and nearby cities. When he was in his eighties, Christian even received a season pass to all the National League ballparks for several years. This love of baseball extended to his children. George Christian Jr. enjoyed the game so much that he contemplated joining a group that made a bid to buy the Cleveland Indians in the 1920s. When he felt too old to attend many games in 1929, Christian Sr. sent his pass to his grandson Warren, who lived in Long Island, New York. National sports fandom, especially for baseball, exploded in the 1920s, when players such as Babe Ruth dominated the athletic world. Historians have observed that baseball represented a shared national space where people of distinct ethnicities and classes gathered to celebrate their almost religious dedication to the national pastime. Sporting events also helped set new definitions of strength and masculinity. In their fandom, the Christians connected with each other and with baseball lovers around the country.[32]

The Christians also enjoyed collegiate football. One family rivalry involved the games between the University of Illinois, Chester Roberts's alma mater, and the United States Military Academy, from which Christian's grandson Warren had graduated. University of Illinois football attracted national attention in the mid-1920s, when All-American Harold "Red" Grange, also nicknamed "The Galloping Ghost," became a national superstar after rushing for 263 yards and four touchdowns in the first twelve minutes of a game versus the University of Michigan. The United States Military Academy also maintained a large national fan base among its graduates and their subordinates in the army. Chester Roberts and Warren Christian maintained a friendly wager on the outcome of the game whenever the two teams met, and the rest of the family enjoyed goading the team loyalists.[33]

Sports represented one outlet for helping the family cope with the grief over their fallen matriarch. Christian tried to find other ways to stay busy as well. In August of 1930, he and a few of his fellow veterans from Marion County traveled to Cincinnati, Ohio, for the sixty-fourth national encampment of the GAR. Christian estimated that more than 2,500 Civil War veterans from throughout the country attended the encampment along with more than 15,000 of their sons and grandsons. The highlight of the event was a ticker-tape parade through the streets of Cincinnati, where residents showered the men with various kinds of paper and confetti out of building windows.[34] Colonel Ulysses S. Grant III, grandson of the former Union general, addressed the crowds alongside the governor of Ohio. A few days later, many of the veterans made a pilgrimage to the gravesite of President Grant in Point Pleasant, Ohio. Christian reported on the event for the *Marion Star*, and his final words proved prescient: "I feel that the sixty-fourth encampment may be considered to have been a swan song for the forty odd thousand survivors of the two and quarter million men who served the union in the great civil war."[35] He was probably referring to both the gatherings and the participants in an abstract sense, but he fulfilled his own prophecy when he died several weeks later.[36]

Fig. 120. Ulysses S. Grant III, grandson of the Civil War commander, spoke at the sixty-fourth national encampment of the Grand Army of the Republic that Christian attended in the last month of his life. (Courtesy of the Archive of U.S. War Department)

Christian fell sick after his return to Marion in early September, and he remained in bed for a week and a half. Occasionally he appeared to recover, but eventually he started to fade. The family summoned George B. Christian Jr. from Washington to see his father one last time, but he never made it. At 3:40 a.m. on September 15, 1930, Christian passed away, surrounded by most of his family at the age of eighty-three. Christian Jr. arrived a few hours too late, though he stayed to help arrange his father's affairs. Christian's death certificate blamed his demise on heart valve problems and heart disease. A stroke or heart attack was probably responsible for the sudden nature of his decline—though no autopsy was ever performed and medicine of the time often misdiagnosed such conditions. Christian's family held a short funeral service on the afternoon of September 17, 1930. Pastor Howard L. Olewiler of the local Presbyterian church officiated the ceremony, as he had done when Lydia Christian passed away. Christian's nephews served as pallbearers, and his colleagues from the GAR provided a gun salute, taps, and a flag for the occasion. After the service, Christian was interred in the Marion cemetery next to his beloved wife of sixty-nine years, who had preceded him in death less than two years earlier.[37]

Because of George B. Christian Sr.'s business success, public service, and personal connection to former president Warren G. Harding, tributes to the Colonel began to pour in from newspapers and friends alike. On the afternoon of Christian's death, George Van Fleet, editor of the *Marion Star*, printed a lengthy obituary with a giant headline on the *Star*'s front page. He also honored the fallen soldier in a personal editorial when he wrote:

> Looking backward over the record of his life of eighty-three years we read the story of one who was a brave soldier; an upright businessman, fair and honest in his dealings with his fellow-men; a good citizen, a true friend to his friends, a fine husband and an indulgent father—a man of good counsel in the community's life and one charming in his home. Profound regret must follow the passing of such a man.[38]

The next day, the *Cleveland Plain Dealer* published a notice about Christian's funeral and listed his most notable accomplishments, including his place as one of "Ohio's old-time journalists." The *Washington Post* also ran an obituary highlighting Christian's role as the father of a former presidential secretary.[39]

Ohio governor Myers Cooper sent a letter that the state librarian read at Christian's funeral. In it, the governor paid tribute to Christian's "fine, rugged character." Cooper recounted recent interactions with Christian at the GAR encampment and after a speech in Marion, and he observed that one of the Colonel's most attractive traits was "a charm that is rare in men. . . . It was magnetic." The governor's strongest praise came in a one-sentence summation: "Colonel Christian was a true Christian gentleman."

The tradition of the Christian gentleman holds a weighty place in Western thought. In the 1500s, Dutch Renaissance humanist Desiderius Erasmus Roterodamus first coined the term to describe the man who devotes himself to God and education, the perfect Christian knight. By the mid-1800s, clergy also used the expression to invoke a selfless man. Twentieth-century preachers added elements of competence and strength to the archetype. By using the "Christian gentleman" label, Cooper evoked many of the

Fig. 121. Ohio governor Myers Y. Cooper was a personal friend of George B. Christian Sr., and he reverently eulogized Christian after he passed away. (Reprinted by permission of the Ohio History Connection)

most prized aspects of American manhood. While the governor might have overemphasized his friendship with Christian in order to offer the best possible eulogy, his letter proved that he genuinely respected Christian and felt that his death was sufficiently important to merit his personal attention and accolades.[40]

The Christian children designated Fred Dombaugh as the executor of their father's estate. Christian left a very modest amount of money to his children. He was not a wealthy man at the end of his life. Each child received about $600 in cash and an equal share in their father's half of the McGruder Building. While the stock market crash in the fall of 1929 and the ensuing Great Depression seemed to affect Christian very little during his lifetime, they hit his heirs hard, because they kept the McGruder Building from turning much of a profit.[41]

Christian spent the fast-paced years of the late 1920s trying to make sense of his own life. In his writing, he worked to understand the history through which he had lived and to share this understanding with the world. Christian's relative youth and health for a veteran of the Civil War made him feel responsible for helping Marion remember its fallen soldiers. He became a spokesman for the living and the dead, and he served as a link to the heroic military feats of the past. Christian also tried to draw his family close together to cope with the death of his wife. He prepared for his own inevitable passing and tried to provide his family with the best possible scenario for settling his affairs. When Christian died, his children and grandchildren witnessed a profound outpouring of love and respect from the community, the state, and even the nation. While most recognized him for his connection to the former president, his friends identified other important character traits that they had admired. Perhaps the best record of the way his fellow Marionites viewed Christian came from a poem by Alice Showers. Showers was an acquaintance of the Christians rather than a close friend, but her short poem described the extent of Christian's relationship with the people of Marion—especially when he met them on the street. She praised his service on behalf of veterans. In her final line, Showers proclaimed that "Soldier, Christian, and Friend, he proved his worth."[42] From the governor himself to everyday acquaintances, many acknowledged the force of George B. Christian's legacy.

Colonel George C. Christian, Sr.

Daily he walked our city's streets,
Proud head erect with kindly grace;
And paused the while each friend he greets,
With handclasp true and smiling face.

We marched behind him on that day
We honored at church our soldier dead;
"For some, we are singing the swan song today,
Who knows which one?" were the words he said.

As he stood upright at the pulpit there,
Facing his Comrades in numbers so few;
Did the Master looking down on the scene so fair,
Whisper to him?" I choose to take you."

We were glad to meet him on our way.
To us, he was a much loved friend;
His greeting brightened all our day,
Must love like this come to an end?

No! His kindly spirit still is here,
Though his cheery greetings we shall miss;
Memories live in hearts of friends so true,
Of a gallant soldier such as this.

Christian in name, and in nature too,
A brave hearted soldier and true good man;
Trying ever the Master's work to do,
Keeping in mind Our Savior's plan.

Under the shade of the arching trees,
We stood as Commander Wiley said:
"I place this flag upon your breast,"
But we could not think of our friend as dead.

Still he fares on in the better land,
Greeting his friends as he did on earth;
At his resting place now we often stand,
Soldier, Christian, and Friend, he proved his worth.

Alice M. Showers
Marion, Ohio.[43]

Conclusion

"To be what we are, and to become what we are capable of becoming, is the only end of life." Robert Louis Stevenson, *Familiar Studies of Men and Books* (New York: Charles Scribner's Sons, 1895), 143.

George B. Christian Sr. lived a conspicuous life. Within his circle of family, friends, and acquaintances, he was an unforgettable force of love, loyalty, and support. To those with whom he disagreed, he served as a fierce critic. In his hometown of Marion, Ohio, Christian was known for his contribution to public life. Though he never achieved national fame, despite his longstanding relationship with Warren G. Harding, and many records of his life have been lost, Christian's biography offers a unique window for understanding the history through which he lived. The story of Christian's military service explores the relationship between the battlefield and the development of soldiers' and veterans' identities. His attempts to find a viable career path in the years after the Civil War reveal the perils of the post-war economy and the effects of the boom and bust cycles associated with the growing industrial-based financial system. Christian's initial voyage to the isolated coast of Florida in 1877 is a first-rate adventure story. In a different vein, his time as an editor with the *Marion Democratic Mirror* illustrates the duties and struggles faced by small-town newspapers and their role in promoting economic growth during the Gilded Age. He eventually became a manufacturer as he built a thriving limestone business. In addition, Christian's political adventures and his relationship with Harding reveal the nature of Ohio and national politics at the turn of the century. The Christian family developed a personal portrait of President Harding, an assuredly flawed president, but one whom they loved and defended. In the last decade of Christian's life, retirement gave him the opportunity to help construct his legacy.

George B. Christian Sr.'s lifetime extended over eight decades of some of the most dynamic years in the history of the United States. While he was alive, twenty new states joined the nation. U.S. troops fought a bloody Civil War. They violently pushed the nation's indigenous peoples onto reservations. Americans also engaged in imperial conflict in the Philippines, Cuba, Guam, and Puerto Rico. This terrible march toward the horrors of total war found one of its most shocking expressions in the trenches of the First World War.

In the years between Christian's birth in 1846 and his death in 1930, the U.S. population changed from being primarily rural to mostly urban. The country was rapidly becoming a world power. Such influence emerged out of economic, technological, and industrial growth. Many of the world's most transformative technologies were invented during Christian's lifetime. Telephones, incandescent light bulbs, motion pictures, radios, automobiles, and airplanes created economic, social, and cultural possibilities unimaginable to previous generations. Innovations in travel and communication converged with determined explorers to make the planet less vast and unknowable. By his final years, Christian lived in a world almost inconceivably different from that of his youth.

Over the same period of time, Marion expanded from a tiny village to a city. The city grew in size and population as it annexed new neighborhoods and the workers who moved into them. Its residents gradually switched from agriculture to manufacturing. Industrial development and wage work attracted chain stores, and Marion became world renowned for the production of steam shovels and other heavy machinery. By the time of Christian's death, his neighbors had access to many of the same conveniences available to residents of larger cities throughout the country. Marion never became a major metropolitan center like Chicago or Detroit, but it harnessed its industrial success to become a regional manufacturing and shipping hub. Even though many of the older residents might have bemoaned the drastic changes to the cityscape, most, like Christian, embraced modern conveniences. The Great Depression would hit the city hard, but in the meantime Marion reaped the benefits of economic growth and prosperity.

The balance Marion struck between industrial growth and adherence to small-town values made it the perfect setting for Harding's presidential campaign in 1920. The surging economy gave the city's elite the resources to host the hundreds of thousands of visitors who passed through Marion, while the city's small size and cohesiveness presented the perfect picture of the heartland that helped make Harding an attractive candidate. Over his lifetime, Christian both observed and participated in the kinds of growth that made Harding's campaign possible. In addition, his relationship with Harding as a neighbor, friend, mentor, confidant, supporter, and admirer helped him add to the nostalgia built around Harding's candidacy.

On a more personal level, Christian and his wife lived long and full lives and raised a successful family. Their son, George Christian Jr., served as Harding's secretary during the president's entire time on the national stage. In the years after Harding's death, Christian Jr. bounced around various civil service and corporate appointments until, tragically, he began to suffer early blindness. One of his sons became a successful career military officer and another became a lawyer—though neither had any children. Christian's elder daughter, Mamie, lived the rest of her life near Marion. She and her husband managed the Harding home and museum until they retired to a rest home in Springfield, Ohio, in 1948. Both of her children died early: Ruth as a girl and George as a young man. Finally, Christian's youngest daughter, Mildred, and her husband raised a family in the Marion home that had belonged to her parents. Even after her husband died of a heart attack in 1945, Mildred remained active in the public life of her beloved town. Her three children left Ohio, but Marion remained her home until 1970, when she left to live in a retirement facility closer to two of her children in Illinois.

George B. Christian Sr. lived a full and impactful life. He raised a family and found a variety of ways to make a living. Although he received little formal education beyond high school, he spent his life studying the world around him and helping those he cared for. While prone to heated debate and influenced by the prejudices of his time, Christian worked to leave a positive mark on his nation, his city, and his family. He happened to have befriended a president, but, more importantly, his life offers a profound example of someone who lived a full life and did so with gusto.

Notes

Introduction

[1] "Mass Meetings Held Sunday: Celebrate the 'Dry' Victory in Marion," *Marion (OH) Daily Mirror*, Nov. 29, 1909.

[2] Thomas R. Pegram, *Battling Demon Rum: The Struggle for Dry America, 1800–1933* (Chicago: Ivan R. Dee, 1998).

[3] K. Austin Kerr, "Organizing for Reform: The Anti-Saloon League and Innovation in Politics," *American Quarterly* 32, no. 1 (1980): 37–53; Ranjit S. Dighe, "Reversal of Fortune: The Rockefellers and the Decline of Business Support for Prohibition," *Essays in Economic & Business History* 31 (2013): 69–88.

[4] *Marion (OH) Independent*, Nov. 21, 1878; *Marion (OH) Democratic Mirror*, May 4, 1882; Warren G. Harding to Lydia Christian, Dec. 22, 1916, Warren G. Harding Papers, microfilm, roll 249, panel 32, Ohio Historical Society Archive/Library, Ohio Historical Society, Columbus, OH; Kerr, "Organizing for Reform," 39–40; "Mass Meetings Held Sunday."

[5] Howard E. Huston, "An Industrial History of Marion, Ohio, 1865–1895" (master's thesis, The Ohio State University, 1963), 24–51.

[6] Department of the Interior, *Seventh Census of the United States: 1850* (Washington, DC: GPO, 1853); Huston, "An Industrial History," 74–93.

[7] Macadam is a term that refers to crushed stone sold for a variety of purposes.

[8] Huston, "An Industrial History," 122–47.

[9] Department of the Interior, *Population of the United States in 1860: Compiled from the Original Returns of the Eighth Census Under the Direction of the Secretary of the Interior* (Washington, DC: GPO, 1864); Department of the Interior, *Ninth Census, Volume I, The Statistics of the Population of the United States* (Washington, DC: GPO, 1872); Department of the Interior, *Compendium of the Tenth Census* (Washington, DC: GPO, 1885); Department of the Interior, *Report on Population of the United States at the Eleventh Census: 1890, Part I* (Washington, DC: GPO, 1895); Census Bureau, *Fifteenth Census of the United States, 1930, Population, Volume I: Number and Distribution of Inhabitants* (Washington, DC: GPO, 1931).

Chapter 1, Roots and Branches

[1] The Isle of Man is a small island located in the Irish Sea, with Ireland to the west, Scotland to the north, England to the east, and Wales to the south. Throughout its history, the Celts, Romans, and Vikings have inhabited it. Its mixed heritage has left the people of the island with an interstitial place in the British Empire. Writer Edward Callow once stated that the island was connected geologically and geographically with Scotland, culturally and linguistically with Ireland, and politically with England. Edward Callow, *From King Orry to Queen Victoria: A Short and Concise History of the Isle of Man* (London: Elliot Stock, 1899), 6.

[2] Eunie V. Christian Stacy, *Christian of Charles City: An Account of the Antecedents and Descendants of Charles Christian of Virginia and Allied Families, Mainly Found in the Southern States* (Shreveport, LA: Insty-prints, 1982), 1–10; Michael W. Berry and Ann Arsell Wheat Hunter, "Collier and Christian of Charles City and New Kent Counties," *The Virginia Genealogist* 34, no. 2 (1990): 83–88; Kevin Frazier, "A List of the Names and Some of the Residences of the Rebel Participants in Bacon's Rebellion of 1676 in Colonial Virginia," *Rootsweb*, accessed Sep. 15, 2013, http://freepages.genealogy.rootsweb.ancestry.com/~fraz/BaconsRebels.

[3] Stuart Lee Butler, *A Guide to Virginia Militia Units in the War of 1812* (Athens, GA: Iberian Publishing Company, 1988), 34–38, 150–51.

[4] Adam Pratt, "The Cavalier in the Mind of the South, 1876–1916" (master's thesis, Louisiana State University, 2007), 2–4; John H. Christian, 1820 census, New Kent, Virginia, M33, Roll 133, page 201, image 240, last modified 2010, http://www.ancestry.com.

[5] Therese Fisher, *Vital Records of Three Burned Counties: Births, Marriages, and Deaths of King and Queen, King William, and New Kent Counties, Virginia, 1680–1860* (Bowie, MD: Heritage Books, 1995), 45–46; Beverly Fleet, *Virginia Colonial Abstracts* (Baltimore, MD: Genealogical Publishing Company, 1988), 1:603, *Marion (OH) Daily Mirror*, Apr. 30, 1874; C.B. Galbraith, ed., *History of Ohio* (Chicago: American Historical Society, 1925), 5:335–36. The portrait of the Millers is located in the True-Stengel Museum found in Marion, Ohio.

[6] Historical sources spell the name of Busby's birthplace as either Darston or Derrstown depending on the source. Both refer to the same town, which later became the city of Lewisburg, Pennsylvania. This is a correction to other confused sources such as the *Biographical Database of the United States Congress, 1775–2005*, which placed Busby's birth in Davistown, which is located on the other side of the state.

[7] The title Old Northwest refers to the territory ceded to the United States by the British in the Treaty of Paris that ended the Revolutionary War. The U.S. Congress, under the Articles of Confederation, officially created the governance structure and requirements for statehood for this territory through the Northwest Ordinance passed in 1887. The region consisted of the territory west of the Appalachians, north of the Ohio River, and east of the Mississippi River. It included parts of the present-day states of Ohio, Indiana, Michigan, Illinois, Wisconsin, and Minnesota. The territory was named for its orientation in reference to the original U.S. colonies as well as the mythical Northwest Passage that promised to offer access to the Pacific Ocean. Northwestern University in Chicago still references this antiquated regional name.

[8] Charles Lanman, ed., *Dictionary of the United States Congress: a Manual of Reference for the Legislator and Statesman* (Washington, DC: GPO, 1864), 63; I. H. Mauser, *Centennial History of Lewisburg: Containing Also a Chronological History of Union County,* (Lewisburg, PA: self published, 1886); Soldier's Certificate No. 792,832, George B. Christian, Private, Company B, Fifth Battalion Ohio Cavalry; Case Files of Approved Pension Applications of Veterans Who Served in the Army and Navy Mainly in the Civil War and the War with Spain, 1861-1934, Civil War and Later Pension Files, Records of the Department of Veterans Affairs, Record Group 15, National Archives I, Washington, DC; James R. Averill, *Fort Meigs: A Condensed History of the Most Important Military Point in the Northwest, Together with Scenes Incident Connected with the Sieges of 1813, and a Minute Description of the Old Fort and Its Surroundings, as They Now Appear* (Toledo, OH: Blade Printing and Paper Co., 1886), 22–35.

[9] Soldier's Certificate No. 792,832; Averill, *Fort Meigs*, 22–35; *Marion (OH) Independent*, Aug. 9, 1883.

[10] Tacy A. Arledge, "Some Ross County, Ohio Records," *The Fountain . . . Welch-Welsh-Walsh: A Surname Newsletter* 15, no. 2 (1998): 37–38; Iris Carter Jones, "The Children of Zachariah Welch of Ohio," *The Fountain . . . Welch-Welsh-Walsh: A Surname Newsletter* 15, no. 3 (1998): 50–51.

[11] Leggett, Conaway, & Co., *History of Marion County: Containing a History of the County; Its Townships, Towns, Churches, Schools, Etc.; General and Local Statistics; Military Record; Portraits of Early Settlers and Prominent Men; History of the Northwest Territory; History of Ohio; Miscellaneous Matters, Etc., Etc.* (Chicago: Leggett, Conaway & Co., 1883), 242–43.

[12] Leggett, Conaway, & Co., *History of Marion County*, 311–40.

[13] The Fugitive Slave Act of 1850 required local law enforcement officers to return escaped slaves to their masters. It also compelled people in free states to cooperate with southern efforts to retrieve runaway slaves.

14 "32nd Congress (1851–1853)," Office of the Historian of the House of Representatives, *History, Art, & Archives: United States House of Representatives*, accessed Sep. 30, 2013, http://history.house.gov/Congressional-Overview/Profiles/32nd/.

15 Leggett, Conaway, & Co., *History of Marion County,* 242–43; *Marion (OH) Weekly Star,* Feb. 7, 1891; "Miscegenation," *Marion (OH) Democratic Mirror,* Feb. 18, 1869.

16 Historians have designated the bank as the Second Bank of the United States to distinguish it from the First Bank of the United States, which was closed during the presidency of Thomas Jefferson.

17 Leggett, Conaway, & Co., *History of Marion County,* 560–61; Alfred James Morrison, *The Beginnings of Public Education in Virginia, 1776–1860: Study of Secondary Schools in Relation to the State Literary Fund* (Richmond, VA: Superintendent of Public Printing, 1917), 141–42; Edward E. Baptist, "Toxic Debt, Liar Loans, and Securitized Human Beings: The Panic of 1837 and the Fate of Slavery," *Common-Place* 10, no. 3 (2010), http://www.common-place-archives.org/vol-10/no-03/baptist.

18 Baptist, "Toxic Debt."

19 Leggett, Conaway, & Co., *History of Marion County,* 242–43; Galbraith, *History of Ohio,* 335–36.

20 John Haller, *The History of American Homeopathy: The Academic Years, 1820-1935* (New York: Haworth Press, 2005), 1–44.

21 Leggett, Conaway, & Co., *History of Marion County,* 242–43; John M. Christian, 1850 census, Union, Madison County, Ohio, M432, Roll 706, page 1865A, image 375, last modified Sep. 17, 2013, http://www.ancestry.com

22 "Democratic County Convention," *Marion (OH) Democratic Mirror,* Sep. 16, 1858; "Meeting of the Dem. Cen. Committee," *Marion (OH) Democratic Mirror,* Sep. 29, 1859; "Ratification Meeting, At the Court House, July 7th," *Marion (OH) Democratic Mirror,* Jul. 12, 1860; "Democratic Club at Big Island," *Marion (OH) Democratic Mirror,* Aug. 2, 1860; "Dr. J.M. Christian," *Marion (OH) Democratic Mirror,* Oct. 4, 1860; "Meeting at Waldo," *Marion (OH) Democratic Mirror,* Oct. 11, 1860.

23 "Knights of the Golden Circle," *Lima (OH) Allen County Democrat,* Oct. 9, 1861.

24 Ibid.; The term filibuster came from the Spanish word *filibustero,* which referred to piracy. In the 1850s and 1860s the term became synonymous with Southern adventures into Latin America that tried to capture additional territory for the expansion of slavery. One famous filibusterer was John Quitman, who attempted to lead an expedition to conquer Cuba in 1850. Perhaps the most famous was William Walker, who attempted to conquer Mexico in 1853 and Nicaragua in 1855. The current legislative use of the term came later and co-opted the term to criticize the hijacking of debate.

25 Frank L. Klement, "Ohio and the Knights of the Golden Circle: The Evolution of a Civil War Myth," *Cincinnati Historical Society Bulletin* 32 (Spring-Summer 1974): 7–11.

26 Ibid., 12–13; "Knights of the Golden Circle"; "A 'Castle' of the Knights of the G.C. Arrested by the U.S. Marshal—The Records Seized—A 'Commander' Taken," *Burlington (IA) Daily Hawk Eye,* Oct. 15, 1861.

27 "A 'Castle'"; Klement, "Ohio and the Knights," 12–13.

28 Klement, "Ohio and the Knights," 12–13; "Knights of the Golden Circle."

29 "Carson League," *Marion (OH) Democratic Mirror,* Jul. 29, 1858; "Democratic Corporation Nominations," *Marion (OH) Democratic Mirror,* Apr. 2, 1868; "Election in Marion County," *Marion (OH) Democratic Mirror,* Apr. 9, 1868; "Election of School Directors," *Marion (OH) Democratic Mirror,* May 7, 1868; "Democratic State Convention," *Marion (OH) Democratic Mirror,* Jul. 15, 1869.

30 *Marion (OH) Democratic Mirror,* Jan. 20, 1876.

31 *Marion (OH) Independent,* Jul. 31, 1879; *Marion (OH) Independent,* Jul. 24, 1879; *Marion (OH) Democratic Mirror,* Feb. 3, 1876; *Marion (OH) Democratic Mirror,* May 9, 1878.

32 "Democratic County Convention," *Marion (OH) Independent,* Aug. 21, 1879; *Marion (OH) Democratic Mirror,* Jul. 6, 1882.

33 "Remarks of Rev. E. B. Raffensperger at the Funeral of Doctor J. M. Christian, June 30th, 1882," *Marion (OH) Democratic Mirror*, Jul. 6, 1882.

34 *Marion (OH) Democratic Mirror*, Jul. 13, 1882.

35 Department of the Interior, *Population of the United States in 1860: Compiled from the Original Returns of the Eighth Census Under the Direction of the Secretary of the Interior* (Washington, DC: GPO, 1864), 386; "School Boys' Reunion: The Boys of the Grammar School of 1859 Hold an Impromptu Reunion," *Marion (OH) Daily Star*, Feb. 21, 1889; "Re-Union of Grammar School Boys Who Attended School from 1857 to 1860," *Marion (OH) Democratic Mirror*, Sep. 13, 1883; "Programs of the Closing Exercises of the Marion High School, for the Winter Term of 1860," *Marion (OH) Democratic Mirror*, Mar. 29, 1860.

36 William Daniel Overman, *Ohio Town Names* (Chicago: Atlantic Press, 1958), 54; Leggett, Conaway, & Co., *History of Marion County*, 796–97.

37 "Married," *Marion (OH) Democratic Mirror*, Oct. 21, 1869; "Reminiscent: John R. Morris Tells a Story of the Day of Fleeing Slaves," *Marion (OH) Daily Star*, May 31, 1897; "Relics of Mound Builders," *Marion (OH) Daily Mirror*, Jul. 30, 1874.

38 Linda K. Kerber, "Separate Spheres, Female Worlds, Women's Place: The Rhetoric of Women's History," *Journal of American History* 75, no. 1 (1988): 9–39.

39 Ibid.

40 *Marion (OH) Democratic Mirror*, Dec. 25, 1890; *Marion (OH) Democratic Mirror*, Mar. 5, 1891.

41 Eric Homberger, *Mrs. Astor's New York: Money and Social Power in a Gilded Age* (New Haven: Yale University Press, 2002), 38; *Marion (OH) Daily Mirror*, Dec. 8, 1909; *Marion (OH) Daily Mirror*, Dec. 9, 1909.

42 While the historical record offers no reason for this nickname, it might have referenced some literary character or a visible public or historical figure.

43 Warren G. Harding to Lydia Christian, Dec. 22, 1916, Warren G. Harding Papers, microfilm, roll 249, panel 32, Ohio Historical Society Archive/Library, Ohio Historical Society, Columbus, OH; Warren G. Harding to Lydia Christian, Aug. 8, 1907, quoted in Edwin K. Gross, *Vindication for Mr. Normalcy* (Buffalo, NY: The American Society for the Faithful Recording of History, 1965), 23; Warren G. Harding to Lydia Christian, Feb. 14, 1909, Roberts Family Library, Sycamore, IL; Warren G. Harding to Lydia Christian, Dec. 25, 1920, Roberts Family Library, Sycamore, IL.

44 Warren G. Harding to Lydia Christian, Dec. 25, 1920, Roberts Family Library, Sycamore, IL.

45 George B. Christian Sr. to George B. Christian Jr., Nov. 8, 1928, Warren G. Harding Papers, microfilm, roll 249, panels 685–86, Ohio Historical Society Archive/Library, Ohio Historical Society, Columbus, OH; Marion County Deed Records, Oct. 27, 1895, 139:140, County Recorder, Marion, OH.

46 Thomas Edward Powell, ed., *The Democratic Party of the State of Ohio: A Comprehensive History of Democracy in Ohio from 1803 to 1912, Including Democratic Legislation in the State, the Campaigns of a Century, History of Democratic Conventions, the Reverses and Successes of the Party, Etc.,* (Columbus: Ohio Publishing Co., 1913), 2:129–30; "Marriage Altar: Miss Stella Farrar and George B. Christian Are Wed," *Marion (OH) Daily Star*, Jun. 10, 1897.

47 *Marion (OH) Democratic Mirror*, Jun. 20, 1894; "Strong Competition in Stone Business: George B. Christian Jr., Quits the Ohio & Western to Join the Allied Christian Interests," *Marion (OH) Weekly Star*, Jun. 26, 1909.

[48] "Heart and Hand: United Amid a Beautiful Marriage Ceremony, Dombaugh-Christian Nuptials," *Marion (OH) Daily Star*, Oct. 8, 1897; "Only Daughter Called by Death," *Marion (OH) Star*, May 13, 1905; *Marion (OH) Daily Mirror*, Jul. 1, 1909; George B. Christian Jr. to J. F. Dombaugh, Oct. 30, 1931, Warren G. Harding Papers, microfilm, roll 249, panels 685–86, Ohio Historical Society Archive/Library, Ohio Historical Society, Columbus, OH.

[49] *Marion (OH) Democratic Mirror*, Feb. 12, 1891; *Marion (OH) Democratic Mirror*, Jan. 23, 1895; *Marion (OH) Democratic Mirror*, May 7, 1901; *Marion (OH) Democratic Mirror*, May 28, 1901; *Marion (OH) Daily Mirror*, Jan. 4, 1909; *Marion (OH) Daily Mirror*, Apr. 4, 1911; "A Military Wedding Late This Afternoon: Miss Mildred Christian and Captain Roberts, Principals," *Marion (OH) Daily Mirror*, Apr. 20, 1918; Mark Walston, "The Reincarnation of National Park Seminary," *Bethesda Magazine* (January–February 2010), http://www.bethesdamagazine.com/Bethesda-Magazine/January-February-2010/The-Reincarnation-of-National-Park-Seminary.

[50] "A Military Wedding"; June Roseberry, "People We're Proud to Know: Mrs. Chester C. Roberts," *Marion (OH) Star*, Jun. 5, 1958.

Chapter 2, Christian Plays the Soldier

[1] James M. McPherson, *Battle Cry of Freedom: The Civil War Era* (New York: Oxford University Press, 1988), 858.

[2] Edison H. Thomas, *John Hunt Morgan and His Raiders* (Lexington: University of Kentucky Press, 1985), 72–86; George B. Christian Sr., "The Fifth Independent Battalion Ohio Volunteer Cavalry," in Howard Aston, ed. *History and Roster of the Fourth and Fifth Independent Battalions and Thirteenth Regiment Ohio Cavalry Volunteers: Their Battles and Skirmishes, Roster of the Dead, Etc.* (Columbus, OH: Press of Fred J. Hber, 1902), appendix, 34–36.

[3] "Marion County, with 1,775 Men in Ranks, Had Notable Civil War Record, Local Veteran Relates," *Marion (OH) Star*, Apr. 18, 1928; David M. Rosen, *Armies of the Young: Child Soldiers in War and Terrorism* (New Brunswick, NJ: Rutgers University Press, 2005), 5–6.

[4] "Marion County, with 1,775 Men in Ranks."

[5] "New Year's Day Reminds Marion War Vet of 25-Below Zero Blast 66 Years Ago: Union Troops Caught in Cold as Mercury Drops 93 Degrees in 24 Hours," *Marion (OH) Star*, Jan. 1, 1930; Ohio Meteorological Bureau, *Sixth Annual Report of the Ohio Meteorological Bureau* (Columbus, OH: Westbote Company State Printers, 1889), 211; John Uri Lloyd, *Stringtown on the Pike: A Tale of Northernmost Kentucky* (New York: Dodd, Mead, and Company, 1901), 81–88.

[6] Soldier's Certificate No. 792,832.

[7] James David Hacker, "The Human Cost of War: White Population in the United States, 1850–1880" (PhD diss., University of Minnesota, 1999), 13.

[8] Christian, "The Fifth Independent," appendix, 37.

[9] "Ten Marion Boys: As They Were When Cruel War Was Raging," *Marion (OH) Star*, May 29, 1897.

[10] Christian, "The Fifth Independent," appendix. 37.

[11] In the Battle of the Crater, General Ambrose Burnside attempted to blow a hole in the Confederate defenses of the area around Richmond. Both sides were deeply entrenched and fighting had almost reached a standstill that would become more common during World War I. This first attempt at breaching enemy lines with munitions failed miserably as Union troops charged forward into the hole created by the explosion and were devastated by the Confederate soldiers looking down on them; Christian, "The Fifth Independent," appendix, 37; "Ten Marion Boys."; "Marion County, with 1,775 Men in Ranks."

[12] Soldier's Certificate No. 792,832.

[13] "Army Pensions: Instructions and Forms to Be Observed in Applying for Them, Under the Act of July 14, 1862," *New York Times*, Aug. 12, 1862.

[14] Soldier's Certificate No. 792,832.

[15] *Marion (OH) Democratic Mirror*, Aug. 26, 1880; *Marion (OH) Democratic Mirror*, Apr. 24, 1879; *Marion (OH) Democratic Mirror*, Jul. 29, 1880.

[16] Robert Burns Beath, *History of the Grand Army of the Republic* (New York: Bryan, Taylor, & Company, 1888), 45; "Marion County, with 1,775 Men in Ranks"; David B. Blight, *Race and Reunion: The Civil War in American Memory* (Cambridge, MA: The Belknap Press of Harvard University Press, 2001), 71–73.

[17] Christian, "Fifth Battalion Events," in Aston, *History and Roster*, appendix, 55.

[18] "Cooper Post Memorial Exercises Held Today: Colonel George B. Christian Pays Dead Beautiful Tribute, Not Forgetting to Praise the Living," *Marion (OH) Daily Star*, Dec. 6, 1915.

[19] William Henry Glasson, *History of Military Pension Legislation in the United States* (New York: Columbia University Press, 1900), 114–15; Soldier's Certificate No. 792,832.

[20] Soldier's Certificate No. 792,832.

[21] Francis George Gosling, *Before Freud: Neurasthenia and the American Medical Community, 1870–1910* (Urbana: University of Illinois Press, 1987), 82–87.

[22] Ibid.

[23] Soldier's Certificate No. 792,832.

[24] Ibid.

[25] Ibid.

Chapter 3, Christian Becomes the Colonel

[1] Soldier's Certificate No. 792,832.

[2] Leggett, Conaway, & Co., *History of Marion County*, 202, 377; Huston, "An Industrial History," 79–93; Mark Twain and Charles Dudley Warner, *The Gilded Age: A Tale of Today* (Hartford, CT: American Publishing Company, 1880).

[3] Twain scholars share the belief that Sellers was Twain's creation invented for the parts of the novel that he wrote.

[4] Lucius M. Lampton, "Colonel Sellers," in *The Mark Twain Encyclopedia*, ed. J. R. LeMaster and James Darrell Wilson (New York: Routledge, 1993), 668–70.

[5] Richard White, *Gentlemen Engineers: The Working Lives of Frank and Walter Shanly* (Toronto: University of Toronto Press, 1999), 28–35.

[6] Leggett, Conaway, & Co., *History of Marion County*, 242–43; *Marion County Commissioners' Journal*, 1867, 6:46–50, Ohio Historical Society Archive/Library, Ohio Historical Society, Columbus, OH.

[7] "Poultry and Game," *Marion (OH) Democratic Mirror*, Dec. 6, 1866; Marion County Mortgage Records, Jan. 8, 1870, 6:488, County Recorder, Marion, OH; Marion County Deed Records, Mar. 10, 1868, 36:118–20, County Recorder, Marion, OH; Marion County Deed Records, Jan. 21, 1871, 39:285–86, County Recorder, Marion, OH; Marion County Deed Records, Mar. 1869, 35:526, County Recorder, Marion, OH.

[8] "A Friend," *Marion (OH) Democratic Mirror*, Mar. 4, 1869; "The Infirmary," *Marion (OH) Democratic Mirror*, Jul. 14, 1870.

9   *Marion (OH) Democratic Mirror*, Mar. 4, 1869; *Marion (OH) Democratic Mirror*, Apr. 8, 1869; *Marion (OH) Democratic Mirror*, Oct. 14, 1869; "Married," *Marion (OH) Democratic Mirror*, Oct. 21, 1869; *Marion (OH) Democratic Mirror*, Jun. 1, 1871.

10 "Co-Partnership," *Marion (OH) Democratic Mirror*, Jan. 12, 1871; George W. King, *The Marion Steam Shovel Company Family: History, Biography, Autobiography* (New York: The Century History Company, 1915), 91–94.

11 "Lumber," *Marion (OH) Democratic Mirror*, Jul. 13, 1871.

12 "The Berwickian Backswoodsman," *Marion (OH) Daily Mirror*, Jan. 18, 1872.

13 Marion County Deed Records, Apr. 18, 1871, 39:481–82, County Recorder, Marion, OH; Robert Sahr, "Inflation Conversion Factors for Years 1774 to Estimated 2024, in Dollars of Recent Years," *Oregon State University Political Science Department*, accessed Apr. 22, 2014, http://oregonstate.edu/cla/polisci/sahr/sahr; *Marion (OH) Democratic Mirror*, Apr. 27, 1871; Marion County Mortgage Records, May 28, 1874, 9:109–10, County Recorder, Marion, OH; George B. Christian Sr. to G.H. Griswald, Jan. 16, 1874, Griswold Family Papers, MSS 193, Folder 1870–1879, Worthington Historical Society, Worthington, OH; Marion County Deed Records, May 23, 1874, 42:428–29, County Recorder, Marion, OH; "Transfer," *Marion (OH) Daily Mirror*, Jun. 18, 1874; *Marion (OH) Democratic Mirror*, Oct. 15, 1875.

14 *Marion (OH) Daily Mirror*, May 9, 1872; *Marion (OH) Daily Mirror*, Jun. 26, 1873; *Marion (OH) Daily Mirror*, Jan. 1, 1874; *Marion (OH) Democratic Mirror*, Mar. 12, 1874; *Marion (OH) Democratic Mirror*, Aug. 10, 1876.

15 "George B. Christian," *Marion (OH) Democratic Mirror*, Jan. 22, 1874.

16 "County Surveyor," *Marion (OH) Democratic Mirror*, Aug. 14, 1873; "Geo. B. Christian," *Marion (OH) Daily Mirror*, Aug. 21, 1873; *Marion (OH) Daily Mirror*, Oct. 23, 1873; *Marion (OH) Daily Mirror*, Oct. 30, 1873; *Marion County Commissioners' Journal*, 1867, 6:313, 324–25, 367–69, 423–28, Ohio Historical Society Archives/Library, Ohio Historical Society, Columbus, OH; "Notice to Contractors: Road Builders Take Notice," *Marion (OH) Democratic Mirror*, Apr. 23, 1874.

17 Marion County Mortgage Records, Sep. 14, 1874, 9:206–7, County Recorder, Marion, OH.

18 "Marion's Latest Enterprise," *Marion (OH) Democratic Mirror*, Dec. 10, 1874; *Marion (OH) Democratic Mirror*, Jan. 7, 1875; *Marion (OH) Daily Star*, Jan. 14, 1875; *Marion (OH) Democratic Mirror*, Dec. 9, 1875.

19 "Greenhorns Wanted: A Proposition That Will Open Their Eyes," *Cincinnati Post*, Oct. 19, 1883.

20 It is unknown whether this was a print of Raphael's famous painting or some other depiction.

21 "The Art-ful Dodger: The Way He Cultivates a Taste for the Beautiful, Thereby Filling His Coffers with Cash," *Cincinnati Enquirer*, May 2, 1878.

22 George B. Christian Sr., "Our European Letter," *Marion (OH) Democratic Mirror*, Jun. 8, 1876.

23 "Gone to Europe," *Marion (OH) Democratic Mirror*, Mar. 4, 1876; Christian, "Our European Letter," Jun. 8, 1876.

24 George B. Christian Sr., "Our European Letter: An Interesting and Descriptive Letter from G.B.C.," *Marion (OH) Democratic Mirror*, Jun. 15, 1876.

25 George B. Christian Sr. to Warren G. Harding, Sep. 27, 1918, Warren G. Harding Papers, microfilm, roll 20, panels 916–17, Ohio Historical Society Archive/Library, Ohio Historical Society, Columbus, OH.

26 "Guy Webber Dead: A Famous Former Marionite Passes Away at a Hospital in New York City," *Marion (OH) Star*, Oct. 20, 1900.

Chapter 4, A Trip to Summerland

[1] Historians generally recognize the election of Rutherford B. Hayes in 1876–77 as the end of Reconstruction in the South.

[2] Jeffrey Alan Melton, *Mark Twain, Travel Books, and Tourism: The Tide of a Great Popular Movement* (Tuscaloosa: University of Alabama Press, 2002), 16.

[3] Ibid., 16–58.

[4] George B. Christian Sr., "Correspondence: A Trip to Summerland," *Marion (OH) Democratic Mirror*, Feb. 8, 1877.

[5] Melton, *Mark Twain*, 16–58.

[6] Galbraith, *History of Ohio*, 5:335. Unfortunately, Christian's memoirs, if they evolved beyond the planning stages, have not survived.

[7] Hoover easily defeated Smith in 1928 and carried Florida. On the other hand, he lost in many Southern states which remained a Democratic stronghold.

[8] Christian, "Correspondence: A Trip."

[9] Ibid.

[10] George B. Christian Sr., "A Trip to Summerland," *Marion (OH) Democratic Mirror*, Feb. 15, 1877. Christian's comments here bear significant resemblance to the ideas of Theodore Roosevelt almost twenty-five years later. Both seemed to be influenced by the evolutionary theories of Jean-Baptist Lamarck, who argued that species evolved through the inheritance of acquired characteristics.

[11] Ibid.

[12] Ibid.

[13] Ibid.; William B. Astor Sr. was one of the richest men in the United States, with a family fortune that he had expanded through New York real estate investment.

[14] George B. Christian Sr., *My Lost Millions* (Marion, OH: Marion Printing Company, 1926), 6–8; George B. Christian Sr., "A Trip to Summerland," *Marion (OH) Democratic Mirror*, Feb. 22, 1877.

[15] Christian, "A Trip," Feb. 22, 1877.

[16] Ibid.; Christian, *Millions*, 7. The parakeet in question was probably the Carolina Parakeet, the only such bird native to North America, which has since become extinct.

[17] Christian, *Millions*, 10–11.

[18] See Chapter 1, note 23.

[19] George B. Christian Sr., "A Trip to Summerland," *Marion (OH) Democratic Mirror*, Mar. 1, 1877.

[20] These coastal islands today serve as the location for NASA's Cape Canaveral facility.

[21] Christian, *Millions*, 11–12.

[22] Ibid., 13–14.

[23] George B. Christian Sr., "A Trip to Summerland," *Marion (OH) Democratic Mirror*, Mar. 8, 1877.

[24] Christian, *Millions*, 15–16; George B. Christian, Sr., "A Trip to Summerland," *Marion (OH) Democratic Mirror*, Mar. 8, 1877.

[25] Christian, *Millions*, 19–21. The story perhaps sounds a little exaggerated, but such is the nature of fish stories.

[26] Ibid., 22–23.

[27] The title *My Lost Millions* referred to the opportunity Christian had missed to invest in Florida land during his first trip to the state. More than once during his life, Christian bemoaned his failure to invest. He felt that he had missed out on securing a fortune.

Chapter 5, The Mirror Man

1   W. David Sloan and Lisa Mullikin Parcell, eds., *American Journalism: History, Principles, and Practice* (Jefferson, NC: MacFarland and Co., 2002), 361–64.

2   *Marion (OH) Democratic Mirror,* Mar. 16, 1882.

3   *Marion (OH) Democratic Mirror,* Mar. 9, 1882.

4   The Union Pacific Company had constructed the western side of the transcontinental railroad, and its problems revealed organizational weaknesses in the entire industry.

5   Eric Foner, *Reconstruction: America's Unfinished Revolution, 1863–1877* (New York: Harper and Row Publishers, 1988), 512–15.

6   The First Party System refers to the divide between Jefferson's Democratic Republicans and Hamilton's Federalists. This period ended when the Federalists fell apart after the War of 1812, ushering in the Era of Good Feelings under James Monroe. The Second Party System entails the polarities between the Jacksonian Democrats and the Whigs that prevailed until the disintegration of the Whig Party in the years leading up to the Civil War. The Third Party system refers to the rivalry between the Democratic and Republican Parties that emerged in the wake of the Civil War.

7   Michael E. McGerr, *The Decline of Popular Politics: The American North, 1865–1928* (New York: Oxford University Press, 1986), 14.

8   Ibid.

9   "Business Notice," *Marion (OH) Democratic Mirror,* Aug. 17, 1876.

10   *Marion (OH) Democratic Mirror,* Jan. 18, 1877; "The Bogus Compromise," *Marion (OH) Independent,* Jan. 25, 1877; *Marion (OH) Democratic Mirror,* Feb. 1, 1877; *Marion (OH) Democratic Mirror,* Mar. 8, 1877; *Marion (OH) Independent,* Feb. 15, 1877.

11   *Marion (OH) Independent,* Mar. 22, 1877; Leggett, Conaway, & Company, *History of Marion County,* 422–24.

12   *Marion (OH) Democratic Mirror,* Jan. 18, 1877; Leggett, Conaway, & Co., *History of Marion* County, 422–24.

13   *Oxford Dictionary,* 2nd ed., s.v. "yellow dog."

14   "Charity," *Marion (OH) Democratic Mirror,* Apr. 12, 1877; *Marion (OH) Independent,* Apr. 19, 1877; "That Yellow Dog," *Marion (OH) Democratic Mirror,* Apr. 26, 1877; "That Yellow Dog Again," *Marion (OH) Independent,* May 3, 1877; "That 'Yellow Dog' Lie," *Marion (OH) Democratic Mirror,* May 10, 1877; *Marion (OH) Independent,* May 17, 1877; *Marion (OH) Democratic Mirror,* May 27, 1877.

15   Foner, *Reconstruction,* 583–85; *Marion (OH) Independent,* Aug. 9, 1877; *Marion (OH) Democratic Mirror,* Jul. 26, 1877.

16   Kathy Foreman Griffith, *Home Town News: William Allen White and the Emporia Gazette* (New York: Oxford University Press, 1989), 6.

17   "Our Chances for a New Railroad," *Marion (OH) Independent,* May 16, 1878.

18   "Card—Change," *Marion (OH) Democratic Mirror,* Oct. 31, 1878. The "we" in this quotation is the royal we which means that Newcomer thinks his position as leader of the paper and its partisans merits a plural pronoun.

19   Leggett, Conaway, & Co., *History of Marion* County, 429; *Marion (OH) Independent,* Nov. 7, 1878; *Marion (OH) Democratic Mirror,* Nov. 14, 1878.

20   "Opera House Meeting," *Marion (OH) Democratic Mirror,* Nov. 28, 1878; "Communicated," *Marion (OH) Daily Star,* Dec. 2, 1878; "To the People of Marion," *Marion (OH) Democratic Mirror,* Dec. 5, 1878.

21   *Marion (OH) Independent,* Jan. 30, 1879; *Marion (OH) Independent,* Feb. 13, 1879.

[22] "Fourth of July Meeting," *Marion (OH) Independent*, May 22, 1879.

[23] *Marion (OH) Independent*, Jul. 24, 1879; *Marion (OH) Independent*, Aug. 7, 1879; *Marion (OH) Independent*, Sep. 18, 1979; *Marion (OH) Democratic Mirror*, Sep. 25, 1879; *Marion (OH) Daily Star*, Oct. 4, 1879.

[24] *Marion (OH) Independent*, Nov. 21, 1878; *Marion (OH) Independent*, Sep. 25, 1879.

[25] *Marion (OH) Independent*, Dec. 25, 1879; James C. Mohr, *Abortion in America: The Origins and Evolution of National Policy* (New York: Oxford University Press, 1978), 147–225.

[26] *Marion (OH) Democratic Mirror*, Jan. 1, 1880; *Marion (OH) Independent*, Jan. 8, 1880; *Marion (OH) Independent*, Jan. 15, 1880; *Marion (OH) Democratic Mirror*, Jan. 22, 1880.

[27] *Marion (OH) Independent*, Jun. 10, 1880.

[28] *Marion (OH) Democratic Mirror*, Jun. 3, 1880; *Marion (OH) Democratic Mirror*, Jun. 17, 1880.

[29] *Marion (OH) Democratic Mirror*, Feb. 5, 1880; "Taxes—Who Pays the Taxes," *Marion (OH) Democratic Mirror*, Feb. 26, 1880; *Marion (OH) Independent*, Feb. 26, 1880; *Marion (OH) Democratic Mirror*, Apr. 28, 1881.

[30] *Marion (OH) Democratic Mirror*, May 20, 1880.

[31] *Marion (OH) Democratic Mirror*, May 27, 1880. Isaac Walton was a well-known sixteenth-century English writer who wrote the *Compleat Angler*, an early manuscript that explored the joys of fishing. Izaak (or Isaac) Walton, *The Complete Angler; or, Contemplative Man's Recreation, Being a Discourse on Rivers, Fishponds, Fish, and Fishing* (London: Henry Washbourne, 1842).

[32] *Marion (OH) Democratic Mirror*, Apr. 22, 1880.

[33] *Marion (OH) Democratic Mirror*, Aug. 12, 1880; *Marion (OH) Democratic Mirror*, Dec. 16, 1880; *Marion (OH) Democratic Mirror*, Dec. 23, 1880; *Marion (OH) Democratic Mirror*, Mar. 10, 1881; *Marion (OH) Democratic Mirror*, Jul. 2, 1881; *Marion (OH) Democratic Mirror*, Mar. 22, 1883; Leggett, Conaway, & Co., *History of Marion County*. The company indeed ended up publishing the history in 1883.

[34] *Marion (OH) Democratic Mirror*, Apr. 22, 1880; Vincent P. De Santis, *The Shaping of Modern America, 1877–1920*, 3rd ed. (New York: Harlan Davidson, 1973), 52–53.

[35] *Marion (OH) Democratic Mirror*, Jul. 1, 1880; *Marion (OH) Independent*, Jul. 15, 1880; *Marion (OH) Democratic Mirror*, Aug. 26, 1880; *Marion (OH) Democratic Mirror*, Sep. 2, 1880; *Marion (OH) Democratic Mirror*, Oct. 28, 1880.

[36] *Marion (OH) Independent*, Jul. 15, 1880; *Marion (OH) Independent*, Jul. 22, 1880; *Marion (OH) Independent*, Aug. 5, 1880; *Marion (OH) Independent*, Aug. 26, 1880; *Marion (OH) Independent*, Sep. 2, 1880; *Marion (OH) Independent*, Sep. 16, 1880.

[37] *Marion (OH) Democratic Mirror*, Nov. 4, 1880.

[38] "Hancock Hung in Effigy," *Marion (OH) Democratic Mirror*, Nov. 11, 1880; *Marion (OH) Independent*, Nov. 25, 1880; *Marion (OH) Independent*, Nov. 4, 1880.

[39] "Announcement," *Marion (OH) Democratic Mirror*, Dec. 2, 1880.

[40] *Marion (OH) Independent*, Dec. 23, 1880.

[41] *Marion (OH) Democratic Mirror*, Dec. 23, 1880.

[42] *Marion (OH) Democratic Mirror*, Dec. 2, 1880; *Marion (OH) Independent*, Dec. 30, 1880.

[43] One of the major issues facing the rapidly industrializing nation involved the role of tariffs in U.S. economic and diplomatic relations. Republicans generally supported higher tariffs as a protection for U.S. industries while Democrats favored lower tariffs in order to foster agricultural exports and keep the cost of produced goods low in the United States.

[44] *Marion (OH) Independent*, Dec. 23, 1880.

[45] *Marion (OH) Democratic Mirror*, Jan. 6, 1881. Christian's use of the term *abortion* in this context referred not to the act of prematurely ending a pregnancy, but to a lack of coherent thought or argument. Christian wanted to portray his rival as a Neanderthal.

[46] *Marion (OH) Democratic Mirror*, Jan. 20, 1881.

[47] *Marion (OH) Independent*, Oct. 28, 1880; *Marion (OH) Independent*, Jan 13, 1881.

[48] By patriarchy, I mean the system of male dominated households in the antebellum world.

[49] *Marion (OH) Democratic Mirror*, Sep. 30, 1880; Gail Bederman, *Manliness and Civilization: A Cultural History of Gender and Race in the United States, 1880–1917* (Chicago: University of Chicago Press, 1996), 5–20; *Marion (OH) Independent*, Feb. 10, 1881.

[50] *Marion (OH) Democratic Mirror*, Jan. 20, 1881; *Marion (OH) Democratic Mirror*, Mar. 10, 1881; *Marion (OH) Democratic Mirror*, May 26, 1881; *Marion (OH) Democratic Mirror*, Feb. 17, 1881.

[51] *Marion (OH) Democratic Mirror*, Feb. 3, 1881.

[52] *Marion (OH) Democratic Mirror*, Apr. 14, 1881; "New Court House," *Marion (OH) Democratic Mirror*, Feb. 10, 1881; "Opera-House and Water-Works," *Marion (OH) Democratic Mirror*, Feb. 17, 1881; *Marion (OH) Democratic Mirror*, Jan. 27, 1881.

[53] *Marion (OH) Democratic Mirror*, Jun. 23, 1881; *Marion (OH) Democratic Mirror*, Jul. 14, 1881; "A Visit to North Land," *Marion (OH) Democratic Mirror*, Jul. 21, 1881; "A Visit to North Land," *Marion (OH) Democratic Mirror*, Jul. 28, 1881.

[54] The Stalwarts were a faction of the Republican Party who opposed ending the policies and priorities of Reconstruction. They also opposed civil service reform and free trade. At the 1880 Republican National Convention, the so-called "half-breeds" opposed the Stalwarts. Longtime leaders of the Republican Party gave half-breeds their nickname because they were perceived as only half Republican. The half-breeds, with whom Garfield sympathized, favored civil service reform and reconciliation with the South.

[55] *Marion (OH) Democratic Mirror*, Jul. 7, 1881; *Marion (OH) Independent*, Jul. 7, 1881; *Marion (OH) Democratic Mirror*, Sep. 1, 1881; Allan Peskin, *Garfield: A Biography* (Kent, OH: Kent State University, 1978), 582–614; "Apologizing for Guiteau," *Marion (OH) Independent*, Nov. 17, 1881.

[56] "Citizens' Memorial Meeting," *Marion (OH) Independent*, Sep. 22, 1881; *Marion (OH) Democratic Mirror*, Sep. 22, 1881; "The Election," *Marion (OH) Democratic Mirror*, Oct. 20, 1881; *Marion (OH) Democratic Mirror*, Dec. 8, 1881.

[57] *Marion (OH) Democratic Mirror*, Nov. 3, 1881; *Marion (OH) Democratic Mirror*, Nov. 24, 1881; "$2,000 Reward," *Marion (OH) Democratic Mirror*, Dec. 1, 1881; *Marion (OH) Democratic Mirror*, Dec. 8, 1881.

[58] *Marion (OH) Democratic Mirror*, May 4, 1882; *Marion (OH) Democratic Mirror*, Jun. 22, 1882; *Marion (OH) Democratic Mirror*, Jul. 6, 1882; *Marion (OH) Democratic Mirror*, Jul. 13, 1882.

[59] James Vaughan, "First Words," *Marion (OH) Democratic Mirror*, Sep. 7, 1882.

Chapter 6, The Rise and Fall of a Limestone Tycoon

[1] Andrew Carnegie, "Wealth," *The North American Review* 148, no. 391 (1889): 653–65.

[2] "Colonel Geo. B. Christian as Seen by a Trade Publication," *Marion (OH) Weekly Star,* Apr. 23, 1904; Randolph C. Downes, *The Rise of Warren Gamaliel Harding, 1865–1920* (Columbus: Ohio State University Press, 1970), 11; *Marion (OH) Democratic Mirror,* Jan. 1, 1880.

[3] Marion County Deed Records, Nov. 29, 1882, 55:40–41, County Recorder, Marion, OH.

[4] Marion County Mortgage Records, Nov. 29, 1882, 17:292–93, County Recorder, Marion, OH; Sahr, "Inflation Conversion."

[5] The people of Marion used the term *quarry* to reference the actual location from which workers extracted limestone as well as the facilities built around that location to process and transport the stone. In other words, a quarry was a type of business as well as a physical location. This chapter deploys the term in the same way.

[6] Fluxing is a metallurgical process in which limestone with a high percentage of calcium carbonate is introduced into the smelting process to help extract impurities within a metal ore. For example, firing limestone with iron ore helps to extract the silica and aluminum usually present in combination with pure iron. The silica and aluminum bonds with the calcium carbonate, leaving a much purer metal for processing. Railroad ballast is the crushed stone placed around railroad ties and tracks that helps hold the infrastructure in place and assists in the drainage of the tracks. Department of Commerce, Bureau of Mines, *Metallurgical Limestone: Problems in Production and Utilization* (Washington, DC: GPO, 1929), 8.

[7] Edward Orton Jr. and Samuel Vernon Peppel, *The Limestone Resources and the Lime Industry in Ohio* (Columbus, OH: The State Geologist, 1906), 158–66.

[8] *Marion (OH) Democratic Mirror*, May 3, 1883; *Marion (OH) Daily Star*, Jun. 5, 1883; *Marion (OH) Democratic Mirror*, Jun. 21, 1883.

[9] Orten and Peppel, *Lime Industry in Ohio*, 249–65.

[10] *Marion (OH) Daily Star*, Sep. 18, 1883; *Marion (OH) Democratic Mirror*, Sep. 20, 1883; *Marion (OH) Democratic Mirror*, Aug. 2, 1883.

[11] "Local Industries," *Marion (OH) Daily Star*, Jun. 15, 1885; Marion County Deed Records, Oct. 31, 1885, 60:321–22, County Recorder, Marion, OH; *Marion (OH) Daily Star*, Dec. 3, 1887.

[12] "Strike at the Lime Kilns," *Marion (OH) Star*, Jun. 25, 1887; Robert E. Weir, ed., *Workers in America: A Historical Encyclopedia* (Santa Barbara, CA: ABC-CLIO, 2013), s.v. "knights of labor."

[13] *Marion (OH) Star*, May 5, 1888; "Oil Burned Lime," *Marion (OH) Star*, May 12, 1888.

[14] *Marion (OH) Star*, Jun. 23, 1888; *Marion (OH) Star*, Jul. 5, 1888; John M. Hazen, "Crushed Stone the Best Road Material," in *Crushed Stone and Its Uses: Facts of Importance in Connection with Modern Concrete Construction*, ed. W.J. Jackman (Chicago: The Producers Supply Company, 1904); *Marion (OH) Daily Star*, Jan. 30, 1889.

[15] Marion County Deed Records, Feb. 18, 1889, 65:522–23, County Recorder, Marion, OH; Sahr, "Inflation Conversion"; "Lime and Stone: Splendid Oak Hill," *Marion (OH) Daily Star*, Jun. 15, 1895.

[16] *Marion (OH) Democratic Mirror*, Mar. 21, 1889; *Marion (OH) Daily Star*, Apr. 18, 1889.

[17] The township is a geographical division larger than a municipality and smaller than the county. Marion Township encompassed the city and the land surrounding it. Christian was responsible to assess the parts of the township which lay outside the city itself.

[18] "Marion Township," *Marion (OH) Weekly Star*, Nov. 9, 1889; John A. Deindorfer, "Taxation," in *Annual Fifty-first Report of the Ohio State Board of Agriculture* (Norwalk, OH: The Laning Printing Company, 1897), 448–455; *Marion (OH) Daily Star*, Jan. 21, 1890; "The Land Appraisers: Organized for Work," *Marion (OH) Daily Star*, Mar. 16, 1890; *Marion (OH) Daily Star*, Mar. 20, 1890; *Marion (OH) Mirror*, Jun. 19, 1890.

19 *Marion (OH) Mirror*, Jul. 31, 1890.

20 Marion County Deed Records, Feb. 18, 1889, 65:522–23, County Recorder, Marion, OH; "Real Estate Appraisement: Col Christian Unfolds Himself in Regard to the Big Job Before Him—The Appraisement to Be as Low as Consistent with the Law," *Marion (OH) Daily Star,* Jan. 25, 1890; George B. Christian Sr., *Marion Township, Appraisers Book, 1890,* BV9841, State Archives Series 3428, Appraisement of Lands, 1837–1910, Ohio Historical Society Archives/Library, Ohio Historical Society, Columbus, OH; "Mistakes of the Assessor," *Marion (OH) Daily Star,* Mar. 26, 1890; "Inconsistent Kicking: Land Appraiser Christian Has Many Callers—The Final Work of Appraisement Full of Interest," *Marion (OH) Weekly Star,* Jul. 12, 1890.

21 "Important Industries," *Marion (OH) Star,* Aug. 11, 1890.

22 Marion County Deed Records, Oct. 13, 1890, 68:491–92, County Recorder, Marion, OH; "Still Another: The Norris & Christian Stone and Lime Co. Added to Marion's List of Incorporated Industries," *Marion (OH) Star,* Oct. 15, 1890.

23 "Lime and Stone: Some Facts Relating to That Important Industry," *Marion (OH) Daily Star*, May 23, 1891.

24 "Annual Meeting: Of The Norris & Christian Lime and Stone Company Was Held Monday," *Marion (OH) Daily Star,* Jan. 11, 1898; "Lime and Stone: Splendid Oak Hill, It Is Most Important in the Business World, Norris & Christian Lime and Stone Company Has the Largest Lime Plant in the West—Limestone, Macadam and Other Features of the Great Lime and Stone Industry," *Marion (OH) Daily Star,* Jun. 15, 1895; *Marion (OH) Daily Mirror,* Dec. 24, 1909.

25 George B. Christian Sr., "The Stone and Lime Industries," in J. Wilbur Jacoby, ed., *History of Marion County and Representative Citizens* (Marion, OH: Biographical Publishing Company, 1907), 165–66; *Marion (OH) Democratic Mirror,* Nov. 27, 1890; "Half the Night is Consumed by the Council in Its Regular Session," *Marion (OH) Star,* Jun. 6, 1891; "Broke the Combine: Council Accepts the Peters Stone Co.'s Bid," *Marion (OH) Star,* Jul. 11, 1891; *Marion (OH) Star,* Aug. 22, 1891; *Marion (OH) Star,* Aug. 29, 1891.

26 Marion County Deed Records, Jan. 16, 1892, 71:46–47, County Recorder, Marion, OH; Marion County Deed Records, Nov. 5, 1892, 72:200–201, County Recorder, Marion, OH; "Big Stone Crusher: The Norris & Christian Company Completed a Big, New, Modern Plant," *Marion (OH) Daily Star,* Aug. 10, 1893.

27 *Marion (OH) Mirror*, May 16, 1889; "Like a Cannon Ball," *Marion (OH) Democratic Mirror*, Nov. 30, 1892.

28 "Disbanded," *Marion (OH) Democratic Mirror,* Oct. 22, 1892.

29 At the time of the panic of 1893, the United States held reserves of gold and silver to back the dollar. Until the country left the gold standard in 1933, investors could exchange paper currency for an equivalent value of gold or silver.

30 Mark Carlson, "The Panic of 1893," in Randall E. Parker and Robert M. Whaples, eds., *The Routledge Handbook of Major Events in Economic History* (New York: Routledge, 2013), 44–45.

31 Parker and Whaples, *Major Events in Economic History,* 40–49.

32 "Reducing Forces: The Norris & Christian Company Cutting Their Expense Account," *Marion (OH) Daily Star,* Aug. 21, 1893; "They Quit Work: Quarrymen at Oak Hill on Reduced Time," *Marion (OH) Daily Star,* Nov. 22, 1893.

33 "Limestone City: A New Company Incorporated to Plat and Build a Fine Suburb to Marion," *Marion (OH) Democratic Mirror,* May 2, 1894; Marion County Bank Records, vol. 109, "Minutes and Articles of Incorporation of the Limestone City Real Estate Co., 1894–1897," MSS 858, Ohio Historical Society Archives/Library, Ohio Historical Society, Columbus, OH; Marion County Deed Records, May 23, 1895, 77:131–32, County Recorder, Marion, OH.

[34] Marion County Board of Commissioners Journals, 1867–1875, GR3425, Jun. 3, 1894, 12:299, State Archives Series 3404, Ohio Historical Society Archives/Library, Ohio Historical Society, Columbus, OH; Marion County Board of Commissioners Journals, 1867–1875, GR3425, Aug. 6, 1894, 12:310, State Archives Series 3404, Ohio Historical Society Archives/Library, Ohio Historical Society, Columbus, OH; *Marion (OH) Daily Star*, Sep. 26, 1894; "Process of Contracting Paving," *Marion (OH) Daily Star*, Aug. 15, 1894; "Thos. J. Peter Talks: And Tells All About His Bid for Center Street," *Marion (OH) Democratic Mirror*, Aug. 29, 1894; "Too Much Sand and Too Little Cement, Say the Pavement Inspectors," *Marion (OH) Democratic Mirror*, Nov. 14, 1894; "Our Sixth Railroad: The Marion and Northwestern Railroad Company, a Distinctly Marion Enterprise," *Marion (OH) Daily Star*, May 13, 1895; *Marion (OH) Democratic Mirror*, May 16, 1895; "Add Fifty Men," *Marion (OH) Daily Star*, May 25, 1897.

[35] "Lime and Stone," *Marion (OH) Daily Star*, Jun. 15, 1895; "Here's a Good Thing," *Marion (OH) Democratic Mirror*, Jul. 29, 1895.

[36] "Add Fifty Men"; "Old Prosperity Strikes the Industries Squarely at Oak Hill, Lime and Stone Business Booms," *Marion (OH) Daily Star*, Aug. 26, 1897.

[37] "Local Klondike," *Marion (OH) Daily Star*, Oct. 23, 1897.

[38] *Sandusky (OH) Star*, Aug. 15, 1898; *Marion (OH) Daily Star*, May 30, 1899.

[39] "A Big Order Is Booked Today by the Norris and Christian People," *Marion (OH) Daily Star*, May 1, 1900; "Big Contract with the Short Line Being Carried on by Local Company," *Marion (OH) Star*, Jan. 19, 1901.

[40] "200 Acres More Are Purchased by the Norris and Christian Lime and Stone Company, Friday," *Marion (OH) Daily Star*, Jun. 29, 1901; *Marion (OH) Weekly Star*, Jul. 6, 1901.

[41] "A Test Will Be Made of a Lime Burning Device," *Marion (OH) Democratic Mirror*, Aug. 9, 1901; *Marion (OH) Star*, Aug. 16, 1901; "New Device for Burning Lime Is a Great Success," *Marion (OH) Democratic Mirror*, Aug. 27, 1901; "Machine in Operation: Scott and Strahel Have Their Wagon Loader Work at Norris and Christian Stone and Lime Plant," *Marion (OH) Daily Star*, Oct. 19, 1903.

[42] "Differences Are Settled: There Will Be No Strike at the Local Quarries," *Marion (OH) Daily Star*, Jun. 10, 1902.

[43] "Hauling Stone with Locomotive: The Norris & Christian Company Operates One at Quarries," *Marion (OH) Star*, Jun. 10, 1905.

[44] "Dollar a Head for Every Man: Proposition Made by a Local Plant," *Marion (OH) Star*, Jul. 29, 1905.

[45] "Will Double the Capacity: Norris & Christian Company Contract for Machinery, Improvements to Be Made at Once," *Marion (OH) Daily Star*, Mar. 26, 1906; "A Conference at the Commercial Club: Changes to Be Made at the Norris & Christian Quarries," *Marion (OH) Daily Star*, Apr. 5, 1906. The Columbus, Hocking Valley, and Toledo Railroad was reorganized as the Hocking Valley Railroad in 1899.

[46] *Marion (OH) Weekly Star*, Jan. 20, 1908; "Some Recent Experiments with Lime in Agriculture: A Timely Paper by Mr. George B. Christian of This City," *Marion (OH) Daily Star*, Jan. 25, 1902; "A Layman's Views: Regarding Men's Failure to Attend Church Services, Col. Christian in the Pulpit," *Marion (OH) Daily Star*, Jan. 31, 1898; "Mass Meetings Held Sunday: Celebrate the 'Dry' Victory in Marion," *Marion (OH) Daily Mirror*, Nov. 29, 1909.

[47] "Indiana Company: Purchases Three Local Stone Quarries," *Marion (OH) Daily Mirror*, Jan. 1, 1907; "Big Limestone Merger: Three in Marion County Taken; Others to Follow," *Cleveland (OH) Plain Dealer*, Jan. 2, 1907; "Closes Million Dollar Deal," *Hammond Lake County (IN) Times*, Jan. 3, 1907; "Refused to Enter Deal," *Marion (OH) Democratic Mirror*, Feb. 7, 1907; "Half Million Deal," *Cincinnati (OH) Enquirer*, Feb. 8, 1907; Marion County Deed Records, Mar. 13, 1907, 110:553–58, County Recorder, Marion, OH; Sahr, "Inflation Conversion."

[48] "Presented with Watch: Workmen Honor Their Former Employer Colonel Geo. Christian," *Marion (OH) Daily Mirror*, Dec. 16, 1907.

49 "Refused to Enter Deal"; "Presented with Watch"; "Strong Competition in Stone Business: George B. Christian Jr., Quits the Ohio & Western to Join the Allied Christian Interests," *Marion (OH) Weekly Star*, Jun. 26, 1909.

50 James R. Lytle, ed., *20th Century History of Delaware County, Ohio and Representative Citizens* (Chicago: Biographical Publishing Co., 1908), 151; *Marion (OH) Weekly Star*, Jun. 13, 1908; Delaware County Deed Records, Apr. 16, 1908, 132:246, County Recorder, Delaware, OH; Delaware County Deed Records, Nov. 24, 1908, 132:412, County Recorder, Delaware, OH; "Colonel Christian Entertains Party: A Pleasant Affair at Commercial Club-House," *Marion (OH) Weekly Star*, Dec. 19, 1908.

51 Delaware County Deed Records, Dec. 15, 1908, 133:319–20, County Recorder, Delaware, OH; Delaware County Deed Records, Mar. 20, 1909, 133:251–52, County Recorder, Delaware, OH; "Colonel Christian Buys More Stone: Acquires the Smith Quarry at White Sulphur Springs," *Marion (OH) Daily Star*, May 15, 1909; "Strong Competition in Stone Business," *Marion (OH) Weekly Star*, Jun. 26, 1909.

52 "Invent a New Crusher: Marion Men Perfect a New Machine," *Marion (OH) Democratic Mirror*, Nov. 13, 1909.

53 "Sleepy Delaware Objects to the Noise: Council Appealed to By Those Who Love Silence," *Marion (OH) Daily Mirror*, Dec. 16, 1909.

54 Ellis W. Tallman and Jon R. Moen, "Lessons from the Panic of 1907," *Economic Review* 75, no. 3 (1909): 2–12.

55 "Ohio Stone Club Honors Marionite: Colonel G.B. Christian Is Made State President," *Marion (OH) Weekly Star*, Jan. 14, 1911.

56 Demurrage refers to the fees charged by railroad companies to cover the time required to transfer cargo to or from a train car.

57 Charles E. Sawyer to Warren G. Harding, Mar. 19, 1916, Warren G. Harding Papers, microfilm, roll 262, panels 38–40, Ohio Historical Society Archive/Library, Ohio Historical Society, Columbus, OH; "Annual Meeting of Ohio Quarrymen," *Cement and Engineering News* 24, no. 10 (1912): 302–10.

58 William James Cunningham, *American Railroads: Government Control and Reconstruction Policies* (Chicago: A. W. Shaw Company, 1922), 16–33.

59 Ibid., 33–65.

60 George B. Christian Sr. to Warren G. Harding, Jan. 17, 1918, Warren G. Harding Papers, microfilm, roll 20, panel 158, Ohio Historical Society Archive/Library, Ohio Historical Society, Columbus, OH.

61 George B. Christian Sr. to Warren G. Harding, Sep. 27, 1918, Warren G. Harding Papers, microfilm, roll 20, panels 916–17, Ohio Historical Society Archive/Library, Ohio Historical Society, Columbus, OH; The Big Four Railroad reference refers to the Cleveland, Columbus, Cincinnati, and Indianapolis Railroad which ran through all the major cities of the region.

62 George B. Christian Sr. to Warren G. Harding, Dec. 26, 1918, Warren G. Harding Papers, microfilm, roll 249, panel 3, Ohio Historical Society Archive/Library, Ohio Historical Society, Columbus, OH.

63 George B. Christian Sr., "Instructions to Cooper Post of G.A.R.," (unpublished manuscript, n.d.), Warren G. Harding Papers, microfilm, roll 249, panels 40–50, Ohio Historical Society Archive/Library, Ohio Historical Society, Columbus, OH.

64 Ibid.; "George B. Christian Reelected President: White Sulphur Lime & Stone Company's Annual Meeting," *Marion (OH) Daily Star*, Dec. 22, 1920. The name of the company changed from the White Sulphur Stone Company to the White Sulphur Lime and Stone Company sometime in late 1918 or early 1919.

65 Delaware County Deed Records, Jun. 14, 1920, 159:148–51, County Recorder, Delaware, OH; *Pit and Quarry Magazine* 6, no. 11 (1922): 94.

Chapter 7, Christian the Campaigner

1 Leggett, Conaway, & Co., *History of Marion County*, 291.

2 The Populist Party became popular among rural people in the Western and Southern regions of the United States during the 1890s. In some ways it was a reform movement which called for political changes such as the direct election of U.S. senators and the institution of secret ballots in elections. They also wanted the U.S. government to regulate the railroad industry and adopt free silver. By the election of 1896, the movement had begun to falter. Its various constituents coalesced around the free silver issue. And since the William Jennings Bryan had appropriated the issue as part of his campaign, the Populists chose not to run a third-party candidate and threw their support behind him.

3 Jackson Lears, *Rebirth of a Nation: The Making of America, 1877–1920* (New York: Harper Collins, 2010), 186–92.

4 Clifford H. Moore, "Ohio in National Politics, 1865–1896," *Ohio Archaeological and Historical Quarterly* 37, no. 2 (1928): 412–22.

5 Lears, *Rebirth of a Nation*, 186–92.

6 Moore, "Ohio in National Politics," 412–22; Jacoby, *History of Marion County*, 291; "Choose a Victim: Thirteenth District Demmies Nominate a Candidate, Col. Geo. B. Christian the Man," *Marion (OH) Daily Star*, Aug. 31, 1897.

7 "Choose a Victim."

8 "Marion Demmies: Notify Col. Christian of His Nomination for Senator, the Nominee Is Serenaded," *Marion (OH) Daily Star*, Sep. 1, 1897.

9 Ibid.

10 Bob Dumm, *Marion (OH) Daily Star*, Sep. 2, 1897.

11 "Christian for Senator," *Marion (OH) Daily Star*, Aug. 31, 1897.

12 Joseph P. Smith, ed., *History of the Republican Party in Ohio and Memoirs of Its Representative Supporters* (Chicago: The Lewis Publishing Company, 1898), 2:495–96; "Christian for Senator."

13 "Democrats: Are Promised Two Eminent Speakers for Marion During the Campaign," *Marion (OH) Daily Star*, Sept. 10, 1897; "Col. Christian at Kenton," *Marion (OH) Daily Star*, Sep. 25, 1897; "Had to Stand Up: Arnett Meeting Duplicated by the Democrats, Christian Talks to the Crowd," *Marion (OH) Daily Star*, Oct. 28, 1897.

14 "Round the Edges," *Marion (OH) Daily Star*, Nov. 5, 1897.

15 "Voting Is Lively: A Pretty Full Ballot Is Being Gotten Out," *Marion (OH) Daily Star*, Nov. 2, 1897; *Marion (OH) Daily Star*, Nov. 3, 1897; "The Election," *Marion (OH) Daily Star*, Nov. 4, 1897; *Sandusky (OH) Star*, Aug. 15, 1898; "What It Cost Them: Expense Accounts of Candidates are All Filed," *Marion (OH) Daily Star*, Nov. 12, 1897.

16 *Sandusky (OH) Star*, Aug. 15, 1898; "Political Observations Made Through the Star's Telescope," *Marion (OH) Daily Star*, Aug. 20, 1898; *Marion (OH) Daily Star*, Jan. 3, 1899.

17 "Here They Are: Governor Bushnell Announces the Centennial Commission, Geo. B. Christianson [sic] of Marion County Will Represent the Thirteenth District at Toledo Exposition," *Sandusky (OH) Star*, Sep. 19, 1899; "Hearty and United Support Is Promised by the Ohio Congressmen for the Promotion of the Centennial Celebration," *Cincinnati (OH) Enquirer*, Jan. 19, 1899; Jacoby, *History of Marion County*, 291.

Chapter 8, Exposition Lost

1 Today we more often use the shortened designation "expo."

2 "President McKinley Favors Reciprocity: Tells People at Buffalo That Treaties Should be Made," *New York Times*, Sep. 6, 1901. This exposition held in Buffalo, New York, was also the site of his assassination.

3 Robert W. Rydell, *All the World's a Fair: Visions of Empire at American International Expositions, 1876–1916* (Chicago: University of Chicago Press, 1987), 8.

4 Robert H. Wiebe, *The Search for Order, 1877–1920* (New York: Hill and Wang, 1966).

5 Martin J. Sklar, *The Corporate Reconstruction of American Capitalism, 1890–1916: The Market, the Law, and Politics* (New York: Cambridge University Press, 1988); Rydell, *All the World's a Fair*, 1–9.

6 "Tennessee's One Hundredth Birthday to Be Celebrated with a Grand Exposition: Arrangements for Which Are Now Being Made," *Cincinnati (OH) Enquirer*, Dec. 8, 1895; "Men and Matters," *Cincinnati (OH) Enquirer*, Dec. 19, 1895; "Cincinnati Will Be a Candidate for the Ohio Centennial Celebration in 1903: Plans Are Now Under Discussion," *Cincinnati (OH) Enquirer*, Aug. 28, 1897.

7 "Cincinnati Will Be a Candidate"; "Memorial Hall Desired for Cincinnati Instead of a Centennial Exposition in 1903," *Cincinnati (OH) Enquirer*, Nov. 8, 1897; "At Sea: Regarding Their Report," *Cincinnati (OH) Enquirer*, Dec. 2, 1897.

8 "Permanent Museum and Library Suggested by the Ohio Centennial Commission," *Cincinnati (OH) Enquirer*, Apr. 7, 1898.

9 "Here They Are"; *Marion (OH) Daily Star*, Oct. 14, 1893.

10 Ohio Centennial Commission, *Report of the Ohio Centennial Commission to the Seventy-Fourth General Assembly of Ohio* (Columbus: Ohio State Printing Office, n.d.), 25–26.

11 "Hearty and United Support Is Promised by the Ohio Congressmen for the Promotion of the Centennial Celebration," *Cincinnati (OH) Enquirer*, Jan. 19, 1899; "There's Too Much Red Tape: Legislature Will Be Asked to Change the Law Authorizing Centennial Bodies," *Cleveland (OH) Plain Dealer*, Apr. 28, 1899; "Not Flattering Will Be the Report on the Centennial Unless the Money Is Up," *Cincinnati (OH) Enquirer*, Nov. 23, 1899.

12 "Not Flattering"; "Hearty and United Support"; Ohio Centennial Commission, *Report to the Seventy-Fourth*, 9–10.

13 Ohio Centennial Commission, *Report to the Seventy-Fourth*, 54.

14 Ibid., 61.

15 Ira Rutkow, *James A. Garfield* (New York: Henry Holt and Company, 2006), 110–13; John Duffy, *The Sanitarians: A History of American Public Health* (Urbana: University of Illinois Press, 1992), 193–98.

16 Ohio Centennial Commission, *Report to the Seventy-Fourth*, 61.

17 Ibid., 16.

18 Downes, *Rise of Warren Gamaliel Harding*, 96–98.

19 Ibid., 98–106.

20 "Secret of Nash's Hostility to Original Plans for Toledo's Centennial Lies in the Desire to Form Powerful Machine Which Will Aid Him in Quarters Where He Is Weak," *Cincinnati (OH) Enquirer*, Mar. 18, 1900.

21 "Defects in the Centennial Bill May Prevent It Becoming Operative if Passed: Supreme Court Will Have to Decide Whether It Is Valid," *Cincinnati (OH) Enquirer*, Mar. 25, 1900.

[22] "Death Blow to Centennial Given by the Senate at Nash's Dictation," *Cincinnati (OH) Enquirer*, Apr. 5, 1900; "Wants the Commission or Nash Will Kill the Bill for the Centennial," *Cincinnati (OH) Enquirer*, Apr. 6, 1900; "Griffin After Nash and Dunham, and Throws Light on Schemes of the Politicians," *Cincinnati (OH) Enquirer*, Apr. 8, 1900; "Conference Refused by the House: Fate of the Centennial Bill Still in Doubt," *Cincinnati (OH) Enquirer*, Apr. 11, 1900; "House Will Confer on the Centennial Bill—The Governor Gains a Point," *Cincinnati (OH) Enquirer*, Apr. 12, 1900; "Tumult in the Closing Hours so Great the Legislature Had to Adjourn," *Cincinnati (OH) Enquirer*, Apr. 15, 1900.

[23] "Enough of the Last Legislature and Nash Will Not Call a Special Session to Help Out the Toledo Centennial," *Cincinnati (OH) Enquirer*, Apr. 21, 1900; "Used by Hanna and Nash Has Aroused a Storm of Wrath and Indignation," *Cincinnati (OH) Enquirer*, Apr. 22, 1900; "Foraker Touched Up the Attorney Who Appeared Against the Centennial Commission," *Cincinnati (OH) Enquirer*, Jun. 16, 1900; "Not Available Says the Supreme Court of the Big Appropriation Made," *Cincinnati (OH) Enquirer*, Jun. 27, 1900.

[24] "Politics Killed the Project to Celebrate 100 Years of Ohio's History," *Cincinnati (OH) Enquirer*, Jun. 27, 1900.

[25] "Hopes to See the Population of Toledo Doubled and Favors a Fair that Will Make Chicago and St. Louis Sick," *Cincinnati (OH) Enquirer*, Oct. 31, 1901.

[26] "Sons of Ohio to Celebrate Centennial of the Province of Statesmen," *Cincinnati (OH) Enquirer*, Nov. 25, 1902.

Chapter 9, Warren G. Harding, From Mentee to Colleague to Senator

[1] Downes, *Rise of Warren Gamaliel Harding*, 1–7; George B. Christian Sr., "Biography of Warren G. Harding" (unpublished manuscript, 1926), Warren G. Harding Papers, box 792, Ohio Historical Society Archive/Library, Ohio Historical Society, Columbus, OH.

[2] *Marion (OH) Democratic Mirror*, Oct. 29, 1874; Jacoby, *History of Marion County*, 810; Christian, "Biography of Warren G. Harding."

[3] "Death of Dr. Harding's Children," *Marion (OH) Democratic Mirror*, Nov. 14, 1878; "Death's Doings," *Marion (OH) Democratic Mirror*, Nov. 21, 1878; "Caledonia Items," *Marion (OH) Democratic Mirror*, Nov. 21, 1878.

[4] Downes, *Rise of Warren Gamaliel Harding*, 8–10; *Marion (OH) Independent*, Oct. 27, 1881; Benson Pratt, "Harding Honesty Illustrated by Col. Christian: Father of Secretary to President Talks of Boy Who Rode into Town on Mule," *New Castle (PA) News*, Aug. 7, 1923; *Marion (OH) Daily Star*, Feb. 28, 1883; Jack Warwick, *Growing Up With Warren Harding* (Marion, OH: Warren G. Harding House, n.d.), 10–12.

[5] Sheryl Hall, *Warren G. Harding & the* Marion Daily Star*: How Newspapering Shaped a President* (Charleston, SC: The History Press, 2014), 17–23.

[6] George B. Christian Jr., "Warren Gamaliel Harding," *Current History* 18, no. 6 (1923): 906; Downes, *Rise of Warren Gamaliel Harding*, 18.

[7] *Marion (OH) Daily Star*, Jan. 20, 1886.

[8] *Marion (OH) Daily Star*, Jun. 29, 1883; *Marion (OH) Daily Star*, Jun. 5, 1883; "Railroad Racket," *Marion (OH) Weekly Star*, Apr. 3, 1886; "Local Industries: The Beginning of a Series of Articles on the Various Local Manufacturers that Prosper in Marion," *Marion (OH) Daily Star*, Jun. 15, 1885; George B. Christian Sr., "A Moving Letter: Our Own George Christian Sends the Star a Meaningful Letter Under the Caption of 'Let Us Have Peace,'" *Marion (OH) Weekly Star*, May 14, 1887; "Choose a Victim."

[9] Christian, "Biography."

[10] Ibid.; Downes, *Rise of Warren Gamaliel Harding*, 19–28.

[11] Gross, *Vindication for Mr. Normalcy*, 48; *Marion (OH) Democratic Mirror,* Feb. 12, 1891; "Rambling Notes: A Joint Contribution of Breezy Paragraphs from the South," *Marion (OH) Star,* Mar. 7, 1891; "A Day's Pleasure: How the Time Is Spent in the Sun in Florida," *Marion (OH) Star,* Mar. 19, 1891; "On to Tampa: Col. Christian Strikes His Old Time Eloquence in Writing of the Glories of Tampa and Its Famous Sights—Reference to the Marionites Seen on the Gulf Coast," *Marion (OH) Star,* Apr. 7, 1891; "The Ancient City: References to Sanford, Winter Park, and Orlando," *Marion (OH) Star,* Apr. 22, 1891.

[12] *Marion (OH) Democratic Mirror,* Jun. 20, 1894; *Marion (OH) Democratic Mirror,* Jan. 23, 1895; *Marion (OH) Daily Star,* Nov. 18, 1903.

[13] Henry J. May to Warren G. Harding, Sep. 13, 1897, Warren G. Harding Papers, microfilm, roll 9, panel 107, Ohio Historical Society Archive/Library, Ohio Historical Society, Columbus, OH; *Marion (OH) Daily Star,* Aug. 31, 1897.

[14] "Here They Are: Governor Bushnell Announces the Centennial Commission, Geo. B. Christianson [sic] of Marion County Will Represent the Thirteenth District at Toledo Exposition," *Sandusky (OH) Star,* Sep. 19, 1898; "Death Blow to Centennial Given by the Senate at Nash's Dictation," *Cincinnati (OH) Enquirer,* Apr. 5, 1900.

[15] George B. Christian Sr. to Warren G. Harding, Feb. 19, 1902, Warren G. Harding Papers, microfilm, roll 10, panel 617, Ohio Historical Society Archive/Library, Ohio Historical Society, Columbus, OH.

[16] Downes, *Rise of Warren Gamaliel Harding,* 112–54.

[17] Warren G. Harding to George B. Christian Sr., Dec. 25, 1904, Roberts Family Library, Sycamore, IL; Warren G. Harding to George B. Christian Sr., Feb. 16, 1906, Roberts Family Library, Sycamore, IL.

[18] Andrew Sinclair, *The Available Man: The Life Behind the Masks of Warren Gamaliel Harding* (New York: Macmillan Company, 1965), 44.

[19] Warren G. Harding to Lydia Christian, Aug. 8, 1907, quoted in Gross, *Vindication for Mr. Normalcy,* 23.

[20] John W. Dean, *Warren G. Harding: The American Presidents Series: The 29th President, 1921–1923* (New York: Macmillan Company, 2004), 27.

[21] George B. Christian Sr. to Warren G. Harding, Sep. 21, 1907, Warren G. Harding Papers, microfilm, roll 13, panels 645–46, Ohio Historical Society Archive/Library, Ohio Historical Society, Columbus, OH.

[22] Dean, *29th President,* 26–27; Warren G. Harding to George B. Christian Sr., Feb. 14, 1910, Roberts Family Library, Sycamore, IL; "Memory of Emancipator," *Marion (OH) Daily Mirror,* Feb. 13, 1909.

[23] Downes, *Rise of Warren Gamaliel Harding,* 155–94.

[24] Ibid., 197–212; Christian Sr., "Biography."

[25] Downes, *Rise of Warren Gamaliel Harding,* 201.

[26] Ibid., 201–202, 212–14.

[27] George B. Christian Jr. to Ray Baker Harris, Sep. 6, 1930, quoted in Donald F. Keller, "George Christian and the Press Relations of Warren G. Harding from Marion, Ohio, to the White House" (master's thesis: University of Wisconsin-Madison, 1972), 34.

[28] Keller, "Press Relations," 33–35.

[29] George B. Christian Sr. to Edward Scobey, May 15, 1915, Warren G. Harding Papers, microfilm, roll 263, panel 41, Ohio Historical Society Archive/Library, Ohio Historical Society, Columbus, OH.

[30] Edward Scobey to George B. Christian Sr., May 20, 1915, Warren G. Harding Papers, microfilm, roll 263, panels 43–44, Ohio Historical Society Archive/Library, Ohio Historical Society, Columbus, OH; Downes, *Rise of Warren Gamaliel Harding,* 250–53.

[31] The paradox of American colonialism was that American leaders believed that U.S. colonial control in the Philippines helped teach principles of Democracy.

[32] Downes, *Rise of Warren Gamaliel Harding*, 216–53; Christian, "Biography of Warren G. Harding."

[33] Christian, "Instructions to Cooper Post"; Downes, *Rise of Warren Gamaliel Harding*, 232–240.

[34] Warren G. Harding to Malcolm Jennings, Jan. 20, 1920, quoted in Sinclair, *The Available Man*, 310; Charles E. Sawyer to Warren G. Harding, Mar. 19, 1916, Warren G. Harding Papers, microfilm, roll 262, panels 38–40, Ohio Historical Society Archive/Library, Ohio Historical Society, Columbus, OH; Warren G. Harding to Charles E. Sawyer, Mar. 23, 1916, Warren G. Harding Papers, microfilm, roll 262, panel 41, Ohio Historical Society Archive/Library, Ohio Historical Society, Columbus, OH; Warren G. Harding to Lydia Christian, Dec. 22, 1916, Warren G. Harding Papers, microfilm, roll 257, panel 626-27, Ohio Historical Society Archive/Library, Ohio Historical Society, Columbus, OH.

[35] Warren G. Harding to Charles E. Sawyer, Feb. 19, 1918, Warren G. Harding Papers, microfilm, roll 262, panels 145–147, Ohio Historical Society Archive/Library, Ohio Historical Society, Columbus, OH.

[36] Downes, *Rise of Warren Gamaliel Harding*, 254–76.

[37] Florence Kling Harding to Alice Mildred Roberts, Apr. 6, 1918, Roberts Family Library, Sycamore, IL.

[38] Warren G. Harding to George B. Christian Sr., May 21, 1918, Roberts Family Library, Sycamore, IL.

[39] "Engagement of Miss Christian Announced: She Will Wed Captain Chester Roberts in April," *Marion (OH) Daily Star*, Mar. 25, 1918; "A Military Wedding Late This Afternoon: Miss Mildred Christian and Captain Roberts, Principals," *Marion (OH) Daily Star*, Apr., 20, 1918; George B. Christian Sr. to Warren G. Harding, May 11, 1918, Warren G. Harding Papers, microfilm, roll 20, panel 633, Ohio Historical Society Archive/Library, Ohio Historical Society, Columbus, OH; Warren G. Harding to George B. Christian Sr., Jul. 10, 1919, Warren G. Harding Papers, microfilm, roll 21, panels 709–10, Ohio Historical Society Archive/Library, Ohio Historical Society, Columbus, OH.

[40] Woodrow Wilson, "Making the World 'Safe for Democracy': Woodrow Wilson Asks for War," *History Matters*, accessed Aug. 27, 2013, http://historymatters.gmu.edu/d/4943/; H. W. Brands, *Woodrow Wilson, 1856–1924* (New York: Henry Holt and Company, 2003), 75–100.

[41] Downes, *Rise of Warren Gamaliel Harding*, 315–44.

[42] Ibid., 315–44.

[43] Ibid., 338–45.

Chapter 10, The Life and Death of a Presidential Friend

[1] Downes, *Rise of Warren Gamaliel Harding*, 345–53; Christian, "Biography of Warren G. Harding."

[2] Warren G. Harding to Hoke Donithen, Dec. 31, 1919, Warren G. Harding Papers, microfilm, roll 21, panel 1400, Ohio Historical Society Archive/Library, Ohio Historical Society, Columbus, OH.

[3] Frederick E. Shortemeier, *Rededicating America: Life and Recent Speeches of Warren G. Harding* (Indianapolis, IN: Bobbs-Merrill Company, 1920), 114.

[4] George B. Christian Sr. to Warren G. Harding, Jan. 12, 1920, Warren G. Harding Papers, microfilm, roll 22, panels 44–52, Ohio Historical Society Archive/Library, Ohio Historical Society, Columbus, OH.

[5] Warren G. Harding to George B. Christian Sr., Jan. 19, 1920, Warren G. Harding Papers, microfilm, roll 22, panels 93–96, Ohio Historical Society Archive/Library, Ohio Historical Society, Columbus, OH.

[6] Harry Daugherty had served as an influential member of the Ohio Assembly during the 1890s but had failed in his many attempts for statewide office. Instead, Daugherty found that his talents were

better spent as a political operative. Harding and Daugherty had met when they both worked to reelect President William Howard Taft in 1912. Even though Taft lost, the two men forged a strong friendship. When Harding decided to run for president, he called on Daugherty to lead the charge.

[7] George B. Christian Sr. to Warren G. Harding, Jan. 12, 1920, Warren G. Harding Papers, microfilm, roll 22, panels 44–52, Ohio Historical Society Archive/Library, Ohio Historical Society, Columbus, OH; Christian, "Biography of Warren G. Harding."

[8] Downes, *Rise of Warren Gamaliel Harding,* 361–376.

[9] Warren G. Harding to George B. Christian Sr., Jan. 19, 1920, Warren G. Harding Papers, microfilm, roll 22, panels 93–96, Ohio Historical Society Archive/Library, Ohio Historical Society, Columbus, OH.

[10] Christian, "Biography of Warren G. Harding."

[11] Downes, *Rise of Warren Gamaliel Harding,* 406–10.

[12] Robert K. Murray, *The Harding Era: Warren G. Harding and His Administration* (Newtown, CT: American Political Biography Press, 2000), 32–41; Christian Jr., "Warren Gamaliel Harding," 906.

[13] Murray, *Harding Era,* 43–54.

[14] George B. Christian Sr. to Warren G. Harding, Jun. 24, 1920, Warren G. Harding Papers, microfilm, roll 60, panels 212–14, Ohio Historical Society Archive/Library, Ohio Historical Society, Columbus, OH.

[15] Ibid.; George B. Christian Jr. to George B. Christian Sr., Jun. 14, 1920, Warren G. Harding Papers, microfilm, roll 60, panel 208, Ohio Historical Society Archive/Library, Ohio Historical Society, Columbus, OH.

[16] Keller, "Press Relations," 83–89.

[17] Downes, *Rise of Warren Gamaliel Harding,* 457.

[18] Murray, *Harding Era,* 44–45; Keller, "Press Relations," 98–99.

[19] Murray, *Harding Era*, 43–54.

[20] Murray, *Harding Era,* 49–54.

[21] Keller, "Press Relations," 108–14.

[22] George B. Christian Jr. to George B. Christian Sr., Jul. 29, 1920, Warren G. Harding Papers, microfilm, roll 60, panel 215, Ohio Historical Society Archive/Library, Ohio Historical Society, Columbus, OH; Zoe Beckley, "Caution Harding's Dominant Quality; Wife Real Helper," *Saginaw (MI) News,* Aug. 1, 1920.

[23] Christian, "Biography of Warren G. Harding."

[24] Keller, "Press Relations," 108–14.

[25] Murray, *Harding Era,* 63–65; Christian, "Biography of Warren G. Harding."

[26] Downes, *Rise of Warren Gamaliel Harding,* 640.

[27] Murray, *Harding Era,* 66; "Celebration Will Be Held Tomorrow Night," *Marion (OH) Star,* Nov. 3, 1920; Christian, "Biography of Warren G. Harding."

[28] Warren G. Harding to Lydia Christian, Dec. 25, 1920, Roberts Family Library, Sycamore, IL.

[29] Christian, "Biography of Warren G. Harding."

[30] George B. Christian Sr. to Warren G. Harding, May 28, 1921, Warren G. Harding Papers, microfilm, roll 229, panels 707–9, Ohio Historical Society Archive/Library, Ohio Historical Society, Columbus, OH.

[31] Murray, *Harding Era,* 93–109.

[32] Christian, "Biography of Warren G, Harding."

[33] Ibid.; Murray, *Harding Era,* 109–12.

[34] George B. Christian Sr. to Warren G. Harding, Jul. 13, 1921, Warren G. Harding Papers, microfilm, roll 229, panel 712, Ohio Historical Society Archive/Library, Ohio Historical Society, Columbus, OH; Warren G. Harding to George B. Christian Sr., Jul. 18, 1921, Warren G. Harding Papers, microfilm, roll 229, panel 714, Ohio Historical Society Archive/Library, Ohio Historical Society, Columbus, OH; George B. Christian Sr. to Warren G. Harding, Jan. 12, 1923, Warren G. Harding Papers, microfilm, roll 229, panels 723–24, Ohio Historical Society Archive/Library, Ohio Historical Society, Columbus, OH; Warren G. Harding to George B. Christian Sr., Jan. 29, 1923, Warren G. Harding Papers, microfilm, roll 229, panels 725–26, Ohio Historical Society Archive/Library, Ohio Historical Society, Columbus, OH; Murray, *Harding Era,* 308–14.

[35] Warren G. Harding to George B. Christian Sr., Dec. 27, 1921, Warren G. Harding Papers, microfilm, roll 229, panels 719–20, Ohio Historical Society Archive/Library, Ohio Historical Society, Columbus, OH.

[36] Murray, *Harding Era,* 150–65.

[37] Christian, "Biography of Warren G. Harding"; Murray, *Harding Era,* 227–58.

[38] Keller, "Press Relations," 143–50.

[39] Warren G. Harding to George B. Christian Sr., Dec. 27, 1921, Warren G. Harding Papers, microfilm, roll 229, panels 719–20, Ohio Historical Society Archive/Library, Ohio Historical Society, Columbus, OH; "Marion's Arms Are Extended to Enfold Distinguished Son; Centennial Celebration Is On," *Cincinnati (OH) Enquirer,* Jul. 4, 1922; W. J. Eads, "Marion En Fete to Receive Harding Party: Home Town Has Warm Greeting Prepared for President on Home-Coming," *Jersey (NJ) Journal,* Jul. 3, 1922.

[40] Christian, "Biography of Warren G. Harding."

[41] Robert T. Small, *Evansville (IN) Courier and Press,* Mar. 25, 1923; *Marion (OH) Daily Star,* Apr. 13, 1923.

[42] George B. Christian Sr. to Warren G. Harding, May 26, 1923, Warren G. Harding Papers, microfilm, roll 229, panel 727, Ohio Historical Society Archive/Library, Ohio Historical Society, Columbus, OH; Warren G. Harding to George B. Christian Sr., May 29, 1923, Warren G. Harding Papers, microfilm, roll 229, panels 728–29, Ohio Historical Society Archive/Library, Ohio Historical Society, Columbus, OH.

[43] Murray, *Harding Era,* 439–51.

[44] Christian, "Biography of Warren G. Harding"; Benson Pratt, "Harding Honesty Illustrated by Col. Christian: Father of Secretary to President Talks of Boy Who Rode into Town on Mule," *New Castle (PA) News,* Aug. 7, 1923; Murray, *Harding Era,* 451–55.

[45] Murray, *Harding Era,* 429–40.

[46] Ibid., 430–37.

[47] Ibid., 461–74.

[48] Christian Jr., "Warren Gamaliel Harding," 903–8.

[49] "Scouts Plant Tree in Honor of Mr. Harding: Memorial Services Held at High School Building," *Marion (OH) Daily Star,* Nov. 2, 1923.

[50] Christian, "Biography of Warren G. Harding."

[51] Murray, *Harding Era,* 492–93; "Harding Building Begun: Ground Is Broken for $800,000 Memorial," *Cleveland (OH) Plain Dealer,* May 5, 1926.

[52] The idea for this inscription came from the grave of George B. Christian Sr.'s grandfather, George H. Busby, whose grave read, "God's noblest work, an honest man." Leggett, Conaway, & Co., *History of Marion County*, 343.

[53] Murray, *Harding Era,* 487–91.

[54] George B. Christian Sr., "An Analysis and Review of a Recently Published 'Best Seller," (unpublished manuscript, n.d.), Warren G. Harding Papers, microfilm, roll 253, panels 317–85, Ohio Historical Society Archive/Library, Ohio Historical Society, Columbus, OH.

[55] Keller, "Press Relations," 75.

[56] "Tell Tales on Nan Britton in Libel Suit: Woman Involved in 'President's Daughter'; Nude Party Revealed," *The Daily Free Press (Carbondale, IL)*, Oct. 29, 1931; George B. Christian Jr. to Mildred Roberts, Oct. 31, 1931, Warren G. Harding Papers, microfilm, roll 250, panel 358, Ohio Historical Society Archive/Library, Ohio Historical Society, Columbus, OH.

Chapter 11, "A True Christian Gentleman"

[1] Glen Gendzel, "1914–1929," in *A Companion to 20ᵗʰ-Century America*, ed. Stephen J. Whitfield (Malden, MA: Blackwell Publishing, 2004), 19–35.

[2] Ibid.

[3] De jure segregation described the racial divisions mandated by law, while de facto segregation referenced the racial separation maintained through tradition and intimidation.

[4] Gendzel, "1914-1929," 19-35; Roger Daniels, *The Politics of Prejudice: The Anti-Japanese Movement in California and the Struggle for Japanese Exclusion* (Berkeley and Los Angeles: University of California Press, 1977).

[5] Galbraith, *History of Ohio*, 5:335–36.

[6] "Miss Carrie Bain Gets Post in City Office," *Marion (OH) Star*, Jan. 28, 1931; "Miss Carrie Bain Is Taken by Death: Former Clerk in City Auditor's Office Is Stricken," *Marion (OH) Star*, Mar. 30, 1942; Soldier's Certificate No. 792,832.

[7] Christian, *My Lost Millions*.

[8] Christian, "Biography of Warren G. Harding."

[9] George B. Christian Sr., "The Democratic Convention of 1868: From the Viewpoint of a Spectator," (unpublished manuscript, 1924) Warren G. Harding Papers, microfilm, roll 253, panels 269–80, Ohio Historical Society Archive/Library, Ohio Historical Society, Columbus, OH; Blight, *Race and Reunion*, 71–73.

[10] George B. Christian Sr., "Suggestions for a Scenario for the Production of a Moving Picture Based Upon the Story of Mazeppa from the Famous Poem of Lord Byron," (unpublished manuscript, 1826), Warren G. Harding Papers, microfilm, roll 253, panels 291–315, Ohio Historical Society Archive/Library, Ohio Historical Society, Columbus, OH; Baron George Gordon Byron, *Mazeppa: a Poem* (London: John Murray, 1819).

[11] Christian, "Suggestions for a Scenario," foreword.

[12] Edward W. Kellogg, "History of Sound Motion Pictures," in Raymond Fielding, ed., *A Technological History of Motion Pictures and Television: An Anthology from the Pages of the Journal of the Society of Motion Picture and Television Engineers* (Berkeley: University of California Press, 1967), 186–87; Christian, "Suggestions for a Scenario."

[13] Fred Dombaugh to George B. Christian Jr., Dec. 20, 1930, Warren G. Harding Papers, microfilm, roll 249, panel 758, Ohio Historical Society Archive/Library, Ohio Historical Society, Columbus, OH; Christian, "An Analysis and Review."

[14] Christian, "Instructions to Cooper Post."

[15] "Fifth Armistice Day Observed by Marion: Exercises Held Under Auspices of American Legion," *Marion (OH) Daily Star*, Nov. 12, 1923.

[16] "Tributes to Willis Voiced by Residents of Marion County, Regardless of Party," *Marion (OH) Star*, Mar. 31, 1928; Blight, *Race and Reunion*, 64–97; "George B. Christian Is Named on Committee," *Marion (OH) Star*, Dec. 16, 1927.

[17] The Cooper Post was the name of Marion's local GAR chapter. It was named after the Cooper brothers. Sturgis Herbert Cooper was Marion's first Civil War fatality. His brother Edward also died in the later years of the conflict. Two other Cooper brothers suffered lasting injuries from their time in the Union army.

[18] "Pittsburgh Plus" referred to the pricing scheme employed by U.S. steel mills in which they set the price of their steel based on the cost of production in Pittsburgh plus the cost of transporting that steel from Pittsburgh to its destination. This procedure divorced the price of steel from actual market conditions, and it created artificially high prices and profits for steel mills but hurt other industries that required raw steel as part of their manufacturing processes.

[19] Christian, "Instructions to Cooper Post"; Frank Emerich, *"Pittsburgh Plus": A Comprehensive and Concise Treatise Upon this Notable Steel-Pricing Controversy, the Most Important Industrial Dispute of the Day, Presenting Fully the Claims and Arguments of Both Sides* (Chicago: Western Association of Rolled Steel Consumers, 1923); Sahr, "Inflation Conversion."

[20] Sahr, "Inflation Conversion"; Marion County Deed Records, Mar. 1, 1907, 110:558–59, County Recorder, Marion, OH; Marion County Mortgage Records, Jan. 7, 1915, 83:275–76, County Recorder, Marion, OH; Marion County Mortgage Records, May 10, 1916, 93:324–25, County Recorder, Marion, OH; Marion County Deed Records, Apr. 16, 1924, 163:102, County Recorder, Marion, OH.

[21] "Young at Eighty," *Marion (OH) Star*, Dec. 29, 1926.

[22] Ibid.; "Social Activities," *Marion (OH) Star*, Dec. 28, 1926.

[23] George B. Christian Sr. to Henry Ford, Jun. 14, 1928, Warren G. Harding Papers, microfilm, roll 249, panel 18, Ohio Historical Society Archive/Library, Ohio Historical Society, Columbus, OH.

[24] Ibid.

[25] George B. Christian Sr. to George B. Christian Jr., Jul. 31, 1928, Warren G. Harding Papers, microfilm, roll 249, panels 695–96, Ohio Historical Society Archive/Library, Ohio Historical Society, Columbus, OH; George B. Christian Jr. to George B. Christian Sr., Aug. 4, 1928, Warren G. Harding Papers, microfilm, roll 249, panel 693, Ohio Historical Society Archive/Library, Ohio Historical Society, Columbus, OH; Blair Coán, *The Red Web: An Underground Political History of the United States from 1918 to the Present Time Showing How Close the Government Is to Collapse and Told in an Understandable Way* (Chicago: Northwest Publishing Company, 1925).

[26] George B. Christian Sr. to George B. Christian Jr., Jul. 31, 1928; George B. Christian Jr. to George B. Christian Sr., Aug. 4, 1928; "Dr. C. J. Nichols, County Republican Committeeman, Resumes Attack on Cooper," *Marion (OH) Star*, Aug. 7, 1928; "Col. Christian Asserts His Political Rights in Reply to Dr. C. J. Nichols," *Marion (OH) Star*, Aug. 11, 1928; George B. Christian Sr. to George B. Christian Jr., Nov. 8, 1928, Warren G. Harding Papers, microfilm, roll 249, panels 685–86, Ohio Historical Society Archive/Library, Ohio Historical Society, Columbus, OH.

[27] George B. Christian Jr. to Chester C. Roberts, Sep. 27, 1928, Warren G. Harding Papers, microfilm, roll 250, panels 419–20, Ohio Historical Society Archive/Library, Ohio Historical Society, Columbus, OH; Chester C. Roberts to George B. Christian Jr., Sep. 19, 1929, Warren G. Harding Papers, microfilm, roll 250, panels 399–400, Ohio Historical Society Archive/Library, Ohio Historical Society, Columbus, OH; Chester C. Roberts to George B. Christian Jr., n.d., Warren G. Harding Papers, microfilm, roll 250, panels 414–16, Ohio Historical Society Archive/Library, Ohio Historical Society, Columbus, OH; George B. Christian Jr. to Chester C. Roberts, Oct. 10, 1928, Warren G. Harding Papers, microfilm, roll 250, panel 413, Ohio Historical Society Archive/Library, Ohio Historical Society, Columbus, OH; Marion County Deed Records, Oct. 8, 1928, 178:267, County Recorder, Marion, OH.

[28] The Kelvinator Company, like many other consumer appliance companies, emerged from the automotive industry when inventor Nathaniel B. Wales pitched an idea for a working electric refrigerator in 1914 to General Motors executives Edmund Copeland and Arnold Goss. The company they formed began testing household refrigerator prototypes in 1917. They named their brand after the Scottish scientist, Lord Kelvin, for whom the Kelvin scale had been named. In 1925, the company created its first self-contained household refrigerator unit, and Chester C. Roberts formed Marion's first company to sell Kelvinator refrigerators in 1926. Jonathan Rees, *Refrigeration Nation: A History of Ice, Appliances, and Enterprise in America* (Baltimore: John Hopkins University Press, 2013); "Chester C. Roberts, Head of Electric Co., Dies Suddenly: Heart Attack Is Fatal to Civic Leader," *Marion (OH) Star*, Nov. 1, 1945.

[29] Chester C. Roberts to George B. Christian Jr., Sep. 19, 1928; Chester C. Roberts to George B. Christian Jr., n.d.; George B. Christian Jr. to Lydia M. Christian, Nov. 6, 1928, Warren G. Harding Papers, microfilm, roll 249, panels 687–88, Ohio Historical Society Archive/Library, Ohio Historical Society, Columbus, OH; George B. Christian Jr. to Harry M. Daugherty, May 23, 1929, Warren G. Harding Papers, microfilm, roll 249, panels 781–82, Ohio Historical Society Archive/Library, Ohio Historical Society, Columbus, OH; Death Certificate for Lydia M. Christian, Feb. 2, 1929, File No. 15990, Marion County, OH; "Mrs. Christian Dies at Home on Church St.: Lifelong Resident of County Taken, Funeral to Be Held Tuesday," *Marion (OH) Star*, Feb. 4, 1929.

[30] George B. Christian Jr. to George B. Christian Sr., Feb. 9, 1929, Warren G. Harding Papers, microfilm, roll 249, panel 675, Ohio Historical Society Archive/Library, Ohio Historical Society, Columbus, OH; George B. Christian Sr. to George B. Christian Jr., Feb. 11, 1929, Warren G. Harding Papers, microfilm, roll 249, panel 674, Ohio Historical Society Archive/Library, Ohio Historical Society, Columbus, OH; George B. Christian Jr. to Lydia M. Christian, Nov. 6, 1928; Marion County Deed Records, May 20, 1947, 254:308–13, County Recorder, Marion, OH.

[31] George B. Christian Sr. to George B. Christian Jr., Apr. 1, 1929, Warren G. Harding Papers, microfilm, roll 249, panel 651, Ohio Historical Society Archive/Library, Ohio Historical Society, Columbus, OH; George B. Christian Sr. to George B. Christian Jr., Apr. 10, 1929, Warren G. Harding Papers, microfilm, roll 249, panels 670–71, Ohio Historical Society Archive/Library, Ohio Historical Society, Columbus, OH; George B. Christian Sr. to George B. Christian Jr., May 2, 1929, Warren G. Harding Papers, microfilm, roll 249, panel 662, Ohio Historical Society Archive/Library, Ohio Historical Society, Columbus, OH.

[32] "Base-ball: Young Heads but Stiff Legs," *Marion (OH) Democratic Mirror*, Oct. 29, 1874; "Say Christian Seeks to Buy Indians' Team," *Sandusky (OH) Register*, Oct. 17, 1923; Kathleen Morgan Drowne and Patrick Huber, *The 1920s* (Westport, CT: Greenwood Publishing Group, 2004), 155–58.

[33] Drowne and Huber, *The 1920s*, 160; George B. Christian Jr. to Warren W. Christian, Jun. 21, 1929, Warren G. Harding Papers, microfilm, roll 249, panel 780, Ohio Historical Society Archive/Library, Ohio Historical Society, Columbus, OH; George B. Christian Jr. to Lydia M. Christian, Nov. 10, 1928, Warren G. Harding Papers, microfilm, roll 249, panel 684, Ohio Historical Society Archive/Library, Ohio Historical Society, Columbus, OH.

[34] The ticker tape parade is an urban tradition which began in New York City in 1886 with a spontaneous celebration inspired by the dedication of the Statue of Liberty. Generally, honorees are showered with copious amounts of confetti and paper from building windows overlooking a parade route. The tradition originated with actual ticker tape, named for the sound stock tickers made as they wrote stock prices on long rolls of paper for stock brokerage firms.

[35] George B. Christian Sr., "Sixty-Fourth G.A.R. Convention," *Marion (OH) Star*, Sep. 3, 1930.

[36] "New Year's Day Reminds Marion War Vet of 25-Below Zero Blast 66 Years Ago: Union Troops Caught in Cold as Mercury Drops 93 Degrees in 24 Hours," *Marion (OH) Star*, Jan. 1, 1930; George B Christian Sr., "Sixty-Fourth G.A.R. Convention"; "Gov. Cooper Pays Tribute to Late Col. Christian," *Marion (OH) Star*, Sep. 18, 1930.

[37] "City Briefs," *Marion (OH) Star*, Sep. 8, 1930; "Death Takes Colonel George B. Christian: Was Prominent in Activities of Home City," *Marion (OH) Star*, Sep. 15, 1930; "Colonel George B. Christian," *Marion (OH) Star*, Sep. 15, 1930; "Salute, Taps, Mark Christian Funeral," *Marion (OH) Star*, Sep. 17, 1930.

[38] "Colonel George B. Christian," *Marion (OH) Star*, Sep. 15, 1930.

[39] "Col. Christian Is Dead: Marion Leader and Old-Time Editor to Be Buried Tomorrow," *Cleveland (OH) Plain Dealer*, Sep. 16, 1930; "Father of Harding's Secretary Dies," *Washington Post*, Sep. 15, 1930.

[40] Myers Y. Cooper to George B. Christian Jr., Sep. 17, 1930, Warren G. Harding Papers, microfilm, roll 249, panels 639–40, Ohio Historical Society Archive/Library, Ohio Historical Society, Columbus, OH; David P. Setran, "Developing the 'Christian Gentleman': The Medieval Impulse in Protestant Ministry to Adolescent Boys, 1890–1920" *Religion and American Culture: A Journal of Interpretation* 20, no. 2 (2010): 165–204.

[41] "Cooper Post G.A.R. to Honor Veteran: Comrades Will Hold Memorial Services for George B. Christian," *Marion (OH) Star*, Oct. 4, 1930; Fred Dombaugh to George B. Christian Jr., Dec. 9, 1930, Warren G. Harding Papers, microfilm, roll 249, panel 761, Ohio Historical Society Archive/Library, Ohio Historical Society, Columbus, OH.

[42] George B. Christian Jr. to Alice M. Showers, May 19, 1931, Warren G. Harding Papers, microfilm, roll 250, panel 461, Ohio Historical Society Archive/Library, Ohio Historical Society, Columbus, OH.

[43] Ibid.

Index

All subentries that mention Christian refer to George B. Christian Sr. unless otherwise indicated.

327

East Church Street home, 258, 282; Lydia Christian ownership of, 46, 287; location of, 15; Mildred Christian wedding in, 230–31; Harding campaign and, 244, 246

Eighteenth Amendment, 230

electoral commission of 1876, 113–14. *See also* Hayes, Rutherford B.; Tilden, Samuel

European travel, 45, 84–87, 89, 221–22

Evans, John, 142, 145, 166

expositions, 189–92

Fall, Albert, 251, 263–4. *See also* Teapot Dome scandal

Federal Trade Commission (FTC), 281

Fisher, William, 93

fishing: on Florida trip, 94; in Lake Erie, 124; in Michigan, 133; in ocean, 103; as sign of masculinity, 131; stories, 308n25; *See also* Isaac Walton

filibustering, 33, 101, 303n24. *See also* slavery

Florida, 89–105, 210, 212, 217–18, 258. See also *My Lost Millions*

Foraker, Joseph: Christian compliments about, 186; Harding and, 219–20, 224; before Ohio Supreme Court, 201; Republican politics and, 198

Forbes, Charles, 251, 262–63

Ford, Henry, 272, 283

formal tea parties, 44–45

Fort Meigs, 22–24. *See also* War of 1812

free silver ideology, 156, 182–86, 316n2. *See also* Bryan, William Jennings; Populism

Freshwater, Benjamin Franklin, 175–76

front-porch campaign, 243–45, 247. *See also* Harding, Warren G.; McKinley, William

Galvin, John D., 242

Garberson, John J., 211–12

Garfield, James A., 125–27, 133–35, 196, 311n54. *See also* Arthur, Chester A.; Guiteau, Charles; Republican Party

Garrett, William H., 57–58. *See also* American Civil War; Ohio Fifth Independent Cavalry

Gilded Age: A Tale of Today, The, 73–75. *See also* Twain, Mark (Samuel Clemens)

Gould, Jay, 146

Grand Army of the Republic (GAR), 65–67, 279–81, 289–91

Grange, Harold (Red), 289

Grant, Ulysses S.: on Decoration Day, 66; election of 1880 and, 126; end of Civil War and, 63; on Florida, 104; presidency of, 112–13, 126–27, 276; at Vicksburg, 55. *See also* American Civil War; Reconstruction

Grant, Ulysses S., III, 290

Great Depression, 268, 271, 292

Great Railroad Strike of 1877, 116–18

Great Southwest Railroad Strike, 146–47

Griswald, George, 80

Guerrant, Jean, 21

Guiteau, Charles, 133–34. *See also* Garfield, James A.

Gyp, 215

Hancock, Winfield Scott, 65, 126–27. *See also* Garfield, James A.

Hanna, Mark, 197–99, 219–20. *See also* Republican Party

Hard, Charles, 257

Harding Memorial Association, 265, 286

Harding, Florence Kling: courtship and marriage of, 210–11; friendship with Christians, 212, 215–17, 230–31, 262; illness of, 212, 222, 258; Harding campaign and, 249, 253

Harding, George Tryon, 207–8, 215, 259, 266

Harding, Warren G.: death of, 261–62, 265 ; friendship with Christians, 4, 45–50, 104, 171–72, 174–75, 185, 188, 205–8, 212–22, 228, 230–31, 237, 243, 252, 266, 274; infidelities of, 222, 266–68; Marion home, 15, 81; as newspaper editor, 159, 209–11; political success of, 12–14, 205, 213, 219–20, 222; presidency of, 92, 250–61; presidential campaign of, 235–50; scandals and, 262–68, 284–85; as senator, 223–26, 228, 230–33. *See also* Britton, Nan; Christian, George B., Jr.; front porch campaign; Harding, Florence Kling; Harding, George Tryon; Philips, Carrie

Harmon, Judson, 223

Harrison, William Henry, 22–24. *See also* War of 1812

Hayes, Rutherford B., 92, 113–14, 116, 125–26. *See also* electoral commission of 1876

Haymarket riot, 147
Hays, William, 245
Herrick, Myron T., 220
History of Marion County, 125
Hodder, Thomas, 33–35
homeopathic medicine, 30–31, 207–8. *See also* Christian, John M.; Harding, George Tryon
Hoover, Herbert, 92, 251, 265, 285, 308n7. *See also* Smith, Al
Huber Manufacturing Company, 8–9, 79
Huber, Edward, 79, 206
Hughes, Charles Evans, 227, 243, 251, 255. *See also* Washington Disarmament Conference
hugmaster general, 46, 243, 251. *See also* Christian, George B., Sr.
Huguenot, 21
Indian River, 89, 101–3. *See also* Florida; *My Lost Millions*
Irish immigrants, 115–16
irreconcilables, 232.
Irving, Washington, 90. *See also travel writing*
Isle of Man, 18–9, 301n1
Johnson, Hiram, 238, 240–41
Jones, D. S., 78–79
Jones, Samuel M., 199, 201. *See also* Toledo, Ohio
Kelly, Dave, 147–48. *See also* Norris and Christian Lime and Stone Company
Kilbourne, James, 202. *See also* Ohio Centennial Celebration Commission
Klem, Joseph John (Johnny Shiloh), 57. *See also* American Civil War
Kling, Amos, 211, 221–22. *See also* Harding, Florence Kling
Klunk, Charles A., 268. *See also* Britton, Nan
Knights of Labor, 146–47. *See also* Great Southwest Railroad Strike; Powderly, Terrence
Knights of the Golden Circle, 33–35, 57–58. *See also* Bickley, George
Know-Nothings, 33
Kodak camera, 214. *See also* photography
Ku Klux Klan, 273
La Follette, Robert, 232, 281. *See also* Progressivism
Lasker, Albert, 245. *See also* Wrigley, William
Lawler, Kathleen, 267, 275–76, 278
League of Nations, 226, 231–34, 244, 248, 255–56. *See also* Treaty of Versailles; Wilson, Woodrow
Lee, Robert E., 55–56. *See also* American Civil War
lime and stone industry: consolidation of, 166–67; industrial growth and, 141; labor pressure and, 170–71; limestone processing and, 143–44; macadam and, 147, 153–54; wartime controls and, 172–75
Limestone City Real Estate Company, 158, 163
Lincoln, Abraham, 27, 32, 35; commemoration for, 222; Gettysburg Address and, 54; Tryon Harding and, 266. *See also* American Civil War, slavery
Lodge, Henry Cabot, 232–33, 244
London, Jack, 90. *See also* travel writing
Lord Byron (George Gordon Byron), 276–78. See also *Mazeppa*
Lost Generation, 272
Lowden, Frank, 238, 240–42
lumber industry, 80–81, 160
Mammoth Oil Company, 263. *See also* Sinclair, Henry
manliness and masculinity, 130–31
Marion Academy, 29, 41. *See also* Christian, John M.
Marion and Northwestern Railway Company, 159
Marion Board of Trade, 212
Marion, City of: centennial of, 7, 258, Christian and, 76–87, 81–83, 150–51; during Civil War, 32–36, 57–58, 66–67; front-porch campaign and, 242–47, 249–50; Garfield funeral, 134–35; growth of, 74, 118, 205–6, 272–73, 282, 298–99; Harding funeral and, 262; Harding Memorial Foundation and, 265; history of, 1, 7–9, 14, 25, 29, 50–51, 115; Huber Manufacturing Company and, 79; map of, 15; Memorial Day Celebrations, 279–80 political loyalties of, 183; quarries in, 176–77; social scene of, 43–45, 213–18, 267; street pavement, 153, 158; students in, 163; temperance movement in, 1

Ohio Centennial Celebration Commission, 189–202. *See also* Bushnell, Asa S.; Kilbourne, James; Nash, George K.

Ohio Centennial Company, 194, 200–201. *See also* Toledo, Ohio

Ohio Fifth Independent Cavalry, 57–59, 61–63, 71. *See also* American Civil War

Ohio Stone Club, 171. *See also* lime and stone industry

Ohio state senate election of 1897, 183–87

Ohio University, 29

Old Northwest, 23, 29, 39, 76, 191–92, 302n7

Olewiler, Howard L., 287, 290

O'Ragan, John, 115–16. *See also* Irish immigrants

Palatka, Florida, 99

Palmer, A. Mitchell, 284

Panic of 1837, 28–29

Panic of 1873, 110–11

Panic of 1893, 156–58

partisanship: after Christian changed parties, 285–86; in Civil War era, 35–36; in newspapers, 111–12, 120–22, 128–30, 136–37

pension process: Christian's denial in, 68–69; Harding's struggles with, 254–55; health information for, 60–61; Pension Act of 1862, 63–64; Pension Act of 1890, 67–68; Pension Act of 1920, 70–71

Pershing, John, 246. *See also* Spanish American War; World War I

Philippines, 226, 238, 298, 320n31. *See also* Spanish American War; Wood, Leonard

Philips, Carrie, 222, 266. *See* European travel; Harding, Warren G.

photography, 214. *See also* Kodak camera

Pittsburgh Plus pricing, 281, 324n18

Polk, James K., 95

Populism, 181–82, 316n2. *See also* Bryan, William Jennings

Powderly, Terrence, 146. *See also* Knights of Labor

property appraisal, 76–77, 148–51

quarry accidents, 155, 162. *See also* Norris and Christian Lime and Stone Company; Norris and Christian Stone Company Mutual Aid Society

Railroad Shop Workers' Strike of 1922, 256–57. *See* Daugherty, Harry; Harding, Warren G.

Reconstruction: abandoned projects of, 102; Christian's condemnation of, 64–65, 93–94; history of, 74, 112, 126, 176; perceptions of the South and, 89–90. *See also* Grant, Ulysses S.

Reed, James S., 148. *See also* Norris and Christian Lime and Stone Company

Republican Convention of 1920, 240–42

Republican Party: Christian's perception of, 121, 127–28, 175, 285–86; Civil War and, 32–35; claims of xenophobia and, 116; election of 1920 and, 238–45, 249; fear of William Jennings Bryan, 182; Florida and, 91–92; Great Depression and, 268; internal divides in, 134, 197–99, 211, 219–20, 223, 227, 236, 311n54; John Morris and, 42; law and order and, 118; opposition to League of Nations, 225–26, 231–34; politics of Reconstruction and, 112–13; tariffs and, 310n43; waving the bloody shirt, 64–65, 126, *See also* Harding, Warren G.; *Marion Independent*

Richey, James, 186. *See* White Sulphur Lime and Stone Company

road construction: under Christian's supervision, 81–82, 158, 163; civil engineering and, 76; construction materials, 143, 147, 153–54; creating relationships, 41–42. *See also* civil engineering

Roaring Twenties, 271–73, 277

Roberts, Alice Mildred Christian: birth of, 43; Chester Roberts and, 50, 230–31; Christian and, 287, 299–300; early life of, 49–50; Hardings and, 211; as Harding home caretaker, 251, 286; as hostess, 44–45; Nan Britton and, 266, 268; volunteerism and, 50–51, 300. *See also* Roberts, Chester

Roberts, Chester: background of, 50; football fandom of, 289; Harding campaign and, 249–50; as Harding home caretaker, 251, 286; as Kelvinator dealer, 286, 325n28; marriage of, 50, 230–31; partnership with Christian, 282; Republican Convention of 1920 and, 240; Republican prognostication, 286. *See also* Roberts, Alice Mildred Christian

Rockefeller, John D., 75, 88, 176

Roosevelt, Theodore: death of, 234; election of 1912 and, 223; Progressivism and, 249; thoughts on race, 308n10; Warren Christian costume as, 216; World War I and, 230

Root, Elihu, 246

Rumford Academy, 27–28. *See also* Christian, John M.

sanitation, 195–97